George Lippard

Legends of Mexico

Edited by

Nichol Allen

Patrick Ayres

Scott Both

Brendon Floyd

William Geiger

Aimee Lafrance

Cassandra Lampitt

Shannan Mason

Alice Morgan

Kendyl Schmidt

Phillip Schneider

Jason Stacy

Louis Thuet

Tyler Young

Hastings College Press | Hastings, Nebraska

Introduction and Annotations © 2019 by Hastings College Press

Text © 1847 by T.B. Peterson. This book has fallen into the public domain and is no longer subject to copyright protection.

All rights reserved. No part of this book may be used or reproduced in any manner whatsoever without permission from the publisher, except in the case of brief quotations embodied in critical articles and reviews.

Production Staff
Samantha Alvarez
Lyette Erin
Juliana Hernandez
Jenny Sells
Abigail Shaw

Copy Editor
Bruce Batterson

Designer
Patricia Oman

ISBN-10: 1942885687
ISBN-13: 978-1-942885-68-9

Note on the text: This edition has been reset from the first (1847) edition. Original spelling and grammatical conventions have been maintained, except in the case of publishing errors in the first edition. The original punctuation has been maintained but updated using modern conventions (e.g., eliminating spaces around dashes).

Manufactured in the United States of America.

Contents

	Introduction	vii
	Notes on the Text	xxxviii
	Acknowledgments	xxxix
I	The Crusade of the Nineteenth Century	1
II	The Camp in the Wilderness	11
III	The Dead Woman of Palo Alto	27
IV	Palo Alto	61
V	Resaca de la Palma	109
VI	Monterey	153
VII	Buena Vista	177
Appendix	Contemporaneous Political Cartoons	201
	Index	213

Introduction

> [H]is memory will live, his genius will live, and future ages will recognize his works while here, as a bright and good inheritance.
>
> —*Sunday Mercury* (1854)[1]

When the *Sunday Mercury* eulogized author George Lippard (1822–1854), its prediction seemed a foregone conclusion. Lippard had written some of the most popular works of nineteenth-century America. His most successful book, *The Quaker City* (1845), was the bestselling American novel until *Uncle Tom's Cabin* (1852) and dripped with debauchery, political corruption, and intrigue.[2] Such topics gained him praise and condemnation. Yet Lippard's reputation quickly faded to such an extent that not one generation after his death, a contemporary journalist lamented that it was all but impossible to find Lippard's novels on book shelves.[3]

George Lippard grew up in Germantown, Pennsylvania, where, in his childhood, he heard legends of the American Revolution from his Aunt Mary.[4] Stories of the heroic exploits of the Revolutionary generation tantalized Lippard, who, recounting his youth, remembered, "[t]he orchard ... with its trees, beneath whose roots men of the battlefield were buried.... Now, you who like to read of battles ... can not think how many interests cluttered around our Homestead."[5] Years later, he wrote his own legends of the founding generation and the Revolutionary War for American readers.[6]

In 1837, when the death of Lippard's father left him orphaned, the family experienced financial difficulties and was forced to sell their land.[7]

Introduction

1. Quoted in David S. Reynolds, *George Lippard* (Boston: Twayne Publishers, 1982), 24.
2. George Lippard, *The Quaker City, Or, The Monks of Monk Hall: A Romance of Philadelphia Life, Mystery, and Crime,* ed. David S. Reynolds (Amherst: University of Massachusetts Press, 1995), vii, xii. *Quaker City* first appeared in serial in 1844. It was then published as a complete work in 1845.
3. "A Novelist of the Last Generation Who is Not Known To-Day," *Pittsburg* [sic] *Dispatch,* August 5, 1889.
4. John Bell Bouton, *The Life and Choice Writings of George Lippard* (New York: H.H. Randall, 1855), 7. Originally, there was no author's name attached to this work. Later, Bouton was identified as the author. Emilio DeGrazia, "The Life and Works of George Lippard" (Ph.D. Dissertation, Ohio State University, 1969), 19, 461; Reynolds, *George Lippard,* 3.
5. Quoted in Bouton, *The Life and Choice Writings of George Lippard,* 11.
6. *Washington and his Generals* began as a serialized set of articles starting in 1846. In 1847, this collection was published as a single book. Reynolds, *George Lippard,* 13, 15.
7. DeGrazia, "The Life and Works of George Lippard," 33.

8   Quoted in Bouton, *The Life and Choice Writings of George Lippard,* 11–12.
9   DeGrazia, "The Life and Works of George Lippard," 23–24.
10 Ibid., 31, 38–39.
11 Reynolds, *George Lippard,* 5.
12 Daniel Walker Howe, *What Hath God Wrought: The Transformation of America, 1815–1848* (New York: Oxford University Press, 2007), 563.
13 George Lippard, "Modern Civilization as Locomotive Crushing the Poor," in *George Lippard, Prophet of Protest: Writings of an American Radical, 1822–1854,* ed. David S. Reynolds (New York: Peter Lang, 1986), 46.
14 Ibid.

Reflecting on the experience years later, he bitterly remarked that the men who bought their farm were "vultures of the Law.... I think that I could sit down with a murderer, and be cheerful with him sooner than I could endure the sight of the Destroyer of the Homestead: for he is a murderer of something more than flesh and blood."[8] Though Lippard received a brief education, he was a reluctant student.[9] At the age of fifteen, he attended the Classical Academy in Rhinebeck, New York to become a Methodist minister, but became disillusioned with the profession and moved on to law, which also proved a fruitless venture for the young man.[10] In 1840, he began writing and later published *The Ladye Annabel* (1844), his first novel, which drew heavily from the popular Gothic style. He received his first official position as a writer for the Philadelphia newspaper *Spirit of the Times* in 1842.[11]

As Lippard the writer developed, so too did the nation; the first half of the nineteenth century marked a period of rapid development for the United States. During these years, technological changes transformed the lives of all Americans. For example, railroads were laid throughout the country, uniting village and city and providing greater access to wider markets. By 1840, the United States possessed more than twice the mileage of railroad than the whole of Europe.[12] Lippard recognized the important symbolism of the railroad and claimed, "[M]odern civilization is very much like the locomotive, rolling along an iron track at sixty miles per hour.... What a magnificent impersonation of power; of brute force chained by the mind of man!"[13] And yet, "[W]oe, woe to the weak or helpless who linger on its iron track! and woe to the weak, the crippled, or the poor whom the locomotive of modern civilization finds lingering *in its way.* Why should it care? It has no heart. Its work is to move onward and to cut down all whom poverty and misfortune have left in its path."[14] Lippard's care for those ground down by the wheels of progress motivated his most successful novel, *The Quaker City*, which explored the plight of the poor and "describe[d] all the phases of a corrupt social system, as manifested in the city of Philadelphia."[15]

For the young author, good writing was always reform-minded. "[L]iterature which does not work practically for the advancement of social reform … is just good for nothing at all."[16] For all his reform-minded intentions, the content of *The Quaker City* proved shocking. Lippard's sensualized tales of rape, surreal Gothic scenes, and perverse characters appalled many of his contemporary readers.[17] When adapted for the stage, public reaction against it forced its cancelation.[18]

While Lippard battled against the effects of the early industrial revolution on the poor, the invention of the telegraph proved important to his success. By 1846, telegraph wires connected Boston, New York, Washington and other major cities in the Northeast.[19] Correspondents in Mexico during the U.S.-Mexico War (1846–1848) transmitted news via the telegraph to newspapers that provided timely and detailed information from the battlefields. These reports fueled Lippard's sensationalized accounts of the war and allowed him to mythologize the event in real time.[20]

Inspired by the exploits of General Zachary Taylor, Lippard imagined a new Washington born to advance American democracy. By 1849, Lippard's hero was president of the United States, though it is impossible to say just how much *Legends of Mexico* and Lippard's stumping for "Old Rough and Ready" proved essential to his electoral victory.[21] But the honeymoon did not last, and Lippard's eventual disillusionment with Taylor was perhaps predictable in hindsight. Lippard was a Democrat while Taylor was a Whig and though, as a condition of his support for Taylor, Lippard acquired a guarantee from the General on the nonpartisanship of his appointments, Taylor proved as partisan as any American politician. During the campaign,

15 Quoted in Bouton, *The Life and Choice Writings of George Lippard*, 18.
16 Quoted in Lippard, *The Quaker City*, viii.
17 Reynolds, *George Lippard*, 10.
18 Ibid., 11.
19 Howe, *What Hath God Wrought*, 748.
20 Reynolds, *George Lippard*, 15.
21 Bouton, *The Life and Choice Writings of George Lippard*, 57.

22 "The Appeal of a Taylor Democrat," *Democratic Banner,* June 25, 1849.
23 Ibid., emphasis added by Lippard.
24 Reynolds, *George Lippard,* 17.
25 "The Appeal of a Taylor Democrat."

Lippard wrote to Taylor and "pledged what literary reputation I possess to you in my book—'Legends of Mexico, or *Battles of Taylor*'" and sought assurances from Taylor that he would remain, though a Whig, ultimately nonpartisan in the midst of an era riven by party politics.[22] Taylor, perhaps aware of Lippard's popularity as author of *The Quaker City,* wrote to him, "I am NOT a party candidate, and if elected, shall not *be the President of a party, but the President of the whole people.*"[23] Lippard supported Taylor upon this guarantee, but when Taylor chose a Whig cabinet when taking office, Lippard felt betrayed.[24] Ultimately, the real Zachary Taylor fell far short of the legend Lippard created in *Legends of Mexico.*

Lippard publicly aired his rage in the press shortly after Taylor took office. After recounting Taylor's promise, he declared in an open letter to the president, "I must frankly tell you, that had you not made the declaration embraced in this letter, I, for one, could not have advocated your election, nor given you my vote." He then asked of Taylor, "Have you fulfilled these pledges? ... Answer me! ... You pledged your faith to me, an humble citizen, and I believed you, and told my fellow-citizens that you had never broken your word, and could not forget tomorrow what you pledged to-day," but "now, sir, ... I wash my hands of the last traces of political Taylorism, as I state my regret that I ever acted the part which your pledges made me act." With a twinge of sadness, Lippard lamented, "[T]hose hands which were free at Buena Vista ... are now tied by the trammels which have been fashioned from the very ruins of the whig party."[25]

Disappointed by Taylor's inability to become a new Washington, Lippard turned from politics and placed his faith in the new organization he founded in 1849, "The Brotherhood of the Union," whose goal was to promote the "Truth" that, as Lippard described it, "every man upon [God's] earth [possessed the right] to Life, Liberty, Land and Home ...

to that right of development, compressed in the simple word Progress."[26] After 1849, Lippard devoted much of his time to the Brotherhood, which grew rapidly, though it drove the young author into debt and forced him to sell his copyrights and the stereotype plates of some of his works.[27]

While writing *Legends of Mexico,* Lippard married Rose Newman, a local resident, in a ceremony overlooking Wissahikon creek and officiated by Reverend Charles Chauncey Burr, the man to whom Lippard dedicated his latest book.[28] Lippard's first child, Mima, was born in 1848 and died in 1850. Another child, Paul, was born later that year and died soon thereafter.[29] Tragedy struck Lippard again when Rose died in 1851, prompting him to devote his life almost entirely to the Brotherhood. He succumbed to consumption on February 9, 1854 at the age of 32, a hasty end to a busy life.[30]

Lippard's final days proved to be as controversial as his work. A report from the *Boston Post* claimed that on his deathbed Lippard lay "without proper attendance or care, in the second story of an old house, situated in an unfrequented part of Philadelphia."[31] In this sensationalized article, one Lippard himself would have appreciated for its gusto, the author asked, "Will no one smooth down the pillow of that talented orphan in that gloomy room of the dying? an orphan! no father! no mother! no brother or friend to care for him! Indeed he is alone!"[32] Another correspondent furthered the story of Lippard's degraded state: "Here, in the case of Mr. Lippard we have another awful evidence of the destruction and soul-destroying influence of intoxicating liquors."[33] The *National Democrat* responded by denying the report of "the romancer who wrote the article in the Boston Post" and claimed that Lippard lived comfortably in a "genteel" house.[34] Other papers joined in by repeating similar skepticism of Lippard's degraded end or hinting at more nefarious circumstances.[35] In death, Lippard created another legend.

26 Reynolds, *George Lippard,* 19; George Lippard, "Goals of the Brotherhood of the Union," in *George Lippard, Prophet of Protest,* 208.
27 De Grazia, "The Life and Works of George Lippard," 376.
28 Ibid., 24–25, 236, 247. In his dissertation, De Grazia alternates between "Wissahikon" and the modern "Wissahickon." Lippard himself uses the term Wissahikon to describe this location in his early life. Mark A. Lause, *A Secret Society History of the Civil War* (Urbana: University of Illinois Press, 2011), 23.
29 De Grazia, "The Life and Works of George Lippard," 308, 377–378.
30 Ibid., 378–379, 436. In the nineteenth century, "consumption" was the name for the disease tuberculosis. Howe, *What Hath God Wrought,* 170.
31 "Illness of George Lippard, Esq., the Author," *Wayne County Herald,* February 2, 1854.
32 Ibid.
33 Ibid.
34 "The Late George Lippard," *The Wheeling Daily Intelligencer,* March 1, 1854. It should be noted that Lippard was named as the editor of the *New York National Democrat* in 1852. Reynolds, George Lippard, 22.
35 "Death of George Lippard," *Sumter County Whig,* March 15, 1854.

36 Reynolds, *George Lippard*, 24.
37 Ibid., 25.
38 Ibid.
39 Lea Sitton, "Last Chapter is Nearing For City Writer's Legacy Begun in 1847, The Brotherhood of America is Ready to Fold," *Philadelphia Inquirer*, November 27, 1994. The Brotherhood of the Union had been renamed "the Brotherhood of America." Reynolds, *George Lippard*, 24–25.
40 See Reynolds, *George Lippard*; Elizabeth Kelly Gray, "The World by Gaslight: Urban-Gothic Literature and Moral Reform in New York City, 1845–1860," *American Nineteenth Century History* 10, no. 2 (2009).

Lippard was buried in Odd Fellows Cemetery on February 13, 1854.[36] For over one hundred years, his memory was kept by his fellow members of his Brotherhood, though largely forgotten by most Americans. Later, a large marble monument to honor him was placed by the Brotherhood in the cemetery where he lay.[37] In 1900, a procession led by the Brotherhood paid tribute to his memory. They did so again in 1922, the centennial of his birth.[38] During the twentieth century, the Brotherhood's membership dwindled to a few old die-hards, and the final chapter closed in 1994.[39] By then, Lippard's legendary status among Americans had long passed.

Young American Gothic

While many scholars place Lippard in the broader context of Gothic literature, he also proved a booster for the contemporary ideal of the nation's "manifest destiny" to spread across the North American continent and beyond.[40] In this regard, Lippard's writing fit loosely into the burgeoning literary movement known as Young America, whose style sought to create a uniquely American literature that undermined the popularity of contemporary European writers. Lippard's reliance on the literary Gothic, however, disqualified him from recognition in the movement. Instead, Lippard's writing diverged from Young America in its Gothic overtones, while his notions of manifest destiny proved consistent with it. In this way, Lippard used Gothic tropes to promote American exceptionalism through "legends" that he hoped would nurture a unified national spirit.

The Gothic writing style became popular in Europe during the 1700s and, by the turn of the century, shaped the American literary scene. Originating in Britain, but spreading further to France and Germany, the Gothic style reveled in darkness and nightmare in fantastical and historical settings that sought insight into the human psyche and gave vent to contemporary anxieties and fears. These literary fantasies delved into the ramifications of good and evil and embraced the latent ironies in the pursuit of each.[41] The Gothic often "harbor[ed] unreasonable, uncivilized, and unprogressive customs or tendencies" in active foil to contemporary ideals of progress and modernity.[42] An early example of this literary style is Horace Walpole's *The Castle of Otranto* (1764),[43] which was set in a romanticized medieval landscape and inspired later authors such as Edgar Allan Poe, Mary Shelley, Nathaniel Hawthorne, and others to adapt the Gothic style to settings more contemporary and characters more complex.[44]

The "penny dreadful" in England and the *roman-feuilleton* in France fueled the popularity of Gothic literature.[45] The cost of printing decreased due to the innovation of the steam-powered press, and these stories spread among the general populace.[46] Eugene Sue, a popular French Gothic writer and one of the first to recast the Gothic setting from the medieval castle to dark urban streets, proved strongly influential on George Lippard. Sue's novel *The Mysteries of Paris* (1842) likely inspired the overwrought sensationalism and sinister characters in Lippard's *The Quaker City*, which followed Sue's model by creating a Gothic Philadelphia that challenged Philadelphians' daylight morality with images of darkness, corruption, and vice.[47] The success of works by authors like Lippard was in part due to the shocked and titillated reaction they elicited from their middle- and working-class readers. Ironically, industrial production of inexpensive books by urban publishers made it possible to print cheap sensationalist works that reflected contemporary anxieties about urban growth.[48]

Lippard's historical fictions, such as *Washington and His Generals* (1847) and *Legends of Mexico* (1847), "transferred the blood and savagery from the medieval castle to the American battlefield."[49] While Lippard exhibited Gothic tendencies, he also emulated elements of the popular

41 Elizabeth MacAndrew, *The Gothic Tradition* (New York: Columbia University, 1979), 3–4.
42 Gray, "The World by Gaslight," 140.
43 MacAndrew, *The Gothic Tradition*, 5–7.
44 Reynolds, *George Lippard*, 27–29.
45 The penny dreadful was a serial story, usually published in weekly installments, sold for one penny, that sensationalized the darker and seedier aspects of the human experience and was often set in the city. The *roman-feuilleton* was the French version of the penny dreadful and translates to "serialized novel." Sally Powell, "Black Markets and Cadaverous Pies: The Corpse, Urban Trade and Industrial Consumption in the Penny Blood," in *Victorian Crime, Madness and Sensation,* ed. Andrew Maunder and Grace Moore (Burlington: Ashgate, 2004), 45–58.
46 Reynolds, *George Lippard*, 28.
47 Ibid., 29.
48 Ibid., 143, 139.
49 Ibid., 37.

Young America literary movement, which sought to separate itself from European traditions and form a uniquely American style. Led by writers and journalists such as John O'Sullivan, Evert Augustus Duyckinck, and Cornelius Matthews, Young America promoted a nationalist spirit that celebrated an American culture modeled on republican values as expressed in the founding of the United States, unmoored from European origins. George Lippard may not have fit into Young America's literary style, but his understanding of manifest destiny echoed that of its leading members. In 1845, one founding member of the Young America movement and editor of *The United States Magazine and Democratic Review*, John O'Sullivan, popularized the term "manifest destiny" when his periodical rejected "limiting our greatness and checking the fulfillment of our manifest destiny to overspread the continent allotted by Providence for the free development of our yearly multiplying millions."[50] Writers like Lippard and O'Sullivan, and more broadly, Young America, thereby drew upon "common republican rhetoric … to address issues of U.S. empire building."[51] In this way, both men viewed the United States' role in the Americas as one of superiority and benevolent conquest; the continent belonged to the United States, and Providence led the way toward a hemisphere, or perhaps a world, of republican virtue.

For these writers, Mexico's greatest weakness was its mistake in imitating foreign governments in "legislation, jurisprudence, [and] literature," which was "more reflective of foreign aristocracy than of American democracy" and resulted in plunging their people into "burthens" perpetuated on the people as "national blessings."[52] In contrast, the citizens of the United States "did not inflict evil on ourselves, subverting common right, in violation of common sense and common justice."[53] Thus the argument for manifest destiny, based on expansionist rhetoric, was supported by notions

---

50 John O'Sullivan, "Annexation," *The United States Magazine, and Democratic Review* (New York: J.L. O'Sullivan and O.C. Gardiner, 1845): 5. Current scholarship challenges the idea that O'Sullivan coined the term Manifest Destiny, instead crediting it to one of his writers, Cora Montgomery. Linda S. Hudson, *Mistress of Manifest Destiny: A Biography of Jane McManus Storm Cazneau, 1807–1878* (Austin: Texas A&M University Press, 2001), 46–48, 205–210; Amy S. Greenberg, *Manifest Manhood and the Antebellum American Empire* (Cambridge: Cambridge University Press, 2005), 20.

51 Shelley Streeby, "American Sensations: Empire, Amnesia, and the US-Mexican War," *American Literary History* 13, no. 1 (Spring, 2001): 3.

52 John O'Sullivan, "The Great Nation of Futurity," *The United States Magazine and Democratic Review* 6, no. 23 (November, 1839): 426.

53 Ibid., 428.

of the United States as a nation that left the old world of kings and empires in the past. In this regard, both Young America and George Lippard embraced the "paradoxical idea of a nonimperial US empire."⁵⁴

They also both envisioned a new race born from the creole populations of the United States and their descendants. As the United States had broken from the political tradition of Europe, so too would it break Europe's hold on American culture. America had "no interest in the scenes of antiquity, only the lessons of avoidance of nearly all their examples.... We are a nation of human progress, and who will ... set limits to our onward march?"⁵⁵ Lippard demonstrated this version of progress in *Legends of Mexico*: "As the Aztec people, crumbled before the Spaniard, so will the mongrel race, moulded of Indian and Spanish blood, melt into, and be ruled by, the Iron Race of the North."⁵⁶ By abstracting Native Americans and Mexicans into a moribund "other," Lippard promoted the cultural, racial, and political supremacy of the United States, which justified the American empire latent within manifest destiny's ideology. Ostensibly eschewing European-style empire-building with a missionary's stance, the United States would bring the Mexican people out of the darkness and into the light of Anglo-Saxon civilization, and for those that resisted, domination or extermination was the natural course.⁵⁷ To Lippard and those in the Young America movement, this was merely the will of Providence, as "God Almighty has given the destiny of the Continent, into the hands of the free People of the American Union."⁵⁸

To justify conquest, Lippard and Young Americans like O'Sullivan reframed what an "American" race was rhetorically. Lippard embraced the destitute masses "from all the nations of Northern Europe ... Germany and Sweden and Ireland and Scotland and Wales and England [who would] ... gr[o]w into a new race." This new race proved to be "the American People,"

54 Streeby, "American Sensations," 2.
55 O'Sullivan, "The Great Nation of Futurity," 427.
56 8.
57 Greenberg, *Manifest Manhood and the Antebellum American Empire*, 92.
58 8.

59 9.
60 O'Sullivan, "The Great Nation of Futurity," 429.
61 Thomas A. Bailey, "The Mythmakers of American History" in *Myth and the American Experience,* ed. Thomas A. Bailey (Beverly Hills: Glencoe Press, 1973), 14n. Richard Slotkin provides another interpretation of Lippard's use of legend as "a work that would have the moralizing capability of fable, and the authority of history." Richard Slotkin, *The Fatal Environment: The Myth of the Frontier in the Age of Industrialization 1800–1890* (Norman: University of Oklahoma Press, 1998).

with authority from the divine and "destiny to possess this Continent" to build an "Empire of Men … on the wrecks of shattered empires," and erect in their place the "Brotherhood of Man," an amalgam of Western Europeans that perpetuated enlightenment for more blighted peoples.[59] Likewise, John O'Sullivan and Young America celebrated an emerging American culture distinct from European traditions, as "American patriotism is not of soil; we are not aborigines, nor of ancestry, for we are all nations … for 'where liberty dwells,' … 'there is my country.'"[60] Here, at the intersection of a new race and its gift to the world, we find an ideological marriage between Lippard and Young America. Where Lippard created a past in the present through his legends, Young America created a new identity for a future people. It was in this way that Lippard and Young America, under the banner of manifest destiny, were both emblematic of a nascent type of expansionist nationalism that took hold in the United States during this period. Though steeped in the European Gothic literary style, Lippard's notions of manifest destiny sprung from the same literary aspirations as Young America. By connecting the Gothic style to manifest destiny ideology, Lippard created a hybrid style that borrowed from European literary genres while inhabiting contemporary conceptions of American exceptionalism.

Lippard and Legend

While "myth" or "legend" today implies something "demonstrably untrue, in whole or in substantial part," legend, the way Lippard used the term, contained essential truths that enhanced history.[61] By entitling works "legends of …," he created a link from fiction to historical fact that connected readers viscerally to the past. Each of Lippard's "legends" mixed fact and fiction in a way that upheld the accuracy of some details, while sensationalizing others to enhance the reader's emotional connection to history. Through this mixture of fact and fiction, he "'assimilate[d]' the historical experience that ma[de] popular sensational war literature especially revealing."[62] In this way, legend was more useful and revelatory than pure fiction or fact. In contrast to history, legend was

> One of those heart-warm stories, which, quivering in rude earnest language from the lips of a spectator of a battle, or a spectator of some event of the olden time, fill up the cold outlines of history, and clothe the skeleton with flesh and blood, give it eyes and tongue, force it at once to look into our eyes and talk with us![63]

As Lippard intended it, legend was the living reality often ignored in staid histories. There was, essentially, a distinction in the ways history and legend were created. History was written by the affluent, who, as a byproduct of their leisure, were disconnected from the individuals who took part in past events. Historians deadened the living past with their books, charts, names, and dates. Legend, on the other hand, was the preserve of those who bore witness to the past or heard stories from a reliable but invested source. For Lippard, like many sentimental writers during this period, a story's ability to evoke feeling outweighed cold factuality.[64] He, therefore, did not distinguish between factual history and emotive legend in his own writings, and moved fluidly between both. By engaging the reader in this manner, he left the determination of what was fact and fiction to the reader, and thereby implied a porous membrane between them.

While Lippard celebrated sentimental legend, he was equally averse to history: "It must be confessed that the thing which generally passes for History, is the most impudent, swaggering bully, the most graceless braggart,

62 Shelley Streeby, *American Sensations: Class, Empire, and the Production of Popular Culture* (Berkeley: University of California Press, 2002), 40.
63 27.
64 Bailey, "The Mythmakers of American History," 2–5, 11–12.

65 28.
66 Ibid.
67 Ibid.
68 Ibid.
69 Ibid.
70 George Lippard, *Adonai: The Pilgrim of Eternity* (Philadelphia, 1851), 82, quoted in Larzer Ziff, *Literary Democracy: The Declaration of Cultural Independence in America* (Middlesex: Penguin Books, 1982), 97–98.

the most reckless equivocator that ever staggered forth upon the great stage of the world."[65] History, which depended upon factuality, rendered the past emotionally dead. To remain vital, history had to be imbibed with the rich textual character of legend. "History[,] to speak to the heart, should not lie to us by wholesale, nor deal in vague generalities, which are worse than robust lies, for they only tell half the truth, and leave the imagination to fill the other half with the infinite space of falsehood."[66] The fact-filled reports of newspapers and history books, therefore, provided only partial realities and half-truths.

Sentiment was the essential component of good history, as it elicited emotional resonance in the reader and "[made] us live with the people, fight by them in battle, sit with them at the table, make love, hate, fear and triumph with them."[67] To fully understand historic figures was to empathize with them in moments of triumph and tragedy, in public and in private; history "pictures the cabinet and field, [but] it should not forget the Home. While it delineates the great career of ambition, it should not neglect the quiet but still impressive walk of social life."[68] Here, then, Lippard united history and legend in a way that emotionally moved and simultaneously informed. Legend reanimated history, and gave its political significance a personal potency, thereby inviting the reader to view momentous events from within the interior lives of historical figures. "A legend ... is a history in its details and delicate tints, with the bloom and dew yet fresh upon it ... in the language of passion, of poetry ...!"[69]

Legend also had the ability to elevate mankind and perpetuate symbols of the triumph of good over evil. In *Adonai: The Pilgrim of Eternity* (1851), for example, Lippard wrote, "History ... correctly interpreted ... is the perpetual Revelation of Almighty God."[70] Lippard thus framed history as the battle between the transcendent forces of good and evil. The battle for

Mexico became for Lippard a battle for the glory of God, a "new crusade."[71] Democracy and manifest destiny, therefore, were the handmaidens of God's will, a sentiment echoed in this era in publications like John O'Sullivan's *Democratic Review*.[72]

Lippard similarly utilized legend to work toward social reform and justify the rituals of the secret society he created, the Brotherhood of the Union. The elaborate rites and titles of the organization's leaders evoked both a sense of history and legend. Officers of the Brotherhood had "ritual paraphernalia" and were awarded titles such as Supreme Washington, Supreme Jefferson, and Supreme Franklin.[73] Lippard, himself, was elected the Supreme Washington in 1850, a post he held for the rest of his life. This legend-making proved symptomatic of his desire to intimately connect people to the Revolution, the physical manifestation of God's will to reform the world in democratic and fraternal terms. As Lippard proclaimed, legendary heroes "made our hearts feel warm—they nerved our arms for battle! When we read of the old times of our Flag, we swore in our hearts, never to disgrace it!"[74] With his Brotherhood, Lippard built an organization that sought "great Reform"[75] by working within a framework that connected regular people to the founding generation. After the swift growth of the Brotherhood, he slowed his creation of literary legends and spent increasing amounts of time furthering the organization, whose survival long beyond his lifetime proved the enduring power of Lippard's application of the legend to everyday life.

George Lippard published *Legends of Mexico* during the war it portrayed, and thereby invited his readers to engage legendary historical events as they unfolded before their eyes. Readers studied the daily press for news from the front while simultaneously retreating into *Legends of Mexico*, published serially in the spring of 1847, to know these events in more

71 1.
72 For more on the theory of collective symbols and the role of imagined conceptions of community, see, Benedict Anderson, *Imagined Communities: Reflections on the Origin and Spread of Nationalism* (London: Verso, 1991).
73 Reynolds, *George Lippard*, 20.
74 George Lippard, *The Legends of the American Revolution "1776," or Washington and His Generals* (Philadelphia: T.B. Peterson, 1876), 525.
75 69.

76 Streeby, *American Sensations,* 40.

77 For a thorough account and example of the increasing sensationalization of the press throughout the 1830s and 1840s, see Patricia Cline Cohen, *The Murder of Helen Jewett: The Life and Death of a Prostitute in Nineteenth-Century New York* (New York: Vintage Books, 1999).

emotionally intense and personal terms.[76] These two mediums, news and legend, proved mutually reaffirming in this regard.[77] Through "legend," Lippard grafted fantasy to fact and created a sentimental enhancement of reality itself, where readers transported themselves into the past by feeling very close to it.

Gender Legends

An introduction to the various notions of masculinity and femininity during the antebellum period helps us understand the stock gender roles in *Legends of Mexico*. These roles were largely shaped by the changing economic, political, social, and cultural conditions during the time period. The United States witnessed the beginnings of the collapse of the artisan system and the rise of a wage economy of workers and consumers. These changes stimulated the rise of the myth of the self-made man and the advent of a concurrent feminine ideal, the dutiful and domestic wife.

In *Legends of Mexico,* George Lippard echoed contemporary culture regarding supposedly stable masculine and feminine types and grounded them in a sentimentalized conception of the past. This sentimental myth wrapped masculinity in mythical patriotic machismo and imagined the Founding Fathers, especially George Washington, as the pinnacle of these ideals. Femininity, on the other hand, was recalled through contemporary ideals of "true" womanhood, an unchanging category that stabilized popular conceptions of femininity during a period of flux. He thereby justified contemporary gender roles with an appeal to the past. In *Legends of Mexico,* Lippard applied these stock roles to his characters, and, in turn, purveyed idealized men and women as a way to present gender stability in the face of growing public unease. In effect, he sought to soothe anxieties about gender roles by portraying identifiable masculine and feminine types that expressed—through a patriotic war far from home—simple and clearly demarcated roles for men and women.

Changes in the American economy in the first half of the nineteenth century fostered anxieties about what it meant to be a man or a woman. The antebellum period witnessed the transformation of the artisan system that provided young men with skills that allowed them entry into the world of labor, whereby a willing master craftsman took on a young apprentice to teach him a particular trade or a father passed his economic status to his son. Under the perfect version of this system, a young man lived in the home where he trained for his trade, ate at the table of a master craftsman, prayed with the family, and, ideally, under paternal tutelage, became a moral and productive citizen. As the United States moved toward industrialization and as technological advancements took hold, this paternalistic system broke down, and a masculine ideal of a more "[m]obile, competitive, aggressive in business … Self-Made Man" became the ideal, which in turn bred individuals who were "also temperamentally restless, chronically insecure, and desperate to achieve a solid grounding for a masculine identity."[78]

Many historians have explored how these changes shaped gender roles during this period. Mary Ryan argues that the ideal of success in the antebellum middle-class family lay with the father who went away to work and a mother whose work was narrowed to the household and child rearing. Children gained an education disconnected from the household economy, and the partnership between men and women demanded separate responsibilities. For women, femininity became increasingly grounded in the American home, whereas for men, work increasingly happened elsewhere.[79]

However, these binary roles never proved so easily distinct. Jane H. Pease and William H. Pease, for example, claim that women's roles covered

78 Michael S. Kimmel, *Manhood in America: A Cultural History* (New York: Oxford University Press, 2006), 13.
79 Mary P. Ryan, *Cradle of the Middle Class: The Family in Oneida County, New York, 1790–1865* (New York: Cambridge University Press, 1981).

80 Jane H. Pease and William H. Pease, *Ladies, Women, and Wenches: Choice and Constraint in Antebellum Charleston and Boston* (Chapel Hill: The University of North Carolina Press, 1990).

81 Christine Stansell, *City of Women: Sex and Class in New York, 1789–1860* (Urbana: University of Illinois Press, 1987).

82 Elaine Frantz Parsons, *Manhood Lost: Fallen Drunkards and Redeeming Women in the Nineteenth-Century United States* (Baltimore: The Johns Hopkins University Press, 2003), 9.

83 Elliot J. Gorn, *The Manly Art: Bare-Knuckle Prize Fighting in America* (Ithaca: Cornell University Press, 1986), 132, 133.

a spectrum of activities and that women were not restricted to a life that bonded them to their husband and children.[80] Likewise, Christine Stansell claims that working-class women maintained personal agency by pushing against the role of a passive wife.[81] Elaine Frantz Parson also demonstrates how the category of the profligate male became a symbol for fallen society, where "men became dependents and women were forced to take on traditionally male roles."[82] As alcohol consumption rose in the nineteenth century, women-in-public often assumed the role of reformer and savior of debauched masculinity, thereby transforming the role of nurturing homemaker to that of moral arbiter for society overall.

While women during this period claimed certain public spaces for themselves, the growth of a consumer ethos increasingly provided both men and women with the ability to self-define through public consumption. Historian Elliot J. Gorn examines how billiard halls, brothels, theaters, bars, and gambling halls increasingly served as exclusively masculine spaces actively contrasted with the feminized home, itself a place for conspicuous consumption. According to Gorn, middle class men experienced these masculinized spaces either by defining themselves in opposition to them, through the rituals of family devotion, or by embracing them, as adventurers and thrill-seekers through vice. Most men lived somewhere in the middle, practicing self-restraint while occasionally dabbling in the illicit.[83] This middle position, where men were sometime tourists in exclusively masculine spaces, allowed for an easy reaffirmation of masculinity, especially for those who could not claim to be "self-made" economically. In this light, Amy Greenberg argues that there were two competing masculine tropes during this period: restrained manhood, which was tied to success in business and an adherence to religious values and morals, and martial manhood, which glorified violence, strength, chivalry, and aggression and rejected the "moral standards that guided restrained men."[84] These two competing identities became a simplistic spectrum that men negotiated daily, defining themselves within it as a situation required. Michael Kimmel sums this up succinctly: "Masculinism [was] ... resistance to femininity" in pursuit of self-definition.[85] Manhood, therefore, could be achieved only when proved and validated in the eyes of other men.

The heroic characters in *Legends of Mexico* were overwhelmingly white males who, in their quest for territory, asserted their white masculinity over darker peoples. Lippard's men are inheritors of the heroes who fought for American independence, thereby making the masculine ideals of his generation the timeless guardians of American freedom. In this regard, his sympathetic portrayal of heroic white masculinity melded Greenberg's morally "restrained" and "martial" manhood into an ideal American type. Morally righteous, chivalrous, and prone to violence, Lippard's men, far from the domesticity of home, allowed readers to revel in a fantasy that stabilized contemporary conceptions of manhood, where women proved the perfect partners to the patriotic men who fought and died for them. In this context, Lippard's women exuded the ideals of "true womanhood" and exhibited the "four cardinal virtues [of] piety, purity, submissiveness and domesticity."[86] Hispanic women played the role of foil to white womanhood as a conquest for American virility. In Lippard's hands, these undomesticated Hispanic women were naturally drawn to the civilizing influence of American men. He thereby attached contemporary ideas about masculinity and femininity to his characters as a way to reassure his readers of the natural truth of their contemporary conceptions of gender. For them, his gender legends proved truer than fact.

84 Greenberg, *Manifest Manhood and the Antebellum American Empire*, 11, 12.
85 Michael S. Kimmel, "Born to Run: Fantasies of Male Escape from Rip Van Winkle to Robert Bly," *The History of Men: Essays in the History of American and British Masculinities* (New York: State University of New York Press, 2005), 21.
86 Barbara Welter, "The Cult of True Womanhood: 1820–1860," *American Quarterly* 18, no. 2, (1966): 152.

87 9.
88 Robert P. Hay, "George Washington: American Moses," *American Quarterly* 21, no. 4 (1969): 780, 781.
89 Christopher B. Coleman, "George Washington and the West," *Indiana Magazine of History* 28, no. 3 (1932): 164–167; "From George Washington to Richard Henry Lee, 22 August 1785," Founders Online, National Archives, http://founders.archives.gov/documents/Washington/04-03-02-0183; "From George Washington to Henry Knox, 5 December 1784," Founders Online, National Archives, http://founders.archives.gov/documents/Washington/04-02-02-0137; Reginald Horsman, "The Northwest Ordinance and the Shaping of an Expanding Republic," *The Wisconsin Magazine of History* 73, no. 1 (1989): 28–29, 32.

Legends of Manifest Destiny

In Lippard's *Legends of Mexico,* America's continental ambition lay in the nation's origins. To personify this claim, he recycled a legend of Washington he told in earlier works:

> WASHINGTON ... sat in his Camp at Cambridge ... in 1775, his eyes fixed upon the map of the Continent, his finger laid upon Canada, while his unsheathed sword, reached from Labrador to Patagonia. In the silence of night, even as he planned the conquest of Canada, he recognized this great truth—God has given the American Continent to the free.[87]

Like most of Lippard's legends, there is historical precedent here—Washington was in Cambridge in 1775—but surrounding that core was a fantasy that communicated something truer to Lippard than mere historical fact: Washington fought not only for the independence of the thirteen colonies, but for all of the Americas. In this regard, Lippard shaped his legendary Washington to better reflect the values of the 1840s and projected claims of the nation's manifest destiny onto the past, a literary strategy not particular to Lippard during this period.[88] A look at Washington's actual interest in the territories west of the Appalachian Mountains, and those of policy-makers after him, presents a more nuanced story of the changing motives behind American expansion.

In the midst of the American Revolution, George Washington's most immediate fear was that settlers in the west might be drawn away by foreign powers—to Spain or Great Britain—if the territories were not securely tied to the United States through commerce.[89] In this regard, Washington's desire to secure the west proved primarily defensive. In the decade after the Revolution, Thomas Jefferson justified western settlement in similar terms.⁹⁰ While Jefferson did not fear, necessarily, that the territory beyond the Appalachians would become a separate nation—"Whether we remain in one confederacy, or form into Atlantic and Mississippi confederacies, I believe not very important to the happiness of either part."—he fretted that western settlers would turn to foreign powers for access to commercial networks along the Mississippi River and through New Orleans.⁹¹ Many of Washington's and Jefferson's contemporaries were equally concerned about the damage rapid expansion might do to their nascent republic by making these western settlements susceptible to commercial overtures by rival powers in North America.⁹² The chosen remedy was to stave off foreign interference in the west by financing internal improvements, organizing land sales, and constructing plans for the organization of territorial governments, through the Land Ordinances of 1784 and 1785 and the Northwest Ordinance of 1787.⁹³ This was done with the intention of binding these lands to the eastern states through commercial ties while offering an eventual path to statehood and political equality with the original states.⁹⁴ In so doing, the United States began to slowly redefine itself as an expanding republic, rather than independent former colonies.⁹⁵ This newly established principle of creating states out of territory already controlled by the United States abided until the presidency of Thomas Jefferson, who purchased Louisiana from the French. This set the stage for future acquisitions from foreign powers, though under very different circumstances.⁹⁶

Jefferson's initial goal was to purchase either or both New Orleans and the Floridas for incorporation into the American republic, though he was willing to settle for commercial access to New Orleans.⁹⁷ In the end, he gained more than intended by purchasing the whole of the Louisiana

90 Bernard W. Sheehan, "Jefferson's 'Empire for Liberty,'" *Indiana Magazine of History* 100 (December 2004): 349; Joseph J. Ellis, *His Excellency: George Washington* (New York: Alfred A. Knopf, 2005), 53–56, 154–157, 209.

91 Sheehan, "Jefferson's 'Empire for Liberty,'" 350, 352–353; "From Thomas Jefferson to Joseph Priestley, 29 January 1804," Founders Online, National Archives, http://founders.archives.gov/documents/Jefferson/01-42-02-0322.

92 Peter S. Onuf, "Liberty, Development, and Union: Visions of the West in the 1780s," *The William and Mary Quarterly* 43, no. 2 (1986): 179–183, 204–207.

93 "From George Washington to Thomas Jefferson, 29 March 1784," Founders Online, National Archives, http://founders.archives.gov/documents/Washington/04-01-02-0179; Horsman, "The Northwest Ordinance," 30–32; Lyon Rathbun, "The Debate over Annexing Texas and the Emergence of Manifest Destiny," *Rhetoric and Public Affairs* 4, no. 3 (2001): 459–462; Albert Shaw, "The Monroe Doctrine and the Evolution of Democracy," *Proceedings of the Academy of Political Science in the City of New York* 7, no. 2 (1917): 280.

94 Coleman, "George Washington and the West," 153–154, 156–159; William Deverell and Anne Hyde, *Shaped by the West, Volume 1: A History of North America to 1877* (Oakland, California: University of California Press, 2018), 131, 137–139; Ellis, *His Excellency: George Washington,* 53–56, 154–157; Horsman, "The Northwest Ordinance," 26–27, 30, 32; Frederick Merk, *Manifest Destiny and Mission in America: A Reinterpretation* (New York: Vintage Books, 1966), 5–6.

95 Onuf, "Liberty, Development, and Union," 180–182, 200, 207–209.

96 Merk, *Manifest Destiny,* 6–8; Onuf, "Liberty, Development, and Union," 211–213; Sheehan, "Jefferson's 'Empire for Liberty,'" 352, 359–360.

97 Ibid., 350.

98 Merk, *Manifest Destiny,* 8–10; Sheehan, "Jefferson's 'Empire for Liberty,'" 354.

99 Amy S. Greenberg, *Manifest Destiny and American Territorial Expansion: A Brief History with Documents* (Boston: Bedford/St. Martin's, 2011), 2–5.

100 Merk, *Manifest Destiny,* 8; "From Thomas Jefferson to Archibald Stuart, 25 January 1786," Founders Online, National Archives, http://founders.archives.gov/documents/Jefferson/01-09-02-0192. Filibustering expeditions, such as with William Walker and his multiple failed efforts, were privately funded and officially unsupported, if not outright opposed, by the United States government. Tom Chaffin, "'Sons of Washington': Narciso López, Filibustering, and U.S. Nationalism, 1848–1851," *Journal of the Early Republic* 15, no. 1 (1995): 79–82; Greenberg, *Manifest Destiny and American Territorial Expansion,* 26–27; Greenberg, *Manifest Manhood and the Antebellum American Empire,* 32–33, 41–42, 54, 96, 135–137; Robert E. May, "Young American Males and Filibustering in the Age of Manifest Destiny: The United States Army as a Cultural Mirror," *The Journal of American History* 78, no. 3 (1991): 857–858, 861, 864–870.

101 Sheehan, "Jefferson's 'Empire for Liberty,'" 354; Bradford Perkins, *The Cambridge History of American Foreign Relations: Volume 1, The Creation of a Republican Empire* (Cambridge: Cambridge University Press, 1993), 171–172.

102 "From Thomas Jefferson to George Rogers Clark, 25 December 1780," Founders Online, National Archives, http://founders.archives.gov/documents/Jefferson/01-04-02-0295; "Thomas Jefferson to James Madison, 27 April 1809," Founders Online, National Archives, http://founders.archives.gov/documents/Jefferson/03-01-02-0140; John O'Sullivan, "The Great Nation of Futurity," 427; Shaw, "The Monroe Doctrine," 280–282.

territory from France, which doubled the size of the nation. As Jefferson came to realize how large the United States had become, he expressed the opinion that a strong federal authority could not extend beyond the Rocky Mountains, as the distance was too great. Any relationship between the United States and the eventual settlements established on the western edge of the continent would follow the natural order as Jefferson understood it—demonstrated in the United States' own history—by becoming independent republics which bore resemblance to the Union without being under its authority.[98]

Despite the addition of such a large tract of land by the Jefferson administration, there was no thoroughgoing plan to reach across the rest of continent. The territorial debate during this period dealt primarily with how to manage the unsettled lands already in hand.[99] Later, the War of 1812 disabused the U.S. of any notion of bringing English-speaking Canada into the Union and, while Central and South America were discussed as fertile ground for emigration and perhaps as future receptacles of republican ideals, there was little attempt to add them to the Union by U.S. policymakers.[100]

Nevertheless, Jefferson "expected that American settlers, nurtured in the principles of republican society, would move west and recreate there the enlightened system that their ancestors had established in the New World."[101] While he used the phrase "empire of liberty" in discussing the settling of the continent, his meaning was more akin to the *Democratic Review*'s "The Great Nation of Futurity," which described a future "Union of many Republics, comprising hundreds of happy millions, calling, owning no man master, but governed by God's natural and moral law of equality, the law of brotherhood."[102] The earliest discussions of national expansion, therefore, were ideological and abstract, predicting an inexorable tide of republicanism that would spread liberty—and commerce—across the hemisphere, even the world.[103]

By contrast, the territorial acquisitions of the early nineteenth century, including the Louisiana Purchase, were "haphazard" and unplanned.[104] Such was the case of Spanish Florida, which was taken by the U.S. piece by piece, until the whole of Florida was purchased through the Adams-Onís Treaty. This result was, in part, achieved by the pressure put upon Spain by Andrew Jackson's invasion and occupation of the territory in a military campaign that was conducted, supposedly, to recapture runaway slaves but actually amounted to a protracted series of land grabs.[105] This method of statecraft at the expense of foreign governments and justified by dubious grievances marked a turn toward a more aggressive expansionism, one that justified invasion of sovereign states in the name of American interests and was exemplified in the U.S.-Mexico War.

In 1845, the *Democratic Review* published an article entitled "Annexation" in support of the annexation of the Republic of Texas as the twenty-eighth state.[106] The article's appeal to Providence and the United States' manifest destiny to possess the entire continent was a subtle but important difference from Jefferson's naturalistic and, in theory, peaceful process. A more salient rationale for expansion was the fear that, should the United States not take western lands such as Texas or Oregon, European powers would.[107] In essence, this shifting ideology of expansion echoed the fears of Washington and Jefferson regarding the West but leavened their limited expansionism with an overt belief in white supremacy and religious zeal. This change marked the rising confidence in the nation's power over the as-yet unconquered continent.

While the rapid and extralegal migration of American citizens into the Trans-Appalachian West prompted concerns among the first generation of

---

103 "From Thomas Jefferson to William Ludlow, 6 September 1824," Founders Online, National Archives, http://founders.archives.gov/documents/Jefferson/98-01-02-4523; "From George Washington to The States, 8 June 1783," Founders Online, National Archives, http://founders.archives.gov/documents/Washington/99-01-02-11404; Greenberg, *Manifest Destiny and American Territorial Expansion*, 20.

104 Greenberg, *Manifest Destiny and American Territorial Expansion*, 8, 14.

105 William S. Belko, "The Origins of the Monroe Doctrine Revisited: The Madison Administration, the West Florida Revolt, and the No Transfer Policy," *The Florida Historical Quarterly* 90 (2011): 174–178, 184–187; Howe, *What Hath God Wrought*, 28, 97–102, 108–111; William Nester, *Age of Jackson and the Art of American Power, 1815–1848: The Art of American Power During the Early Republic* (Dulles: Potomac Books Inc., 2013), 51–57; Rathbun, "The Debate over Annexing Texas," 462–463.

106 John O'Sullivan, "Annexation," 5–6, 9–10.

107 Perkins, *The Cambridge History of American Foreign Relations: Volume 1*, 180; Belko, "The Origins of the Monroe Doctrine Revisited," 157–158, 174–178, 184–187; Harlan Hague, "James K. Polk and the Expansionist Spirit," *Journal of the West* 31, no. 2 (1992): 52.

108 Horsman, "The Northwest Ordinance," 2.
109 Belko, "The Origins of the Monroe Doctrine Revisited," 157–158.
110 Greenberg, *Manifest Destiny and American Territorial Expansion*, 20; Timothy J. Henderson, *A Glorious Defeat: Mexico and Its War with the United States* (New York: Hill and Wang, 2007), 38–39, 41, 54–59; Perkins, *The Cambridge History of American Foreign Relations: Volume 1*, 175–180; Howe, *What Hath God Wrought*, 658–662.
111 Frederick Merk, *Albert Gallatin and the Oregon Problem: A Study in Anglo-American Diplomacy* (Cambridge: Harvard University Press, 1950), 12–13, 70, 84n, 89; Greenberg, *Manifest Destiny and American Territorial Expansion*, 8–10, 20.
112 Edward P. Crapol, "John Tyler and the Pursuit of National Destiny," *Journal of the Early Republic* 17, no. 3 (1997): 477–478, 481–482; Hague, "James K. Polk," 51, 53; Perkins, *The Cambridge History of American Foreign Relations: Volume 1*, 174; Jesse S. Reeves, *American Diplomacy under Tyler and Polk* (Baltimore: The Johns Hopkins Press, 1907), 258.

American leaders, settlement west of the Mississippi inspired expansionist enthusiasm decades later.[108] American migrants in Spanish West Florida, for example, prompted the United States to claim the territory for itself.[109] American migration to Mexico's Tejas resulted in a short war between American settlers and Mexican troops and an independent, but soon to be annexed, Republic of Texas.[110] It seemed that common Americans, in search of land and opportunity in territories outside the United States, were driving American expansionist policy.[111]

Lippard's legend of Washington's sword was intended as an origin story of the national policy of continental expansion. However, U.S. expansion was piecemeal, often led not by the nation's leaders but instead by land-hungry settlers. A consistent policy of expansion was not officially adopted among American leaders until the administrations of Tyler and Polk, both presidents in Lippard's lifetime who were enthusiastic about the United States' destiny in general and its expansion in particular. Polk campaigned in 1844 for the annexation of Texas, while Tyler began the annexation process in his last weeks in office. Both men were also eager to see California fall away from Mexico. They hoped to control the ports along the western coast, which would give the U.S. access to trade in Asia.[112]

Lippard's legend tells us more about his time than Washington's. It was Zachary Taylor who held the sword of continental conquest and fulfilled the nation's manifest destiny. While Lippard wanted Taylor to be Washington and the U.S.-Mexico War to be the culmination of a grand dream of the Founders, it was the insatiable desire of nineteenth-century Americans for more land and the actions of Tyler and Polk that fueled expansion. While Lippard dreamed of a continent of republics, he, in effect, endorsed a continent beholden to one nation's authority.

The U.S.-Mexico War and Its Aftermath

The U.S.-Mexico War began on April 25, 1846, with military activity in the disputed territory between the two nations. Though the last American troops left Mexico on July 15th, 1848, the footprint of the war lingered for decades.[113] In the years preceding the war, Americans resided in Texas as colonists under loose Mexican governance—a relationship that ultimately dissolved following the Texan declaration of independence in 1835 and victory over Mexican troops in 1836.[114]

In 1845, after nine years of failed rule and contention with Mexico, the independent republic of Texas was annexed by the U.S. to general acclaim by the Anglo-Americans who resided there, though no Mexican government recognized the legality of the annexation.[115] Disagreement over the border of the respective nations—the U.S. claimed the Rio Grande as the border while Mexico claimed the Nueces River, about 150 miles to the north—culminated in violence when Polk ordered General Zachary Taylor and his troops into the disputed territory, prompting Mexican forces to cross what the U.S. deemed the American border, kill three American troops, and provide Polk with a justification for war.[116] The Battle of Palo Alto on May 8, 1846, followed immediately by the Battles of Resaca de la Palma on May 9 and Monterrey from September 20 to 24, resulted in a string of decisive American victories.[117] The coverage of these battles in contemporary newspapers and wired by telegraph to the northeastern cities of the U.S. served as Lippard's inspiration for *Legends of Mexico* and lent the foundation upon which the young author built his legend. The remaining major battles of the war coincided with troop movements that progressed further into Mexican territory, including Buena Vista (February 20–24, 1847), Veracruz (March 9–29, 1847), Cerro Gordo (April 18, 1847), Contreras and Churubusco (August 20, 1847),

---

113 Henderson, *A Glorious Defeat*, xv.
114 Ibid., 84–98.
115 See David M. Pletcher, *The Diplomacy of Annexation: Texas, Oregon, and the Mexican War* (Columbia: University of Missouri Press, 1973); Joel H. Silbey, *Storm over Texas: The Annexation Controversy and the Road to Civil War* (Oxford: Oxford University Press, 2005).
116 Richard Griswold del Castillo, *The Treaty of Guadalupe Hidalgo: A Legacy of Conflict* (Norman: University of Oklahoma Press, 1990), 11; Ronald C. Lee, "Justifying Empire: Pericles, Polk, and a Dilemma of Democratic Leadership," *Polity* 34, no. 4 (2002): 517.
117 There were two battles of nearly identical names during the war—the Battle of Monterey occurred in the California territory in July, while the Battle of Monterrey occurred in Mexico in September. Spencer C. Tucker, ed., *The Encyclopedia of the Mexican-American War: A Political, Social, and Military History, Volume I* (Oxford: ABC-CLIO, 2013), 438.

118 Ibid., 126.
119 Appointments of leadership positions during the war were politically motivated and contentious. See John C. Pinheiro, *Manifest Ambition: James K. Polk and Civil-Military Relations during the Mexican War* (Westport: Praeger Security International, 2007).
120 Griswold del Castillo, *The Treaty of Guadalupe Hidalgo*, 7.
121 K. Jack Bauer, *The Mexican War, 1846–1848* (Lincoln: University of Nebraska Press, 1974), 358–370.
122 See Chapter V of *Legends of Mexico*.
123 The total number of Mexican casualties is unknown due to poor record keeping by the Mexican government. Tucker, *Encyclopedia of the Mexican-American War*, 126; Henderson, *A Glorious Defeat*, 179.
124 Bauer, *The Mexican War*, 101.

and Molino del Rey (September 8, 1847).[118] While Taylor gained repute for his leadership during the first half of the war, the second half saw Winfield Scott lead American forces to victory, culminating with his occupation of Mexico City on September 14, 1848.[119]

But conflict was not isolated to the battlefield, as both the U.S. and Mexico experienced internal conflict at home. A legacy of political instability and class warfare followed Mexico into the conflict, as nearly every president elected since independence in 1821 had been overthrown.[120] In the U.S., some, such as the young Whig representative from Illinois, Abraham Lincoln, contended that the war was both unconstitutional and a ploy to expand the institution of slavery westward. Others followed John O'Sullivan's support for the war and hoped for the acquisition of part or all of Mexico at its resolution.[121] Closely following these debates, Lippard included a lengthy annotation in his coverage of the Battle of Resaca de la Palma that described these domestic squabbles.[122]

In total, the United States mobilized 104,556 troops and lost nearly 14,000, of which 87% died from disease. Mexico, by contrast, mobilized 82,000 troops and suffered 5,000 deaths as a direct result of combat and an unknown number of deaths from disease, though estimates range from 25,000 to 50,000.[123] These figures demonstrate in part the military devastation experienced by Mexico, but they do not shed much light on the trauma imparted on the civilian population both during and after the conflict. With the U.S. fighting force predominately comprising untrained volunteers who carried notions of Mexican inferiority into battle, the statistical records of the war elided attacks on the lives and property on Mexican civilians by American soldiers.[124] The Mexican Republic also lost a significant amount of territory in defeat. On February 2, 1848, the United States negotiated the Treaty of Guadalupe Hidalgo with the defeated Mexican government and gained territory comprising what are now the modern states of Texas, Oregon, California, Arizona, Utah and New Mexico, resulting in the greatest expansion of American territory to date.[125]

While the treaty ostensibly ended conflict between the two nations, it also bred internal conflicts in its aftermath. Mexico experienced ongoing political as well as economic instability, with liberals and conservatives deeply divided over whom to blame for the war and its outcome. These factors ultimately culminated in the "War of Reform" (1858–1861) with attendant volatility continuing to the end of the nineteenth century.[126] Mexican citizens who resided in the territory acquired by the U.S. legally became citizens under the conditions of the treaty, but many were denied land rights previously recognized under the Mexican government and suffered *de facto* second-class status and harassment by white settlers.[127]

In the U.S., General Zachary Taylor rode his reputation as the "Hero of Buena Vista" to the White House in 1848, despite the looming issue of the status of slavery in the new territories.[128] While the Compromise of 1850 admitted California as a free state into the Union and abolished the slave trade in Washington D.C., it did not adequately address the issue of slavery in New Mexico and Utah, leaving the debate to future settlers. According to Senator and future U.S. Supreme Court Justice Salmon P. Chase, "The question of slavery in the territories has been avoided. It has not been settled."[129] The question was ultimately settled by civil war.

The decade after the war U.S.-Mexico War was filled with divisions between Americans over the expansion of slavery into the newly acquired territories, coming to a temporary head in 1854 with the Kansas-Nebraska Act, which overturned the free status of territories closed to slavery by the Missouri Compromise and led to open warfare between pro- and anti-slavery forces in the Kansas Territory.[130] In this regard, "Bleeding Kansas"

125 Howe, *What Hath God Wrought*, 805.
126 Henderson, *A Glorious Defeat*, 186.
127 Howe, *What Hath God Wrought*, 810.
128 Ibid., 828.
129 Quoted in William L. Barney, *The Oxford Encyclopedia of the Civil War* (Oxford: Oxford University Press, 2011), 80–81.
130 John R. Wunder and Joann M. Ross, eds., *The Nebraska-Kansas Act of 1854* (Lincoln: University of Nebraska Press, 2008), 1.

proved to be one legacy of the U.S.-Mexico War. The next war fought by the United States proved an ever more bitter legacy. Several of the men who began their military careers in Mexico ended them fighting each other on American soil: for the Confederacy, Jefferson Davis, Robert E. Lee, Pierre Gustave Toutant Beauregard, Braxton Bragg, Thomas "Stonewall" Jackson and James Longstreet; for the Union, Ulysses S. Grant, George McClellan, George Meade, Joe Hooker, and William T. Sherman.[131] In a twist of fate, the skills each of these men honed with each other on the battlefields of Mexico early in their military careers were later used against each other on American soil. What was successful in defending each other in the 1840s proved successful in defeating each other in the 1860s—a legacy that is too often forgotten.

The Legacies of a Legend Manifest

Legends of Mexico is indicative of the ethos of manifest destiny. For individuals like Lippard, America represented the height of human civilization and, therefore, it was America's duty to spread across the continent in order to create republics of freedom. In *Legends of Mexico,* Lippard wrote:

> We are the American People. Our lineage is from that God, who bade us go forth, from the old world, and smiled us into an Empire of Men. Our destiny [is] to possess this Continent, drive from it all shreds of Monarchy, whether British or Spanish or [Portuguese], and on the wrecks of shattered empires, buil[d] the Altar, second to the BROTHERHOOD OF MAN.[132]

In this way, *Legends of Mexico* displayed the U.S.-Mexico War as an extension of the Revolutionary War by using the imagery of "Washington's

---

131 For further information regarding the military influence of the U.S.-Mexico War on the Civil War, see Kevin Dougherty, *Civil War Leadership and Mexican War Experience* (Jackson: University of Mississippi Press, 2007), viii–ix.
132 9.

sword" to connect notions of manifest destiny to the founding of the United States.

After the Civil War, the desire for expansion continued to animate American policymakers. According to Paul Kramer, "[T]he United States in the post-Civil War era was an empire-building nation in which state and settler colonial conquest and the territorializing of the continent were fundamental to an increasingly confident national self-definition."[133] Starting with the 1867 purchase of the Alaska territory from Russia and President Grant's unsuccessful efforts to annex Santo Domingo (the modern day Dominican Republic), the United States pursued expansionist policies into the late nineteenth century in the Spanish-American War (1898), which was justified by President William McKinley and his Assistant Secretary of the Navy Theodore Roosevelt in terms that framed conquest as a benevolent enterprise. While many Americans were uncomfortable that their republic had become an empire, in the aftermath of the Spanish-American War President McKinley declared that "[n]o imperial designs lurk in the American mind. They are alien to American sentiment, thought and purpose."[134] According to Anders Stephanson, American expansion "looked remarkably like European colonialism or imperialism, which was not an idea easily digested in a former colony."[135] This cognitive dissonance led to the creation of a new lexicon to justify conquest. Phrases such as "empire of peace, empire of love, empire of the intellect, empire of liberty [borrowed from Jefferson in a very different context], and other poetic recodings" emulated European claims of benevolence and paternalism.[136] These qualities were justified by America's supposed dedication to liberty, freedom, and republicanism.

The rhetoric of American empire-building during the late nineteenth century turned "colonialism into *tutelage* [and] preparation for republican self-government at some suitable future date."[137] By this argument,

[133] Paul Kramer, "Power and Connection: Imperial Histories of the United States in the World," *American Historical Review* 116, no. 5 (December, 2011): 1371.
[134] William McKinley, *Speeches and Addresses of William McKinley* (New York: Doubleday & McClure Co., 1900), 192.
[135] Anders Stephanson, *Manifest Destiny: American Expansion and the Empire of Right* (New York: Hill and Wang, 1995), 90.
[136] Ibid.
[137] Ibid.

conquered peoples, such as the residents of the former Spanish colony of the Philippines, welcomed the opportunity to study democratic government under the direction of the United States. As Senator Albert Beveridge rhetorically asked in 1898, would not the Filipinos "prefer the just, humane, civilizing government of this Republic to the savage, bloody rule of pillage and extortion from which we have rescued them?"[138]

The spread of democracy in this era was carefully managed by the expansionist policies of the American government. Nations such as the Hawaiian Islands in 1898, the Philippines in 1899, and Haiti in 1915 were controlled by the United States for decades. In the case of the Philippines, "[f]or the most part ... Americans ... made it clear in their writings that they did not consider Filipinos ready for independence," even though they appeared "to have placed great importance on *seeming* to consider the possibility."[139] These arrangements allowed the United States to extract resources from these lands as well as to establish strategic military bases without having to settle these countries or bring them into the Union on the model of state-making practiced in the continental United States. Expansion and intervention in sovereign countries was further justified under the 1904 Roosevelt Corollary, whereby, in the event of unsatisfactory foreign governance, "the Monroe Doctrine may force the United States ... in flagrant cases of such wrongdoing or impotence, to the exercise of an international police power."[140]

During both world wars, American policy-makers applied the idea of the United States as the harbinger of democracy to Europe. On the eve of the U.S. entry into World War I, President Woodrow Wilson, echoing O'Sullivan in the *Democratic Review* seventy-five years before, claimed that "the world must be made safe for democracy" to "make the world at last free."[141] Wilson later explicitly quoted O'Sullivan in his 1920 address to

---

138 Albert Beveridge, *The Meaning of the Times: And Other Speeches* (Indianapolis: The Bobbs-Merrill Company, 1908), 49.

139 Megan Elias, "The Palate of Power: Americans, Food and the Philippines after the Spanish-American War," *Material Culture* 46, no. 1 (Spring 2014): 44–57.

140 "Theodore Roosevelt: Fourth Annual Message," The American Presidency Project, University of California Santa Barbara, accessed October 31, 2018, https://www.presidency.ucsb.edu/documents/fourth-annual-message-15.

141 Woodrow Wilson, *Americanism: Woodrow Wilson's Speeches on the War, Why He Made Them, and What They Have Done,* ed. Oliver Marble Gale (Chicago: The Baldwin Syndicate, 1918), 42–43.

Congress, when he described the "purity" and "spiritual power" of democracy: "It is surely the manifest destiny of the United States to lead in the attempt to make this spirit prevail."[142]

The United States' refusal to join the League of Nations, the "isolationist" policies of the 1920s, and the economic problems caused by the Great Depression in the 1930s all contributed to America's focus on domestic policy in the post-World War I period. This ostensibly "isolationist" period lasted until the rise of Nazi Germany and Imperial Japan in the 1930s and the return of world war in the 1940s. The onset of World War II prompted President Franklin Roosevelt to make his "Four Freedoms" speech in 1941, in which he described America's role in protecting its democratic allies and called for an "[a]rmed defense of democratic existence."[143] After elaborating on the potential threats to the United States, Roosevelt argued for American intervention by claiming that "the future of all the American Republics is today in serious danger."[144] He concluded by claiming that since America's inception, it had been "engaged ... in a perpetual peaceful revolution," since "[t]he world order which we seek is the cooperation of free countries, working together in a friendly, civilized society."[145] The "world order" Roosevelt described closely mirrored O'Sullivan's own, as both envisioned a future of a "Union of many Republics, comprising hundreds of happy millions."[146]

At the end of each world war, the United States led the international community in the creation of regulatory organizations that ideally had the power to peacefully resolve future conflicts. The first attempt to actualize this ideal, at the end of World War I, led to the creation of the League of Nations. Its mission sought "a system of collective security [by] states [that] were democratic in their internal form of government, ... made up of people who had implicitly or explicitly exercised the principle of self-determination."[147] While the League proved to be ineffective, its mission

142 Woodrow Wilson, *A Compilation of the Messages and Papers of the Presidents, Volume 1: Supplement to the Messages and Papers of the Presidents covering the second term of Woodrow Wilson, March 4, 1917, to March 4, 1921* (Bureau of National Literature, Inc., 1921), 8882.
143 "Franklin D. Roosevelt, 1941 State Of The Union Address 'The Four Freedoms' (6 January 1941)," Voices of Democracy: The U.S Oratory Project, University of Maryland, accessed October 29, 2018, http://voicesofdemocracy.umd.edu/fdr-the-four-freedoms-speech-text/.
144 Ibid.
145 Ibid.
146 John O'Sullivan, "The Great Nation of Futurity," 426–430.
147 Paul Taylor and A.J.R. Groom, *The United Nations at the Millennium: The Principal Organs* (London: Continuum, 2000), 7.

formed the basis of the United Nations. One significant change to this revised version of the League allowed the "responsibility for action to protect international security [to be] given to the Security Council [of which the United States was a permanent member], and is not attached equally to all states."[148] Unlike with the League of Nations, the United States took on a leadership role in this global organization devoted to spreading democracy and preventing another world war.[149]

After World War II, U.S. policymakers perceived a new international threat to democracy stemming from the Soviet Union. George Kennan's proposal to contain communism, coupled with President Harry Truman's doctrine that the U.S. would intervene in other nations for the sake of democracy, shaped American foreign policy until the end of the Cold War. In pursuit of this end, the U.S. sent troops to nations in Asia, Central and South America, and Africa for two generations and often supported anti-communist governments whose devotion to democratic practices were weak at best. Specific instances of this intervention include the Korean War, the Vietnam War, and U.S. support for the Taliban during the Soviet invasion of Afghanistan.

With the fall of the Soviet Union and the end of the Cold War in 1989, American expansionist ideology evolved, justified with the language of democracy, as "American leaders chose not to conceive of security in the strict sense of territorial integrity, political autonomy, and economic viability, but in the broader sense of a congenial world filled with ideological kindred devoted to optimizing economic exchange and resolving disputes through the rule of law."[150] U.S. policymakers equated the spread of democracy with national security, since "if other countries are given a fair chance, American exceptionalism should evolve into universal Americanism, or at least Western liberal democracy of some sort in tune with the United States."[151]

---

148 Ibid.
149 President Wilson lobbied for the United States to become a member of the League of Nations, but Congress refused.
150 Richard K. Betts, "From Cold War to Hot Peace: The Habit of American Force," *Political Science Quarterly* 127, no. 3 (2012): 355.
151 Ibid., 358–359.

As the nation moved into the twenty-first century, the "peaceful" idea of expansion was challenged by international terrorism and the rise of rival powers like China and Russia, whose devotion to democracy fell short of American democratic rhetoric. With the Global War on Terror at the forefront of national domestic and foreign policies, the notion of expansion, in the name of democracy, was again repackaged to fit contemporary international politics. The invasion of Iraq, under the pretense of finding and stopping the production of weapons of mass destruction, presented U.S. policy makers with an opportunity to rebuild Iraq on the model of Western democracy. President George W. Bush advocated a "Freedom Agenda"[152] that sought to spread democracy throughout the Middle East. According to Bruce Gilley, the Bush administration attempted to accomplish this goal by "building functioning democracies in Afghanistan and Iraq as part of the U.S. occupations of those countries."[153] According to this new ideal of a world comprising western-style democracies, regime change in Iraq was to "produce diffusion effects to the region."[154] Indeed, during a speech in 2003, President Bush proclaimed, "The establishment of a free Iraq at the heart of the Middle East will be a watershed event in the global democratic revolution."[155]

While American expansionism has evolved in practice since Lippard's day, the democratic rhetoric that supports it has remained surprisingly stable. Its effects have shaped American policy for over 150 years, even as resistance—from Whigs like Abraham Lincoln, from the Anti-Imperialist League during the Spanish-American War, through protests during the Vietnam War, and in the disillusion following the prolonged Iraq War—challenged the assumptions of American expansionist rhetoric. In this regard, Lippard's impassioned call to arms leaves us with a mixed legacy.

152 According to Bruce Gilley, the term "Freedom Agenda" was created by the Bush administration following President Bush's 2003 speech at a National Endowment for Democracy event. Bruce Gilley, "Did Bush Democratize the Middle East? The Effects of External-Internal Linkages," *Political Science Quarterly* 128, no. 4 (2013): 659.
153 Ibid., 662.
154 Ibid., 659.
155 "President Bush Discusses Freedom in Iraq and Middle East: Remarks by the President at the 20th Anniversary of the National Endowment for Democracy United States Chamber of Commerce," White House Archives, last modified November 6, 2003, https://georgewbush-whitehouse.archives.gov/news/releases/2003/11/20031106-2.html.

Notes on the Text

> "An historical methods seminar that required completion of a group of edited documents ... would produce better historians and better editors."
>
> —Charles T. Cullen, "Principles of Annotating in Editing Historical Documents; or, How to Avoid Breaking the Butterfly on the Wheel of Scholarship." (1981)

Students at Southern Illinois University Edwardsville introduced and annotated this edition of *Legends of Mexico* in a course entitled "History of American Ideas." Students at Hastings College published this edition in a course entitled "Book Production." Jason Stacy (Southern Illinois University Edwardsville) and Patricia Oman and Bruce Batterson (Hastings College) taught these courses respectively.

Legends of Mexico first appeared serially in spring of 1847 in two Philadelphia newspapers, *Scott's Weekly* and the *Saturday Courier,* and was published as a book by T.B. Peterson in August 1847. An expanded version, published in 1849 by J.S. Pratt, added a section entitled "Anecdotes of Old 'Rough and Ready,'" largely taken from contemporary newspapers. Since the 1849 edition of *Legends of Mexico* contains so much text from sources other than George Lippard, we chose the 1847 Peterson edition to serve as our copy-text for this annotated version of the book.

In this edition, we have sought a balance between fidelity to the 1847 edition with readability. Throughout, we note variant spellings of common words and silently revise likely compositor errors of punctuation and spelling.

Acknowledgments

Thanks to Southern Illinois University Edwardsville's College of Arts and Sciences, the Department of Historical Studies, and especially the Excellence in Undergraduate Education program for supporting our work. We are also grateful to Hastings College Press for making a beautiful book in record time.

And thanks to our families, who make the good we do possible.

I

The Crusade of the Nineteenth Century

"Ho! for the New Crusade!"

It was in the spring of 1846, that this cry, thundering from twenty-nine states, aroused a People into arms, and startled Europe, its Kings and Slaves, into shuddering awe.

It was in the dawn of the year, when the blossoms of spring were upon the trees, and the Promise of a golden harvest on the fields, that a fiery blast came from the far south, scattering the blossoms of battle over the hills of our land, and darkening the sky with clouds of lurid grandeur—clouds that gave Promise of a harvest of blood.

In the spring of 1846, from the distant south, there came echoing in terrible chorus, a Cry, a Groan, a Rumor! That Cry, the earnest voice of two thousand brave men, gathered beneath the Banner of the stars in a far land, encompassed by their foes, with nothing but a bloody vision of Massacre before their eyes. And the Cry, wrung from two thousand manly hearts, said the People of the Union.—'We are in danger, but the Banner of the Stars floats above us. An army, twice our number surrounds us, Assassins hung like vultures, in the shadows of our camp, a Plague broods in the poisonous air, of the swamp and chaparral.[1] Come—help us—fight with us! Or if you cannot fight, Come, and behold us die, for the flag of Washington!'

That groan! It was the incoherent yell, of the first American soldier, who with the knife in his back, and the hot blood gurgling from his throat, fell at the Assassin's feet on the shores of Rio Grande.[2]

Chapter I

1. During the U.S.-Mexico War, the term "chaparral" became widely used. A contemporary source describes chaparral as "a series of thickets of various sizes, from one hundred yards to a mile ... with bushes and briars, all covered with thorns, and so closely entwined together to prevent the passage of anything larger through than a wolf or hare." John Russell Bartlett, *Dictionary of Americanisms: A Glossary of Words and Phrases, Usually Regarded as Peculiar to the United States* (New York: Bartlett and Welford, 1848), 71.

2. Before the U.S.-Mexico War, the exact border between the two countries was disputed. Expansionists in the United States claimed the boundary was at the Rio Grande. In 1836, the Treaties of Velasco signed by detained Mexican President Antonio López de Santa Anna (1794–1876) and a Texas delegation marked the boundary as the Rio Grande. The Mexican government never ratified the agreement and claimed the boundary was still at the Nueces River. This difference eventually sparked conflict between the two nations. Daniel Walker Howe, *What Hath God Wrought: The Transformation of America, 1815–1848* (New York: Oxford University Press, 2007), 667–69.

The Rumor! Like the hurricane of the tropics it came. First, a small cloud in a serene sky, far on the horizon it was seen, and no one wondered to behold it. Then darkening up the zenith, it shut the southern sky in a wall of ebony, and flashed its quivering lightnings far over the snow mountains of the north. And it rolled on, that brooding Rumor, and it gathered, and it grew, until its shadow darkened the Nation, and its thunder and lightning spoke to the hearts of fifteen millions people.

For that Rumor spoke of a battle, fought by American soldiers, amid the sands and thorns of the hot chaparral; it spoke of hideous charges, made through the darkness of yawning ravines, by men heroic to despair; it spoke of a contest, lengthening its bloody trail over the course of two long days; of a brave foe, fighting while there was a hope, and then crowding in heaps of wounded, through the lone desert, and choking the calm river with their mangled dead.

As thunder at once, convulses and purifies the air, so that Rumor did its sudden and tempestuous work, in every American heart. At once, from the People of twenty-nine states, quivered the Cry—

"To Arms! Ho! for the new crusade!"

Never since the days of Washington, had an excitement, so wild and universal, thrilled in the souls of freemen. From the mountains of Maine—they are yonder, rising ruggedly in their stern grandeur, with snowy mantles, bound about their granite brows—to the prairies of the Texas—blossoming for hundreds of miles, a wilderness of flowers—that cry startled a People into action, and sent the battle-throbs palpitating through fifteen millions hearts.

Long after we are dead, History will tell the children of ages yet to come, how the hosts gathered for the Crusade, in the year 1846.

From the mountain gorges of the north, hardy birds of freemen took their way, turning their faces to the south, and shouting—Mexico! In the great cities, immense crowds assembled, listening in stern silence, to the stories of that far-off land, with its luxuriant fruits, its plains of flowers, its magnificent mountains overshadowing calm lakes and golden cities, and then the cry rung from ten thousand throats—Mexico! The farmhouses of the land, thrilled with the word. Yes, the children of Revolutionary veterans, took the rifle of '76 from its resting place, over the hearth, and examined its lock, by the light of the setting sun, and ere another dawn, were on their way to the south, shouting as they extended their hands toward the unseen land—"Mexico!"

Even now I see the panorama of that wild excitement spread varied and bewildering before me. I see the workshop, give forth its hardy Mechanic—I see, the sturdy mountaineer, come from his gorge—the embrowned farmer from his fields—the pale student from his desk—and all join the army of the New Crusade, and pour with arms glittering and banners waving upon the plains of Mexico.

The world beheld the sight and wondered. Old Germany, festering under her chains, looked up in awe, at this strange spectacle—*an every day people suddenly transformed into a disciplined army*.³ France, saw it too, and sighed as she turned her eyes to the grave of Napoleon.⁴ But England, hypocritical and ferocious, at once the fox and the hyena, crouching on her trophies,—the skulls of Irish starvation⁵ and the corses⁶ of Hindoo Massacre⁷—England, whom we hurled from our shores in the Revolution, and chased, ignominiously from our seas, in the second war,⁸ England, that Carthage of Modern History,⁹ brutal in her revenge and Satanic in her lust for human flesh, behold the American People, in arms, with trembling, and recognized their victorious march to the south, with niggardly¹⁰ praise.

It must be confessed that the great national excitement of 1846, this transformation of a plain working people, into a formidable, yes, an

3   Lippard refers to the German Confederation, a loose grouping of Germanic states composed largely of the former Holy Roman Empire. In 1848–1849, France and the Germanic states were rocked by a series of democratic revolutions. The modern state of Germany was formed in 1871.
4   Napoleon Bonaparte (1769–1821), French general and later emperor who reigned from 1804 to 1814. He returned to power in 1815 before being defeated at Waterloo in Belgium in June, 1815.
5   Starting in 1845, Ireland suffered years of severe famine brought on by a potato blight. It was a common belief among anti-British groups that the British exacerbated the effects of the famine.
6   A contemporary source defines "corse" as "[a] corpse; the dead body of a human being." Noah Webster, *An American Dictionary of the English Language: Exhibiting the Origin, Orthography, Pronunciation, and Definitions of Words* (New York: Harper & Brothers, 1844), 196.
7   Between 1845 and 1846, the British fought with the Sikh Empire known as the First Anglo-Sikh War. Tensions and conflict eventually culminated with the bloody Sepoy Rebellion of 1857–1858.
8   Lippard refers to the War of 1812 between Great Britain and the United States between 1812 and 1815.
9   The Roman Republic and Carthage fought a series of conflicts known as the Punic Wars. In the 2nd Punic War, the Carthaginian general Hannibal (247 BCE–ca. 183–181 BCE) invaded the Italian Peninsula and threatened Rome. Here Lippard compares the British to Carthage and the United States to the Roman Republic.
10 A contemporary source defines "niggardly" as "[m]eanly covetous or avaricious; sordidly parsimonious; extremely sparing of expense." Webster, *An American Dictionary*, 556.

unconquered army, struck the tyrants of the old world with awe. The Man who sits upon the Russian throne, worshipped as a God, and yet never for one moment secure from the assassin's steel, beheld the wondrous sight, and reviewed his armies of slaves, with new anxiety, asking from his satraps[11] an explanation of that magic word—"THE PEOPLE!"

And while the world wondered, the "PEOPLE" of America rushed to arms, and marched by tens and twenties, by hundreds and thousands, by companies, by legions, by armies, to that golden land, which rose to their vision, rich with the grandeur of past ages.

Standing on the mountain tops, the Crusaders of the Nineteenth Century beheld it—that golden and bloody land of Mexico.

A land rich in the productions of every clime, where the fruits are more luxuriant, the flowers more rain-bow like in their dazzling dies, the birds more radiant in their plumage, than in any other land on the wide earth of God. A land where monuments arise, mysterious and awful, with the history and religion, of those solemn ages which melt away in the abyss of time. A land, where every stone bears some tokens of the lost nations and the dead people of ten thousand years.

A land, where in the course of forty-eight hours, you can ascend from the hot plains of the tropics, festering with plague, to the mild clime of eternal spring, strewn with the fruits of the temperate zone; to the snowclad mountains, frozen as with the ice of the Polar waste, and with the volcanoes throbbing with their breasts, like hearts of fire, beneath shrubs of snow! A land, no less beautiful with its flower-framed lakes, than magnificent with its cathedrals, with images and shrines of solid gold, no less gorgeous with its panorama of mountain, pyramid and valley, than bewildering with its City of Cortes and Montezuma,[12] that dream of gold and blood, which men call—Mexico.

---

11 A contemporary source defines "satrap" as "In *Persia*, an admiral; *more generally*, the governor of a province." Webster, *An American Dictionary*, 723. Lippard uses this term to exemplify Russian despotism.

12 Lippard refers to Mexico City, the capital of Mexico. In his conquest of the Aztecs, Hernán Cortés (1485–1547) destroyed Tenochtitlan and captured the Aztec leader Montezuma II (1466–1520). Mexico City was built on the ruins of Tenochtitlan.

"Ho! for the new crusade!"

Yes, against this land, so burdened with awful memories, the American People, marched in deadly and determined crusade.

Why was this?

Because the infant Texas had felt the rude grip of Mexican Massacre? Because the homes of that virgin soil, had been desolated, the men butchered and the women dishonored, by the hordes of military chieftains, trained to kill from childhood, and eager to kill, for so much per day?

Why this Crusade?

Was it because the Alamo, still cried out for vengeance?[13] That gory Alamo which one day, dripped on its stones and flowers and grass with the blood of five hundred mangled bodies—the bodies of brave Texians cut down by Mexican bayonets and pierced by Mexican balls, and hacked by Mexican knives?

Why this Crusade?

Was it because the American People, having borne for a series of years, the insults and outrages of Mexican Military despots,[14] and seen their brothers in Texas, butchered like dogs, at last resolved, to bear insult and outrage no longer, at last, determined to take from the Tomb of Washington the Banner of the Stars, and swore by his Ghost, never to stay their efforts, until it floated over the City of Mexico!

These are some of the reasons of this new crusade, but not all. Here is the truth of the matter—

From the dark cloud of battle was stretched forth the hand of Almighty God, and even from the shock of carnage, an awful voice spoke out: 'I speak to Man in the thunder storm, I speak to him, in the Plague. Now, I speak to him, in the breath of war, and write my lessons in the blackness of the battle-field.'

13 During the War for Texas Independence between Texans and the Mexican government in 1836, the Texan defenders were defeated by the Mexican Army under General Antonio López de Santa Anna.

14 President James K. Polk (1795–1849) sent John Slidell (1793–1871) in 1845 as a minister to negotiate with the Mexican government over the border issue, damages accrued by Mexico to U.S. citizens, and the purchase of other territory for 25 million dollars. Upon arrival, Slidell was not recognized by the Mexican government and did not treat with them, which was perceived as an insult by the Polk administration. Frederick Merk, *Manifest Destiny and Mission in American History* (Cambridge: Harvard University Press, 1995), 84–87.

15. This is likely a reference to the biblical Golgotha or "Place of Skulls." According to the Gospels, Jesus was crucified on Golgotha. John 19:17, *KJV*. Here, Lippard is comparing the innocent death of Jesus with the "unjust" war forced on Americans.
16. "Vallies" was a contemporary plural spelling for valley.
17. "Monterey" is a variant spelling of the city Monterrey. *Oxford English Dictionary*.

Is this false? Does not Almighty God, lead the Nations to civilization, through the reeking Golgothas of War?[15]

But have a care, brave People! The same tide of war, that now sweeps over the vallies,[16] and mounts the pyramids of Mexico, may roll back upon your American land. What Prophet shall dare to read the meaning of yonder portentous Future? While we write our record of the war, that War is still in the hey-day of its tempestuous career. The events that we chronicle, have not yet reached the consummation. They ripen into history, even as we write them down.

Strange and bewildering events!

First we hear of the Battles of the Wilderness, those glorious struggles of the desert and chaparral, where a few hardy Americans beat back and trampled into dust the bravery and chivalry of Mexico. Two battles, fought on two successive days, under a burning sun, the Americans fighting with the certainty of Massacre in case of defeat: The Mexicans looking forward, first to triumph, then to butchery!

Next comes thundering on our ears, the story of a three days' fight, fought by the children of Washington, against walls and bars and bolts, and legions of armed men, a battle which for dogged perseverance and sullen courage has no comparison in history; that glorious battle of the city and mountain, which the Sierra Nevada beheld, and Monterey[17] felt to her most sacred home!

Then, another battle of three days, fought amid the snows of winter, on the desert plain, by the Hero and his Crusaders, against the Mexicans and their leader: a terrible triumph, which drew more tears from the eyes of orphans and made more widows, than any fight of the entire war.

Linked with this battle, in the same breath of glory, comes the story of the conquered fort and the bombarded city, and last of all, the history of the bloody route when the mountains of Cerro Gordo, could scarce afford a hiding place to the dismayed leader of the Mexican legions.—

Take it, all in all, such a Crusade of a civilized People, against a semi-barbarous horde of slaves, has no parallel in history.

There is a deeper reason, in all this, than meets the superficial eye. Beneath the bloody foam of battle, flows on, forever, the serene and awful current of Divine truth.

Do you ask the explanation of this mystery? Search the history of the North American People, behold them forsake the shores of Europe, and dare the unknown dangers of the distant wilderness, not for the lust of gold or power, but for the sake of a Religion, a Home.

An Exodus like this—the going forth of the oppressed of all nations to a new world—the angels never saw before. All parts of Europe, sent their heart-wounded, their down-trodden thousands to the wilds of North America.

The German and the Frenchman, the Swede and the Irishman, the Scot and the Englishman, met in the wild, and grouped around one altar—Sacred to the majesty of God and the rights of man. From this strangely mingled band of wanderers, a new People sprung into birth.[18]

A vigorous People, rugged as the rocks of the wilderness which sheltered them, free as the forest which gave them shade, bold as the red Indian who forced them to purchase every inch of ground, with the blood of human hearts. To this hardy People—this people created from the pilgrims and wanderers of all nations—this People nursed into full vigor, by long and bloody Indian wars and hardened into iron, by the longest and bloodiest war of all, the Revolution, to this People of Northern America, God Almighty has given the destiny of the entire American Continent.[19]

18 During the 1840s, the United States experienced a wave of immigration, especially from Ireland and the Germanic states, due respectively to the Irish famine and political instability. In response, nativist backlash developed. In his public life, Lippard criticized nativist ideas and policies. David S. Reynolds, *George Lippard* (Boston: Twayne Publishers, 1982), 30.

19 Coined in 1845, "manifest destiny" was the belief that the whole continent was given to Americans by God, and they had a duty to settle it. See Amy S. Greenberg, *Manifest Manhood and the Antebellum American Empire* (Cambridge: Cambridge University Press, 2005); Merk, *Manifest Destiny*.

The handwriting of blood and fire, is upon British America and Southern America.

As the Aztec people,[20] crumbled before the Spaniard, so will the mongrel race, moulded[21] of Indian and Spanish blood, melt into, and be ruled by, the Iron Race of the North.

You cannot deny it. You cannot avoid the solemn truth, which glares you in the face.

God speaks it, from history, from the events now passing around us, from every line of the career of the People, who followed his smile into the desert.

As the People of the old Thirteen states, rose like one man, against the Juggernaut of government, the British Monarchy, so the serfs[22] of Canada will rise, trample the thing of blood into dust, and in the gore of the battlefield plant the olive tree of peace and freedom.[23]

Thanks be to God, the time comes, when Niagara, will no longer extend from a free land to a British despotism. Before many years that awful cataract will sing the anthem of a free Continent.

God Almighty has given the destiny of the Continent, into the hands of the free People of the American Union.

Not the Anglo-Saxon race,[24] for such a race has no existence, save in the brains of certain people, who talk frothily about immense nothings. You might as well call the American People, the Scandinavian race, the Celtic race, the Norman race, as to apply to them, the empty phrase, Anglo-Saxon. This ridiculous word, has been in the mouths of grave men, who should know better, for years: it is high time, that we should discard it for some word, with a slight pretence[25] to a meaning.

WE are no Anglo-Saxon People. No! All Europe sent its exiles to our shores. From all the nations of Northern Europe, we were formed. Germany

---

20 The Aztecs were a Mesoamerican people and empire conquered by the Spanish. Lippard's writing on Mexico includes fantastical accounts of characters interacting with lost Aztec tribes. See chapter III for more information on Lippard's portrayal of the Aztec people.

21 "Moulded" is a nineteenth-century variant spelling of the word molded. *Oxford English Dictionary*.

22 A contemporary source defines "serf" as "[a] servant or slave employed in husbandry, and, in some countries, attached to the soil and transferred with it." Webster, *An American Dictionary*, 742.

23 A common belief in the United States is the divine mission of the nation to serve as an example of a republic for the world. According to this ideology, all nations would follow the example of the United States and either join the U.S. or be their own republics. Here, Lippard draws on the peaceful symbolism of the olive tree.

24 Term referring to Germanic peoples that started settling in England in the fifth century. In nineteenth-century America, the term was used to contrast whites of English descent with others. Many nineteenth-century Americans believed ideas essential to American democracy were inherent to Anglo-Saxon peoples. Peoples not designated Anglo-Saxon, including other western European nationalities, were often considered lesser and incapable of participating in American political discourse. Reginald Horsman, *Race and Manifest Destiny: The Origins of American Racial Anglo-Saxonism* (Cambridge: Harvard University Press, 1981), 4; Merk, *Manifest Destiny*, 192.

25 "Pretence" is a nineteenth-century variant spelling of the word pretense. *Oxford English Dictionary*.

and Sweden and Ireland and Scotland and Wales and England, aye and glorious France, all sent their oppressed to us, and we grew into a new race.

We are the American People. Our lineage is from that God, who bade us go forth, from the old world, and smiled us into an Empire of Men. Our destiny is to possess this Continent, drive from it all shreds of Monarchy, whether British or Spanish or Portugese,[26] and on the wrecks of shattered empires, build the Altar, second to the BROTHERHOOD OF MAN.[27]

Then come with me, and look upon our Banner of the Stars, as it goes in glory and gloom over the Continent, freedom's pillar of cloud by day, her pillar of fire by night.[28] Our fathers loved that Banner in the days of old. Its stripes were painted with the blood of martyrs. Its stars flashed through the clouds of Bunker Hill and Brandywine, and Saratoga, and came shining out in the cloudless sky of Yorktown.[29] Let us follow it then, and bid God's blessing on it, as its stars gleam awfully through the bloody mists of Mexico.

Let us not heed the miserable cant of the traitors among us, who advise the Mexicans to give the American soldier a bloody and hospitable grave.[30] Though these traitors increase like vipers under a hot sun, though they poison our air, in the Senate and the Press, let us pass them by, with a simple prayer, that God will be very merciful to the pitiful dastard, who—under the cloak of British or Mexican Sympathy—would turn traitor to a land like ours.

WASHINGTON, you all remember, sat in his Camp at Cambridge,[31] in September, 1775, his eyes fixed upon the map of the Continent, his finger laid upon Canada, while his unsheathed sword, reached from Labrador to Patagonia.[32] In the silence of night, even as he planned the conquest of Canada, he recognized this great truth—God has given the American Continent to the free.

26 "Portugese" was an archaic variant spelling of Portuguese. Ibid.

27 Lippard founded a labor organization named "The Brotherhood of the Union" in 1849. In his own words, the organization sought to promote "the cause of the Masses, and battle against the tyrants of the Social System,—against corrupt Bankers, against Land Monopolists and against all Monied Oppressors." Reynolds, *George Lippard*, 19.

28 A reference to when God led the Israelites through the desert away from Egypt in the Book of Exodus. The original quote reads "And the Lord went before them by day in a pillar of a cloud, to lead them the way; and by night in a pillar of fire, to give them light; to go by day and night." Exodus 13:21 *KJV*. Lippard compares the chosen people of Israel to the newly chosen people of America.

29 Revolutionary battles fought in June, 1775, September, 1777, September–October, 1777, and October, 1781, respectively. Lippard wrote extensively about the Revolutionary War; a year before publishing *Legends of Mexico* (1847), he published *Blanche of Brandywine; Or September the Eleventh, 1777, A Romance*.

30 Leading up to and during the war, the Whig Party was critical of Democratic President James K. Polk's actions and his conduct of the war. Contained in this sentence is an allusion to the remarks of Whig senator Thomas Corwin (1794–1865) of Ohio, in which he derided the U.S.-Mexico War. He placed himself in the position of a Mexican citizen and then declared to Americans, "Have you not room in your own country to bury your dead men? If you come into mine, we will greet you with bloody hands and welcome you to hospitable graves." Merk, *Manifest Destiny*, 93.

31 Cambridge is located near Boston. George Washington's (1732–1799) headquarters were located in Cambridge from July 1775 to April 1776. Kevin J. Hayes, *George*

Washington: A Life in Books (New York: Oxford University Press, 2017), 160, 169.

32　Labrador refers to a province in northeastern Canada. Patagonia is an area in the southern region of mainland South America.

33　A similar scene of Washington planning an invasion of Canada is mentioned in Lippard's *Washington and His Generals*. That account differs in several details. Most notably, the differences include no mention of Washington's sword and the presence of Benedict Arnold. Later, Lippard included a short scene of Washington studying a map of the entire continent. George Lippard, *Washington and His Generals: Or, Legends of the Revolution* (Philadelphia: G.B. Zieber and Co., 1847), 158, 335.

Let us follow then, the American Banner, and while our souls are awed by the thunder flash of battle; while the horrible world of carnage with its shrieks and groans, its dead armies and butchered legions widens and crimsons around us, let us never for one moment forget, that mysterious Symbol of our destiny—THE UNSHEATHED SWORD OF WASHINGTON RESTING UPON THE MAP OF THE NEW WORLD.[33]

II

The Camp in the Wilderness

The Army encamped in the wilderness, a hamlet of white tents, gleaming from the gloom of the boundless prairie, the stars of midnight shining serenely from the dark blue vault, that Banner, with its stars, its belts of scarlet and snow, borne aloft, like a mighty bird, by the summer breeze!

Here, rising from the sod of the prairie, a solitary rock, glooms greyly through the night. Like the fragment of some meteoric shower, like the wreck of some Pre-Adamite[1] world, like a monument, built long ages ago to the memory of the heroic dead, the solitary rock, glooms into the sky.

We will stand near the rock, we will lean upon its rugged front, and gaze upon this strange sight—the camp in the wilderness!

Does not the scene strike your heart with a deep awe?

That boundless prairie, canopied by the midnight sky, with the hamlet of white tents gleaming like altars of snow from the darkness! Far to the south, thick and dense, like a forest blasted in its growth, extends the chaparral; a wall of briers and thorns. Yonder, on the north, like a silver clasp, on a robe of dark velvet, a small lake, shines from the blackness of the prairie.

In front of each tent, the bayonets gleam, like scattered drops of light. Here you behold the cannon, and there, the war-horses, crouching in slumber, on the soft grass of the waste.

A silence like death prevails.

Now it is broken by the voice of the sentinel, pealing suddenly from the camp of the wilderness. Now, the shrill neigh of the war-steed—now the roar of the ocean, breaking on the shore, seven miles away, comes like

Chapter II

[1] During the nineteenth century, the pre-Adamite theory stated there were humans on earth before the biblical Adam and Eve and these pre-Adamite races prepared the planet for the Adamite race. These humans, however, were inferior to the race created by Adam and Eve and, by extension, so were their descendants, including both African and Native American peoples. Lester Stephens D., "The Earth and Humans Before Adam: The Pre-Adamite Theory of Georgia Geologist Matthew Fleming Stephenson," *Georgia Historical Quarterly* 100, no. 1 (2016): 8–35.

the hoarse whisper of a thousand men murmuring over the plain. Now, a stillness like death; in that encampment of two thousand brave men, not a sound is heard.²

Again, hark! The howl of the jackal, comes like a funeral knell over the waste. Hideous, prolonged, distant, that cry chills your heart with dread, for it speaks of a loathsome beast, mangling with grey teeth and fangs, the cold face of the battle dead.

And whether the Ocean's roar comes like a hoarse whisper, or the jackal's howl like a funeral knell, whether the cry of the sentinel breaks along the air, or the neigh of the war-horse, quivers like a battle-shout, or whether a silence like death, comes down upon the camp of the wilderness, still, yonder, above the central tent, floats and swells the Banner of the Stars.

Confess with me, that the scene is invested with a grandeur all its own. Here, you behold no mountains rising from clustered vallies,³ into the region of eternal silence and snow. Here, no undulating hills, crowned with the golden wheat or emerald corn. Here, no awful cliffs, with a narrow passage, winding amid their broken shadows. Only a vast prairie, a hamlet of tents and a midnight sky!

You have seen Washington encamped among the wintry hills of Valley Forge, or amid the sublime cliffs of the Hudson, or in the centre of the Brandywine vallies. Encircled by scenes like these, the American Banner floated on the air, into a background of rocks, or mountains, or undulating woods.⁴ But here, it waves against the sky, alone. Here, man—with nothing to break the awful monotony of the scene—is in truth, alone with the earth and sky.

From the central tent of the encampment, with the mountains, waving to the air, a belt of light streams far along the sod.

Ere, we enter that tent, and gaze upon the Man who watches there, let us remember these important truths:

---

2 Zachary Taylor's forces, or the Army of Occupation, numbered closer to four thousand men. "A Continent Divided: The U.S.-Mexico War," The University of Texas Arlington, accessed October 15, 2018, https://library.uta.edu/usmexicowar.

3 "Vallies" was a contemporary plural spelling for valley.

4 Lippard is connecting Taylor's encampment to George Washington's at Valley Forge during the winter of 1777 after his defeat at the Battle of Brandywine Creek. Though the physical landscape was different from Washington's encampment, Lippard imagines a continuous connection in tradition between the two armies.

It is the seventh of May, 1846.

This little army of two thousand men, slumbering securely on the boundless Prairie, are surrounded by a Mexican army of some six thousand veteran soldiers.[5] Yonder wall of chaparral is black with their faces.

The morrow will bring a battle—and the end of that battle will be Massacre and Butchery.

We enter the central tent of the Camp in the Wilderness.

A solitary light burns there, on the small table, overspread with charts and papers.

In the far corner of this home in the wilderness, with its roof and walls of fluttering canvass, you behold military trunks piled in a mass. Around the light extends an open space of grassy sod.

Four men are gathered there, talking with each other, in low, earnest tones.

The one on the right, dressed in a plain green frock, with a knife in his belt and a rifle in his hand, is a Texian Ranger:[6] a man of iron frame, not so remarkable for his height as for the unpretending resolution, written upon his sunburnt face. Broad cheekbones, an aqualine nose, thin, firm lips, wide forehead and chesnut hair, curling in short locks, complete the picture of his face.

He stands there, erect as the Red Indian, a fine specimen of an iron man, who with but ten hunters, armed with rifles, would deem himself a match for at least a hundred disciplined soldiers.

Next to him, presenting a perfect contrast, you behold a tall young soldier, clad in the blue uniform of the American dragoon,[7] his finely proportioned limbs, narrow waist, and broad chest, his marked face, with hair flowing to the shoulders, and beard waving over the breast—both dark as

5 The Mexican veterans Lippard is referring to most likely would have been veterans of the multiple internal struggles Mexico found itself in during and after its fight for independence. After establishing a federal constitution in 1824, Mexico experienced several revolts and military coups that eventually led to the rise in 1845 of President Mariano Paredes y Arrillaga, who was ousted by López de Santa Anna in July, 1846. Timothy J. Henderson, *A Glorious Defeat: Mexico and Its War with the United States* (New York: Hill and Wang, 2007).

6 The Texas Rangers Division, more commonly known as Texas Rangers, was organized in 1835 to protect American settlers from hostile Native Americans and Mexicans. Walter P. Webb, *The Texas Rangers: A Century of Frontier Defense* (Austin: University of Texas Press, 1935), 89–135.

7 The American dragoon was a mounted soldier with a blue cotton uniform, similar to regular soldiers, with the exception of "yellow piping" on the edges of the coat. The sergeants of the dragoon companies also had stripes down their pant legs. They carried sabers into combat during charges on horseback. Sally J. Ketcham, "Dragoon Soldier—Tools of the Trade," National Park Service, U.S. Department of the Interior, accessed October 17, 2018, https://www.nps.gov/fosc/learn/education/dragoon3.htm.

8   Lippard is referring to Major Ringgold's maternal grandfather, John Cadwalader, who served with George Washington during his New Jersey campaign. David H. Fischer, *Washington's Crossing* (Oxford: Oxford University Press, 2004), 191.
9   Brigadier General Zachary Taylor began his military service in the early nineteenth century and served through the U.S.-Mexico War, after which he began his political career and ascended to the presidency in 1849. By the time of the U.S.-Mexico War, Taylor had received promotions for actions in the War of 1812, The Black Hawk War, and the Seminole War under the command of General Andrew Jackson. John S.D. Eisenhower, *So Far from God: The U.S. War with Mexico, 1846–1848* (Norman: University of Oklahoma Press, 2000), 29–30.
10 Captain Samuel Walker (1817–1847) was a Texas Ranger under the command of Captain Jack Hays during the U.S.-Mexico War. Walker became famous for his contribution to the design of Samuel Colt's "Colt Single Action Army" revolver, better known as the "Walker-Colt" revolver. He was killed in action on October 9, 1847 at the Battle of Huamantla. Bruce Glasrud and Harold Weiss Jr., *Tracking the Texas Rangers: The Nineteenth Century* (Denton, TX: University of North Texas Press, 2012), 87–119.
11 Charles A. May (1818–1864) was, at the time of this battle, a 2nd Lieutenant in the 2nd Regiment of Dragoons. He fought in most major engagements of the U.S.-Mexico War, including the Battle of Buena Vista, where he was wounded and received a promotion to the rank of Colonel for "gallant and meritorious conduct." He retired from military service in 1860 and died in New York City four years later. "New York Obituaries—Col. Charles A. May," *The New York Times,* December 27, 1864.
12 Major Samuel Ringgold (1796–1846) was born in Maryland and attended West Point Military Academy from 1814 to 1818.

night—affording a picture, something like the chivalric crusader of the olden time.

Opposite the young dragoon, stands a man of majestic stature, and imposing presence. His fine figure is clad in the blue and buff uniform which clings to him like a glove to the hand, with the epaulettes on the shoulder, the sword by the side. His dark hair falls back from his broad forehead, his full eye sparkles as with the fire of battle. In his determined face, you may read the lineaments of his great Ancestor, a heroic General of the Revolutionary time.[8]

The centre of the group and the object of every eye!

An old man. An old man, not even clad in the glitter and show of a uniform, but attired in the much-used frock coat of dark brown hues, grey pantaloons, with a wide-brimmed hat in his hand. An old man, with a broad chest, a figure not more than five feet nine inches in stature, a face, bronzed by the sun and toil of thirty eight years of battle service.[9]

His form is somewhat broad and bulky, his face bronzed and seamed by battle toil, his hair whitened by age, and yet there is that about the old man, which interests your eye, and impresses your heart.

His face, in repose, seems only to indicate an overflowing good humor and abundance of social feeling. But now the full grey eye flashes wild deep light, from beneath the strongly defined eye brow, the lips—the lower one slightly projecting—are moulded in an expression of iron resolution, the brow glows in every wrinkle, with the fire of Thought.

Who are these four men gathered at midnight, by the light of the solitary candle, in this Tent of the Wilderness?

They bear names which may become famous before many days. The Texian Ranger, is Captain Walker[10]—the chivalric dragoon, Captain May[11]—the soldier of the majestic figure, Major Ringgold.[12] And the old man in the faded brown coat, with the broad brimmed hat in his hand, stands there with the lives of two thousand men upon his heart, with the honor of the Flag of Washington in his hand.

That plain old man is Zachary Taylor, General of the Continental Army—Yes, let us call this heroic band by the name which Washington made sacred, that name which indicates the destiny of our arms and the course of our civilization—Continental.[13]

Can you tell me the nature of the thought, that stamps the old man's brow?

Even as you gaze in his battle-worn face, he starts—he mutters an ejaculation of surprise. For booming over the waste from afar, comes that hoarse murmur of the Signal gun. Yes, seven days ago, when—with Mexicans swarming over plain and river—he left the Rio Grande, determined to march to Point Isabel, distant some twenty-six miles, there remained in the rude fort opposite Matamoras, the veteran Major Brown, with only three hundred men.[14]

"When you are attacked," said Zachary Taylor, "send me word by your signal gun."

That signal gun has been heard for the last four days and nights. But a few hours ago, driven almost to frenzy by its sound, Taylor, with his men, left Point Isabel, on the sea shore, determined to march to the rescue of his brothers on the Rio Grande—to march twenty-six miles, through that wilderness of chaparral and prairie, swarming with the veteran armies of Mexico.[15] Nor with armies alone, but darkened by the wild assassin horde of rancheros.[16]

And now, encamped for the night, on the desert prairie, he hears once more the signal gun, calling with its thunder throat for aid. As he starts

During the Seminole Wars, he was promoted twice to the rank of Major. On May 8th, he was mortally wounded in the Battle of Palo Alto, and he died three days later. George W. Cullum, *Biographical Register of the Officers and Graduates of the U.S. Military Academy at West Point, N.Y.* (New York: Houghton & Company, 1891), 189.

13 At this point in the war, Taylor's army was referred to as the "Army of Observation." Christopher Conway, ed., *The U.S.-Mexican War: A Binational Reader* (Indianapolis: Hackett Publishing Company Inc., 2010), xix. Lippard, however, is intentionally using the term "Continental Army" to connect Taylor's army to Washington's during the Revolutionary War. In doing this, Lippard espouses the commonly held notion of manifest destiny that views the expansion of the United States across the American continent as a continuation of the Revolutionary War. Frederick Merk, *Manifest Destiny and Mission in American History* (Cambridge: Harvard University Press, 1995), 24–60.

14 Major Jacob Brown (1789–1846) was an officer in the 7th infantry. Born in Massachusetts, Brown was in the military for thirty years and was fifty-six years old by the time of this battle. On the morning of May 5, 1846, Brown made a routine inspection of the fort, was hit by a cannonball, and died of his injuries. Eisenhower, *So Far from God*, 72, 84.

15 Point Isabel was the U.S. Army's depot at the mouth of the Rio Grande River. Ibid., 50.

16 Rancheros both owned and worked on ranches in northern Mexico. After the war, these rancheros lost much of their land to the territory ceded to the United States. Daniel W. Howe, *What Hath God Wrought: The Transformation of America, 1815–1848* (New York: Oxford University Press, 2007), 708–709, 739–740.

17 Matamoras was a port city on the Rio Grande River where the Mexican army encamped during this period of the conflict. Merk, *Manifest Destiny,* 87.

18 By distinguishing this type of architecture in Mexico, Lippard connects the Mexican people and landscape to notions of an antiquated old world "otherness," in this case the Moorish architecture of Spain. In doing so, he upholds the idea of the "martial nature of the American race as providentially selected to subdue the whole favored continent." Amy S. Greenberg, *Manifest Manhood and the Antebellum American Empire* (New York: Cambridge University Press, 2005), 21.

19 Fort Brown was originally named Fort Texas. When Taylor returned to the fort and learned of Major Brown's death, he issued General Order No. 62 renaming it Fort Brown in his honor. Eisenhower, *So Far from God,* 84. According to the National Park Service, it is still "unofficially" known as Fort Texas. "Fort Texas/Fort Brown," National Park Service, U.S. Department of the Interior, accessed October 18, 2018, https://www.nps.gov/paal/learn/historyculture/siegeofforttexas.htm.

20 Fort Brown was a bastion fort, or "star fort," that had extensions from its corners in the shape of a star. These extensions allowed defenders to have multiple ways to fire on attackers assaulting the fort. Additionally, there were trenches dug in front of the fort which provided both more dirt for the walls and further barriers for attackers to navigate. Specifically, Fort Brown had walls over nine feet tall and fifteen feet thick at the base with six bastions, all surrounded by a trench that was eight feet deep. Eisenhower, *So Far from God,* 72–73.

with anxiety, raising his hand to his brow, let us for ourselves behold the danger announced by the Signal gun.

Away to the Rio Grande, that stream which like a huge serpent winds languidly to the sea. Away through these wastes, across these dark ravines, away for eighteen miles, and look upon the peril of the heroic three hundred.

Emerging from the shadows of the chaparral, we stand upon this rock, and witness a wildly beautiful scene. Before us, rolling through the dim shadows like a waving belt of silver thrown down upon a black mantle, gleams the Rio Grande. Yonder through the gloom, we behold the roofs and steeples of Matamoras;[17] a town built in a strange Moorish architecture, embosomed in a country of leaves and flowers.[18]

On this side of the river, the Fort gleams through the night, an immense structure of earth, built by the old General, when he first displayed the banner of the stars on the Rio Grande, and held for the last four days and nights, by the veteran Brown and three hundred men, against thousands of Mexican soldiers.[19]

The night is very dark and still. The sky is obscured by clouds—the clouds of cannon smoke which for four days and nights have veiled sun, moon, and stars.

Suddenly, from the town, a blaze rushes into the dark sky. Is it a Comet, with its head of fire, and long mane of flame? It sweeps over the dark pall, it lights the winding river with a momentary glare, and then hisses down into the rude home of the American soldiers.

All is silent, dark, and dead again.

Not a sound from the fort. Its bastions half-destroyed, its trenches filled with earth, its soldiers standing like spectres, in the shadows, this fort capable of containing six regiments of soldiers, is now silent as the grave.[20]

Where is the commander of these men, where the veteran Brown, who seven days ago, grasped swarthy-faced Zachary by the hand, and pledged himself to keep the fort or die?

Come! While from the centre of the Fort, lashed to the staff, the banner of the Stars waves on the night, as it has waved since first it shone over Rio Grande—Come! Here, we will find the first hero of the fort.

Behold him in his couch. Yes, a couch sheltered by a rude canopy.—Certain barrels, support horizontal pieces of timber, on which sod and clay is laid. In that dismal resting place, thus made, behold all that remains of the hardy soldier. His brow wet with the dews of mortal agony, he writhes there, protected by these barrels from the bomb-shells, which cut the earth and agitate the air on every side.

Only yesterday, with his right leg, in literal words, torn from his body by a shell—only yesterday, while calmly taking his rounds through the besieged fort, he fell, and as he writhed in pain, uttered the memorable words:

"Men go to your duties: stand by your posts: I am but one among you."

As we gaze upon him in his agony—dying here by inches, on the shores of Rio Grande—that solitary streak of fire is followed by another, and another, until the sky is alive with threads of quivering light. It looks like a battle fought in the heavens, by the good and evil angels; the weapons stars and comets.

The town, its roofs crowded with people, its cathedral towers looming over all, comes forth gaily in the red light, Boom—boom—boom—the cannon shout, as they hurl the brazen balls through the heated air.

The winding river glows and burns on every wave. The fort, with its battered walls, its disfigured parapets, its three hundred solders, cowering for want of ammunition by their voiceless guns, stands out in the glare of that fierce cannonade.[21]

21 A contemporary source defines "cannonade" as, "[i]n fortifications, a wall, rampart, or elevation of earth for covering soldiers from an enemy's shot." Noah Webster, *An American Dictionary of the English Language* (New York: Harper & Brothers, 1848), 715.

On either side of the fort, from the river shore to the chaparral, the prospect is terrible. The land swarms with Mexicans. Their gay apparel of gilt buttons, glittering spangles, cloth of many dies, shines brilliantly in the light. Here march the disciplined legions; there skulks the knifed and bearded Ranchero, waiting until the fort is taken, that he may cut throats, and feel hot blood spouting over his hands.

At this moment, when the brave three hundred,—these iron men, who, since last Sabbath morning have stood, with but a few soldiers killed, the incessant bombardment, listen to the groans of the mangled veteran, and behold the universe, blazing with light, the river and the shore and the city, all black with thousands, waiting for the moment of their fall, that they may witness their massacre,—at this moment, when the "great old man," Zachary, is but eighteen miles away, waiting for morning light, when with his two thousand, he will cut his way to the fort or die—at this instant of light and darkness and blood, the torch is applied to the cannon, and that signal gun calls to the General, far over the prairie, and with its fiery throat says, help us or we die!

Let us see what difficulties intervene between the Cromwell of the American Army, and the doomed fortress on the Rio Grande.[22]

Search the chaparral—they gleam with bayonets. Yes, like fire flies the sharp points glitter through the gloom. Look into the ravines—they are black with crouching rancheroes, grim fellows, who cut a throat to give them appetite, and inflict a stab in the back from mere exuberance of animal spirits.

For eighteen miles or more, which extend between Fort Brown and the Camp in the Wilderness, the Mexican forces—the regular veterans, who have fought like wounded tigers in many a battle, and the assassin hordes who follow the disciplined legions, as buzzards flutter in the wake of eagles—the

---

22 Oliver Cromwell was one of the leaders in the English Civil War (1642–1651). He helped lead the English Parliamentarians, or "Roundheads," in a revolt that resulted in the execution of King Charles I and the exile of his son, Charles II. Cromwell ruled as the Protectorate of the Commonwealth of England until his death in 1658. See Robert S. Paul, *The Lord Protector: Religion and Politics in the Life of Oliver Cromwell* (London: Lutterworth Press, 1955).

Mexican forces extend in terrible array, one immense cloud of battle, armed with the thunder of cannon, the lightning of lance and bayonet.

They await the coming of the Morrow! There will be a royal time, by the setting of to-morrow's sun. Whoop! How the vultures will shriek, as by its last ray, they settle on the cold faces of the battle dead, and pick glassy eyes from their sockets.

Through the dusky chaparral, into the camp of the Mexican general!

A splendid tent, fluttering with curtains of silk and gold, and with the light of wax candles, streaming through its crevices, rises in the centre of a grassy glade, near a lakelet of cool, clear water.

Around this tent, all is light, glitter and motion.

Here a tawny Ranchero in his half bandit, half soldier uniform crouches on the grass, playing cards with a soldier of the regular forces: yonder the clatter of the drinking vessel breaks on the air, mingled with the sound of footsteps, rioting in the dance.

And all the while, bands of music, fill the air with a thunder-chorus of rich sounds, or die away through the dark paths of the chaparral, in a low deep murmur, that seems like a requiem for the battle-dead.

And near the lakelet, towers the Marque of the General, surmounted by the gay tri-colored flag of Mexico, typifying the three predominant influences in that golden and bloody clime, Superstition, Ignorance, Crime.[23]

Within the tent, seated on a luxuriously cushioned chair, near a voluptuous bed, glistening with the trappings of oriental taste, you behold a man of warrior presence, his gay uniform thrown open across the breast, while he holds the goblet of iced champaigne to his lips.[24]

By his side, converses the handsome and brave La Vega, and around extends a circle of officers, clad in the most gaudy uniforms, their eyes keeping time with their lips, in the game of careless mirth.[25]

23 The Marque of the General was the commanding general's personal battle flag or standard. This flag signified which general was in command and the location of the general's tent.

24 Lippard here demonstrates example of what Edward Said calls "Orientalism," which "is … a considerable dimension of modern political-intellectual culture, and as such has less to do with the Orient than it does with our world," by the juxtaposition of the image a contemporary reader would have had of an American soldier or general and what Lippard is describing as the Mexican soldier or general. Edward Said, *Orientalism* (New York: Vintage Books, 1978), 13.

25 General Rómulo Díaz de la Vega (1800–1877) was second in command of the Mexican Army under General Francisco Mejía. Eisenhower, *So Far from God*, 56–57.

The fragrance of tobacco—not your miserable weed, which is called Tobacco, because it resembles a compound of brimstone and pitch—but the glorious tobacco, from Cuba, pervades the tent, with a mild and delicious perfume.

The swarthy faces of the Mexican officers, glow with calm satisfaction as the champaigne glass and the Havana cigar, pass from lip to lip.

In the camp of Zachary Taylor, you behold nothing but a plain old man, in a brown coat, conversing earnestly with three of his bravest officers, on the fate of to-morrow's battle:

Here, the blaze of oriental magnificence blinds your sight, here the laugh and the song go round, to the chorus of clattering glasses and applauding hands. In the midst of all, sits the General Arista, that man whom Santa Anna made a soldier, twirling his red mustache, as he presses the delicious champaigne to his lips.[26]

Meanwhile Ringgold, and Walker and May—three heroic men, each the type of a different class—have gone to their quarters and the leader of the American army is alone.

Extended on the rude camp bed he sleeps. His form still attired in his plain apparel, his throat bared, his bronzed face turned to the light. He slumbers for a few brief hours, in order to gather strength for the march of the morrow.

The sentinel—a grim veteran—paces slowly up and down in front of the tent.

All is silent. The distant roar of the Ocean, the howl of the jackal, the neighing of steeds, have died away.

As the moon rises over the distant horizon, flinging the shadow of the tents far over the sod, a dark object moves in the gloom—advances imperceptibly and is still again.

---

26 General Mariano Arista (1802–1855) was the General of the Mexican Army of the North at the beginning of the war and fought in the Battles of Palo Alto and Resaca de la Palma. After, he was recalled by the Mexican government and court-martialed, though acquitted. Arista was the president of Mexico from 1851 to 1853. Henderson, *A Glorious Defeat* (New York: Hill and Wang, 2007), 149, 185, 188.

Is it a jackal in search of a dead body, or a vulture impatient for the feast of the morrow?

Still it moves on, ever keeping in the shadow. Moves on, while the Sentinel paces to and fro, and the May moon rises over the Camp in the Wilderness.

It approaches the tent of the General, glides under the walls, and starts stealthy up to his bed, and stands revealed, in the form of a man of some sixty years, with a broad chest, tawny skin, long hair, grizzled with age and thick beard, descending to the breast of a half-robber uniform.

It is a Ranchero. He stands scowling beside the couch of the General, his white teeth, gleaming beneath his dark mustache, while the sharp knife quivers in his hand.

Hark—a footstep! The sentinel comes, passes the opening of the tent, looks in, and sees nothing but the bronzed face of the sleeping general. For the Ranchero has sunk beside the couch, nestling snake-like in the shadow.

The Sentinel is gone, and that dusky image of Assassination, glooms once more beside the couch, the knife quivering in his hand. The bared throat invites the blow. A muttered ejaculation in barbarous[27] Spanish, and the murderer contemplates his victim.—

An old man, soundly sleeping, as though God protected every one of his grey hairs, and reserved his large brain, for immortal deeds.

One blow of that knife, and the old man is a corse, the American army deprived of its Mind, the Mexicans secured forever from his sword.

Only one blow? The grizzled-haired Ranchero raises the knife, mutters a prayer, kisses a cross, and whirls the knife home, to the victim's heart.[28]

That brawny arm, with sinews like whip cords never failed of its mark, never once, in the perils of darkest battles; why should it now?

27 The use of the word "barbarous" in connection to the Mexican dialect of Spanish further racializes the Mexican people as an inferior race.

28 Anti-Catholic sentiment was particularly strong during this period among Protestant Americans. The Catholic religion was seen as a threat to American security and republicanism. Many Americans blamed what they conceived as Mexico's "laziness and ignorance … on the Catholic Church," Greenberg, *Manifest Manhood,* 21, 98–99.

And yet it does! Hissing through the air, it grazes the General's cheek, and cleaves his pillow.

The face of the Murderer, is convulsed in every feature. As though astonished by his want of success, he folds his hands, bends, prays and then crawls snake-like from the tent.

The knife was found next morning, buried in the pillow.—

Again that dim figure creeping through the ways of the camp—now pausing, now looking like a frightened tortoise from a side, and still cautiously crawling on, he gains the open prairie, where his steed waits for him, with quivering nostrils and waving mane.

And still the moon arises and sheds its calm light over the city of tents, and over the bronzed face of the sleeping old man. And the sentinel, pacing his rounds in front of the old General's tent, feels his senses cheered by the perfume of wild flowers, feels the cool breeze from the ocean upon his brow, feels the throb of the fight, which is to come on the morrow, already palpitate in his veins.

In the dusky shadow of the chaparral, a Ranchero dismounts from his steed.

By the light of the moon, you may see twenty swarthy faces, look from the covert in his face, and the stalwart forms of the band, encircle with a wall of iron-sinewed chests.

The solitary Ranchero, whom we have seen, bending over the couch of Zachary Taylor, advances, and then you hear these fierce whispered words, spoken in barbarous Spanish—

"It is done?" cries the foremost of the band. "The Oath was taken on the Holy Cross. We swore to have the life of the Invader. On you, by lot, devolved the office of Executioner. You have done it. Yes—the blood of the American drips from your steel!"

But the Ranchero with grizzled hair and beard could not reply.

Bending down among his brethren—those stern children of the wild—he veiled his face in his hands.

"I saw him in his sleep—I felt the blood tingle in my veins—I struck home with the knife—but there was something about the old man's face that turned its aim aside. I could not kill him! Sworn to do the deed, sworn upon the holy cross, to destroy the invader, I could not strike, him! There is a Providence about the old man!"

And as the Ranchero—the bloodiest of that bloody band—sank cowering on the sod, not ashamed to confess, that he was afraid to kill the sleeping old man, the brothers of the dark confederacy, gazed upon his tawny face, in silent awe—in wonder—in fear—even as the moonlight played with the blade of his assassin's knife.

In the most fearful hour of battle—that hour, when the hand is weary with slaughter, and the eye sick of seeing forevermore wherever it turns, the faces of dead men—this same Ranchero, with the blood pouring from his death-wound, told the strange story to an American soldier, who knelt by his side, and 'thanked God, that there was a Providence about the old man.'

Up over the prairie, up over the chaparral, up over the city and the fort, rises the moon! The night wears on. Still, from the fort yells the shriek of the signal gun, and in the plaza of Matamoras gather the forlorn hope, who are to storm the refuge of the Americans, and put them all to the mercy of the assassin's knife. The night wears on. Between your vision and the moon, the vulture flaps his wings—from yonder thicket the jackal howls for his dead man feast. The night wears on, the moon rises, the hum of a thousand insects makes the atmosphere alive. The Banner of the Stars still waves from its staff; the Crusaders still soundly sleep beneath its folds.

Sleep on, brave men. To-morrow, perchance, for many of you, a softer couch will be spread by skeleton hands. Dream of your wives, your little ones—of all that Heaven says to us in the word—Home. To-morrow: for many of you, that word will not mean the pleasant fireside of Pennsylvania, nor the quiet room of your wild-wood dwelling, but merely a dark chaparral, a dead body, with a Jackal and Vulture as chief mourners.

Pace your rounds brave sentinel, with your grey moustache and withered cheek.

Even now, in your distant home, your daughter—oh you remember her! how beautiful she looked, when she pressed her warm lips to your mouth and said, playing with your hard hands—Good bye; God bless you Father! Even now in that distant home, just a few paces from the village path, where the old sycamore stands, your daughter comes to the window, and looking upon the very moon which shines upon your face, Prays God that father may come home again, and come soon!

Pace on your rounds brave sentinel, and shout—"All is well!" What matter if the Jackal echoes you, and the Buzzard flaps its wings above your head?

Do you know, brave soldiers, that it makes my heart feel sick, to go among your tents, at this dead hour of the night, and listen to the words you whisper in your dreams?

Home—Wife—Child! These words are on your lips, still you whisper of them all. Here, a beardless boy turns him over in his sleep, and says in one breath, the words, Mother—Glory! A ghostly marriage of a pale face with blue eyes and grey hair, with a hideous skull wreathed with flowers, those words form together—Mother and Glory!

Sleep on, stout old Zachary, nor dream of your Indian wars, nor turn your bronzed face from the moon, nor restlessly reach forth your hand to grasp your sword.[29] Never fear the morrow. God and Destiny watch over your grey hairs, and for you bright words are written, even upon the battle cloud, and brighter forms beckon you on, even across the wilderness of battle graves!

29 Zachary Taylor received notoriety in the Black Hawk War (1832), the Second Seminole War (1835–1842), and as a "peacekeeper among the Cherokees, Creeks, and Seminoles" when he was stationed in western Arkansas. David S. Reynolds, *Waking Giant: America in the Age of Jackson* (New York: Harper Collins Publishers, 2008), 367.

III

The Dead Woman of Palo Alto

And so the night passed in that Camp of the Wilderness!

While it wears on, and ere the morning dawns, let me lead you for a little while, from the prominent personages of history, to those quiet characters, whose destiny is woven into the fate of battles and empires, like threads of silver with a bloody shroud.

Let me tell you a Legend of the war, a legend of the new crusade. Legend? What mean you by Legend? One of those heart-warm stories, which, quivering in rude earnest language from the lips of a spectator of a battle, or the survivor of some event of the olden time, fill up the cold outlines of history, and clothe the skeleton with flesh and blood, give it eyes and tongue, force it at once to look into our eyes and talk with us!

—Something like this, I mean by the word Legend. So many gentlemen have done me the kindness, to write "Legends" since I began it, and in certain cases, to borrow mine, without so much as a bow for common courtesy, that I am forced to define my position. "Legend" may mean what you please, it certainly is not a thing to be stolen from the owner, by all the highwaymen and footpads of literature. These gentlemen meet my Legends of the Revolution in the highway of a book, or the railroad of a newspaper, and on the instant cry, stand! Strip them of all vestiges of the owner's name, and send them forth to the world again, as gipsies do stolen children, with their faces marked and a new name.[1] May I be permitted to hope, that the Rancheros of literature will suffer to pass, without robbing or maiming, my Legends of Mexico?—

Chapter III

1. The myth of child-stealing "gipsies" was a common trope in this period. "Gipsies" is a nineteenth-century variant spelling of gypsies. *Oxford English Dictionary*.

A legend, is a history in its details and delicate tints, with the bloom and dew yet fresh upon it, history told to us, in the language of passion, of poetry, of home!

It must be confessed that the thing which generally passes for History, is the most impudent, swaggering bully, the most graceless braggart, the most reckless equivocator that ever staggered forth upon the great stage of the world.

He tells us a vast deal of Kings and blood, Revolutions and Battles, Murderers by wholesale, but not a word does he say of that Home-life of nations, which flows on, evermore the same, in all ages, whether Kings cut one another's throats, or the throats of their pitiful sheep, the people.

History, for example draws you a picture of a tall man on Horseback, with a cap and sword and feather, and calls it Washington, but what does History say of Washington, the Man, in his home, with the arms of his wife about his neck; or Washington, the Man, in his closet, with the thought of his country's destiny, eating like a silent agony into his great soul?

History, deals like a neophyte in the artist's life, in immense dashes and vague scrawls, and splashy colors: it does not go to work like the master painter, adding one delicate line to another, crowding one almost imperceptible beauty on another, until the dumb thing speaks and lives!

History to speak to the heart, should not lie to us by wholesale, nor deal in vague generalities, which are worse than robust lies, for they only tell half the truth, and leave the imagination to fill the other half with the infinite space of falsehood: No! It should, in narrating the records of an event or age, make us live with the people, fight by them in battle, sit with them at the table, make love, hate, fear and triumph with them. While it pictures the cabinet and field, it should not forget the Home. While it delineates the great career of ambition, it should not neglect the quiet but still impressive walk of social life.

While it eloquently pictures Washington the General charging at the head of his legions, it should not forget Washington the Boy, in his rude huntsman's dress, struggling for his life, on a miserable raft, amid the waves and ice of the wintry flood.[2] At the same time, that it delineates Taylor, the Conquerer of the New Conquest of Mexico,[3] sitting on his grey steed, amid the roar of battle, his grey eye blazing with the anger and rapture of the fight, it should remember, Taylor the man, mingling like a father or brother with his soldiers, sharing crust and cup with them and weeping the heroic tears of manhood, when disease or death, rends them from his side.[4]

Which most touches your heart, Napoleon the Emperor, sharing the imperial purple, with the doll of legitimacy, Maria Louisa, or Napoleon, the Man, stealing to the chamber of his divorced wife, true-souled Josephine, weeping at her feet and sealing his remorse with burning tears?[5]

Let us listen to the Legend of the Dead Woman of Palo Alto.

While in the camp of the wilderness, Zachary Taylor, sleeps the rugged sleep of warrior toil; yonder, in the almost oriental[6] city Matamoras, a young girl in her virgin slumber, with her voluptuous form, couched on soft pillows, dreams a sweet wild dream, amid the war of battle, and hear the angel voices of memory, speak out, amid the hurricane of fiery shells.

Amid all the terrors of that fearful night she slept—a strangely beautiful woman, with her loose white robe, gleaming through the intervals of her long flowing raven hair.

It was a luxurious chamber, paved with mosaic slabs of marble, with a cool fountain, bubbling from a bath, sunken in the centre of the place,

2 Upon returning from negotiating a territorial dispute with the French over the Ohio Valley in 1754, George Washington and Christopher Gist were forced to build their own makeshift raft to cross the Allegheny River. Large pieces of ice and the current made this impossible, and both men were forced to abandon the raft and swim in the freezing river. Kenneth P. Bailey, "Christopher Gist and the Trans-Allegheny Frontier: A Phase of the Westward Movement," *Pacific Historical Review* 14, no. 1 (1945): 45–56.

3 "Conquerer" is a nineteenth-century variant spelling of conqueror. *Oxford English Dictionary*. Lippard likely characterizes Taylor as a "new conqueror" with Hernán Cortés.

4 Disease killed more soldiers in the U.S.-Mexico War than battle. "The Veracruz Expedition of 1847," *Military Affairs* 20, no. 3 (1956): 162–69. See Jack Edward McCallum, *Military Medicine: From Ancient Times to the 21st Century* (Santa Barbara: ABC-CLIO, 2008).

5 Lippard is referring to Napoleon's first wife, Josephine, born Marie Josèphe Rose Tascher de La Pagerie (1763–1814), who reluctantly consented to Napoleon's request for a divorce. Despite having children from a prior marriage, she had no children with Napoleon. The Emperor married Maria Louisa (1791–1847), royalty of the Austrian Empire, in hopes of an heir. Claude-François Méneval, *Memoirs of Napoleon Bonaparte, the Court of the First Empire* (New York: P.F. Collier & Son, 1910), 600–611. See William Hazlit, *The Life of Napoleon Bonaparte* (Boston: D. Estes, 1902).

6 Lippard uses the word "oriental" here to evoke a sense of exoticism by nodding to the cultural influence of the Moors on Spanish architecture.

while four slender pillars supported the ceiling. Toward the river a single large window, with a balcony defended by bars—toward the garden, a wide doorway, concealed by silken curtains, which tossed like a banner to the impulse of the night-breeze. Through the doorway, you pass down steps of cool marble, into garden all shade and bloom, fountains and flowers. Around the walls, were grouped vases of alabaster, blooming with all manner of rare and delicate plants, from the wild blossoms of the prairie to the gaudy cactus, plucked from the steeps of dizzy cliffs, or gathered from the green spots of desert wastes.

But the most beautiful thing in all the place, was the Woman who slumbered there!

Behold her!

A small lamp, suspended from the pillar, flings its rays over her couch; a small bed, covered with folds of dark cloth, edged with gold. Behold her! One of those wild, warm natures, born of the tempests and sunshine of the volcanic south; her cheek a rich, clear brown; her eye-lashes long and dark; her bosom full and passionate, her hair, flowing from the forehead to the waist, a shower of midnight tresses, gleaming and darkening over a robe of snow.

As she slumbers there, her cheek resting upon her left arm, you may see the dark brow, gather in a frown, the ripe warm lips compress with alternate fear and scorn, the bosom, agitated at first with a gentle motion, and then rushing with one wild throb into light. The loose white robe falls aside, and you behold that young breast, beating with violent emotion.

She has passed from the cool waters of the bath, to the agitated slumbers of the couch. A loose robe, flowing from the white shoulders to the feet—shoulders and feet, are naked and white as marble—encircles with its easy folds, her young and voluptuous form.

Let us approach her couch, let us bend over this sleeping woman, and listen to the words which fall quivering, as though each word was a drop of blood, from her young lips.

Strange revelation! Even in her sleep she tells the story of her life.

Even while the lull of the fountain, is heard in the awful intervals of the cannonade, while the perfume of the flowers, mingles with the smell of powder and blood, this beautiful child of the South, in her tempestuous dream, beating gently her breast all the while, with her fingers, reveals to us the history of her heart.

At first the dream bewilders us, with its light and gloom, its pictures of loving beauty and sombre[7] sublimity.

We stand in the shadows of the Cathedral aisle. It is the evening hour. The setting sun flings one broad belt of light, over yonder altar of solid silver, with the candelabra of gold above it, and the balustrade[8] of precious metals, extending on either side. Count the wealth of a fairy legend, and you have it here, in this solemn cathedral. And yonder—smiling sadly over all the display of wealth—stands the golden Image of the Carpenter's Son of Nazareth, and by his side, beams the silver face of his Divine Mother. It is an awful place, confounding us, by its strange, almost gorgeously grotesque architecture, its mingling of the Aztec with the Catholic faith, its almost blasphemous conjunction of Montezuma and Jesus.

This Cathedral of Mexico, in which we now stand, occupies the very spot, where stood hundreds of years ago, the temple of the bloody God of Anahuac. Here, where Jesus smiles, once writhed the human sacrifice, with his heart torn palpitating from his breast.

But hold! A vision breaks upon us now. Even as the shadows of night descend, as the deep serenity of this holy place, is only broken by the bustle

---

7 "Sombre" is a nineteenth-century variant spelling of somber. *Oxford English Dictionary*.

8 A balustrade is "[a] row of balusters, surmounted by a rail or coping, forming an ornamental parapet or barrier along the edge of a terrace, balcony, etc." Ibid.

of the gay plaza without, as the everlasting light, burns near the face of Jesus—behold!

Two figures approach and bend before the altar—a Virgin in the bloom of her southern life, dark in eyes, eyebrows and hair, luxuriant in the fiery tinge of her clear brown cheeks, kneels beside a soldier, dressed in the costume of the northern land, his chesnut hair, curling round a thoughtful brow.

They kneel there, impressive types of widely contrasted races—He, born of the land of Washington, a wanderer from the hills of Virginia—She, a voluptuous daughter of the land of the Aztec, with the old Castilian blood, mingling in her veins with the blood of Montezuma.[9]

They kneel there; the awful cathedral forms their marriage canopy. The Priest in his white robes, scatters from his withered hands, a blessing on the strangely wedded pair. He looks into her face, his clear hazel eye, drinking those eyes of hers, which seem at once to combine, all that is dark and bright, in the whole world.

But at this moment—we are still in the maiden's dream, you will remember—a footstep rings along the aisle, and a stern man, with snowy hair, a bronzed cheek, and a white mustache, strides slowly forward, his eye burning with the wounded pride of an old Castilian.

He tears his child from the embrace of her husband—you see a woman's form flung fainting by the altar, you see the figure of the husband, borne rudely along the aisles by mortal hands, and mists and darkness close the strange sad vision.

Yes, the maiden's dream ends here—with the stern old Castilian, standing in triumphant scorn, alone with the affrighted Priest and the unconscious daughter, alone in that place of religion and gold, the Cathedral of Mexico. Even as the mists close over their forms, the light glitters upon

---

9 For an analysis of the establishment and demographic consequences of the *encomienda* system, see Lesley Byrd Simpson, *The Encomienda in New Spain: The Beginning of Spanish Mexico* (Berkeley: University of California Press, 1982).

his uniform tinselled with stars, and the breeze gently moves the white folds of her bridal dress.

With the dream of the past, the beautiful girl, sleeping in this perfumed chamber of the Matamoras home, moves her round arms and uncloses her dark eyes. She starts to her feet, with her long hair showering half-way down her voluptuous form. She stands with bare feet on the marble floor, and presses her hand to her forehead.

"Only six month ago"—Not in English, but in the rich, sonorous Castilian she speaks—"And I knelt by his side, before the Altar of the grand Cathedral. My father tore him from my grasp; this lover, this husband of mine, rots in prison at this very hour. And I—already married, must by to-morrow's light, wed another. Such is the decree of *my father!* Have a care proud Castilian! The blood of my mother, which flows in my veins, the blood of the Montezumas, may foil you, even yet!"

She paces along the chamber, her white robe flowing to her feet. With one hand she dashes aside the mass of dark hair from her brow, while that face, so passionate in its warm beauty, is softened in every outline by a sad and tender memory.

"Even yet I remember it! Recovering from my swoon, I clung to the arm of my father and passed from the Cathedral; on the threshold a beggar girl started forward and clasped my arm. Even in her rags, she was beautiful—that child of the *Lepero** born in the hut, and nourished into bloom, by hopeless misery. My father started—'*She is the very image of my daughter—of Inez!*' he whispered. Meanwhile that poor girl, still clung to my arm, gazing in my face, with her large eyes as she whispered—'Fear not proud lady! For I do not fear, I do not despair! I, that have nothing but rags

---

* The outcasts of Mexican civilization, swarming by thousands in the hovels of the city, and descended from the old Aztec race, are entitled, *Leperos*.

and misery, the leper's crust and the leper's straw, do not despair, for *I am a daughter of Montezuma!*"

A strange memory! The beggar girl of Mexico and the proud lady Inez—one in rags and the other in lace and gold—and yet resembling each other, like twin copies of some beautiful statue.

You should have seen the proud elevation of this woman's form, as with her dark hair, streaming over her shoulders and down her back, she exclaimed—

"I, I, too am a daughter of the race of Montezuma!"

And all the while, as she paced along in that place of fountains and flowers, the thunder of the cannonade, mingled with the music of the pattering fountains, and the smell of powder, choked the perfume of the flowers.

"There is no hope!"

Terrible words, when spoken by a beautiful and helpless woman, communing with her own heart! No hope! To-morrow, Inez at once a Wife and Virgin, would be dragged to the altar—perchance amid the roar of battle—and married to a man, whom her soul abhorred.

Even as she spoke, the silken curtain, which waved from the window, leading to the balcony, was thrust aside, and a strange form stood there, framed in the curtain folds as in a veil. It was the form of a young man, attired in the plain blue undress of an American officer, which revealed every outline of his slight, yet sinewy frame. His face was very pale, yet strongly featured, the white forehead encircled by clustering curls, and the eyes, gazing with deep and steady light, from beneath the compressed brow!

As silent as a corse, he stood, regarding the maiden with that unvarying gaze.

She sank on one knee, muttering a prayer, and invoking the name of Mary, the Virgin Mother. It was a vision that she saw—a vision of the ghost of her dead Husband.

This beautiful woman, on her knee, the white robe falling from her shoulders, and revealing half the beauty of her bosom—that silent figure, standing in the window, his deep eye glaring from a face pale as death, formed together, with the light and shadow, the fountains and flowers, a strangely impressive picture.

Her senses fled from her, even as the cross which she clasped, glided from her stiffening fingers.

When again she looked up from that death-like trance, she felt her young bosom beating warmly against a manly heart, she felt the smile of her Husband upon her face.

"Come!" said the VIRGINIAN, speaking low in the deep Castilian—"There is no time for a long story—I have dared death to meet you, and we must dare death again, ere we escape from this place."

Girding her gently in his arms,—clasping the waist, which quivered in his embrace—he bore her through the curtain, and they stood upon the balcony, with their eyes dazzled by a picture, at once horrible and sublime.

That mansion of Matamoras, stood but a short distance from the river,[10] from which it was separated by a garden, whose fountains sparkled through arcades of flowers.

The river wound before them, a fiery track of light.

Yonder arises Fort Brown, the Banner of the Stars, waving out in red light, from the background of the midnight sky. Around that beleagued fort, darkens the Mexican army—you see them, Ranchero and Soldier, spread by thousands along the river shore.

10   The reference is to the Rio Grande.

But the sky was the most fearful sight of all. It was like an immense pall, stretched over the universe, with fearful hieroglyphics traced upon it by the blaze of a volcano.

And the light of the blazing sky, was thrown upon the face of the beautiful girl, who clung to the breast of her American husband. His pale face glows with crimson; her olive cheek, as with a burning blush of passion. Even her white robe and black hair, are tinted with fiery gleams of scarlet.

They stand upon the balcony, while the thunder of the cannon shakes the earth, and the hoarse murmur of the Mexican army, swells terribly in each interval of the night battle. That river, crowded with boats, that shore darkened by legions, whose lances glitter like torches of flame, that fort, defended by three hundred men, its banner waving on, through the lightning of battle, it was a sight to fire the blood, and make the heart leap, to mingle in the hurricane.

"They are there, my countrymen—fighting on, when hope is gone!" cried the VIRGINIAN, "Inez, you will go with me? With me, over the river, with me, through the roar of battle, with me into the shades of the chaparral?"

It was a terrible sight, that flashed before the maiden's eyes, and yet with the warm blood, glowing in her cheek, she answered, "I will!"

Down, from the balcony, by the ladder that quivers beneath its burden, down into the shadows of the garden, she girded by his arm, her snowy robe fluttering loosely around her queenly form.

They are lost to sight, but a step resounds within the chamber, and an old man strides madly forth upon the balcony, into the light of the cannonade.

Gaze upon that tall form, clad in the Mexican warrior costume, green faced with gold—upon that bronzed face, wrinkled with age, the white mustache covering the compressed lips, the eyes shooting frenzy from the lowering brow, and pray for the young girl and her lover, her husband!

The old man stands upon the balcony, quivering with rage, the deep curses trembling from his lips. For there is a boat upon the river, a fragile skiff, that glides over the glowing waves bearing two forms to the opposite shore the young Virginian and his Mexican bride!

"Curses! They near the opposite shore! Ha! That shell—it bursts above their heads—it crushes them into the red waves! A cloud of smoke—it is gone! Curses! They are there again, speeding toward the shore! May the fiend drive the bullet to his heart! He leads forth from the bushes by the shore, his black steed—they mount together—rushing through our ranks, he flies!"

And as the old man, sent up from the bitterness of his heart, a curse upon his child, that American on the black horse, dashed through the Mexican ranks, while the white robe of his bride floated over the dark skin of the steed, and wrapped their forms as in a mantle of snow.

"Huzza!" he cried in defiance, as the shot rained like hail about his horse's feet—"Blaze on! I go to the Camp of Taylor; I go to bring succor for the beleagued fort."[11]

It is a glorious thing to feel a battle steed, as black as death, bound beneath you, like a shell hurled from a mortar, it is a glorious thing to see the glare of battle, enfolding you like a curtain, to hear its thunder, yelling like the earthquake from the volcano's throat, but to ride through the fury of a battle, at dead of night, a black steed bounding beneath you, while a beautiful woman quivers in your arms—it makes the heart swell and the blood burn like a flame!

Long upon the balcony, stood the old Mexican Chieftain, gazing—not upon the Fort, which stood boldly out, in the fierce light of the cannonade,

11 Before the Battle of Palo Alto, Taylor and two thousand of his men made camp at Fort Isabel and aided in strengthening the defenses. After Taylor was satisfied with the progress of defenses at Isabel, he moved his troops to provide support at Fort Brown. Daniel Walker Howe, *What Hath God Wrought: The Transformation of America, 1815–1848* (Oxford: Oxford University Press, 2007), 744.

12 Lippard is referring to the anecdote that the Aztecs believed Hernán Cortés (1485–1547) to be the returned serpent god Quetzalcoatl. Buddy Levy, *Conquistador: Hernan Cortes, King Montezuma, and the Last Stand of the Aztecs* (New York: Random House Publishing Group, 2009), 89, 90, 110, 138, 139.

nor upon the shore thronged with the legions of Mexico, nor upon the roof of Matamoras, black with spectators of the midnight battle—but upon the dark chaparral, where his eye had seen the last flutter of his daughter's snowy robe.

Did you ever read of Montezuma?

Did you ever read of that Monarch, with the olive cheek, who sate upon the Throne of Tenochtitlan,* three hundred years ago, the last of a long line of kings, surrounded by kneeling nobles, and served at the festival table, by groups of beautiful women, dark-eyed and passionate daughter of the south?

Did you ever hear of the strange land of Anahuac over which he reigned, a land magnificent with its mountains of snow and fire, its vallies of fruitfulness and bloom, its clear, calm lakes mirroring beautiful cities, its awful Religion, smoking on every altar, with human blood?

How this land fell beneath the Spaniard, how the bloody Prophet, whose coming had been announced by the Aztec priests for hundreds of years, came in the person of the stern bigot, chivalric soldier, Hernan Cortes—you have read it all.[12]

When the empire of Montezuma fell, and the sad emperor, who had been conquered by Fate, not by man, yielded up the last throb of her broken heart, his blood still beat in the veins of his daughters, who were joined in marriage with the proudest of the Castilian nobility.

It is of some of the descendants of these marriages of the Spaniard and the Aztec noble, that we now purpose to speak.

---

* Aztec name of the city of Mexico.

You remember the horrible religion of old Mexico? That creed of blood which raised its vast altar in every city, and led its human victim, to the place of the sacrifice, and flung his quivering heart, torn smoking from the body, in the face of its Devil-God.

A creed in fact, which in its atrocious details, all acted, in the name of a Devil, almost rivals some of those barbarous corruptions of the Christian faith, whose bloody sacrifices of human hearts, have been acted in the name of Jesus and of God.

You remember that eternal flame, which burned on the altar of Montezuma, bearing with its clouds of white smoke and radiant light, a silent testimony to the immortality of the Aztec faith?

That flame, was first lighted, when the Ancestors of Montezuma, hundreds of years before his day, came swarming from the north, upon the fertile valley of Mexico. It burned on for ages, until the time of Cortes, when it was supposed to be forever quenched, in the last baptism of blood, offered by him upon its altar.

But it was never quenched, that awful fire of Montezuma! While the Spaniard, crowded Mexico with his legions, and built his altars upon the ruins of Aztec *Teocalli*,[13] certain tribes of the old people, true to their race and their religion, fled to the mountain and the wilderness, bearing with them, flaming torches, which had been lighted at the eternal fire.

That fire has never once gone out, through the long course of three hundred and twenty-six years. It burns on at the present hour, as it burned in the days of Montezuma.

Where the ravine is dark and horrible, where the mountain threatens you with death, if you dare approach its summit of eternal snow, where the wilderness extends, fenced in from civilization by impenetrable thickets,

13 A teocalli is an architectural "[s]tructure for purposes of worship among the ancient Mexicans and Central Americans, usually consisting of a four-sided truncated pyramid built terrace-wise, and surmounted by a temple." *Oxford English Dictionary.*

14 Miguel Hidalgo y Costilla (1753–1811) was a Catholic priest and revolutionary who fought for Mexican independence from September 16, 1810 until his death in January, 1811. Hidalgo was ultimately captured and killed by firing squad for his revolutionary activities. For more information, see Suzanne B. Pasztor, *The Spirit of Hidalgo: The Mexican Revolution in Coahuila* (Calgary: University of Calgary Press, 2002).

15 The Battle of Palo Alto took place May 8, 1846. For troop movements and an account of the battle, see John D. Eisenhower, *So Far from God: The U.S War with Mexico 1846–1848* (Norman, OK: University of Oklahoma Press, 2000), 75–85. For an analysis of Mexican motivations, see Timothy Henderson, *A Glorious Defeat: Mexico and Its War with the United States* (New York: Hill and Wang, 2007).

swarming with wild beasts—there, may you still discover, the eternal fire of Montezuma.

Torches, lighted at this flame, have been brought forth, to the gaze of the white man, on certain occasions, since the conquest of Cortes.

Whenever danger to the Spaniard, hovers in the air, those torches are seen, flashing from the tops of the mountains, from the shadows of the ravine!

When the Hero-Priest Hidalgo,[14]—descended from the Aztec race,—raised the standard of revolt, and declared the soil of Anahuac, free from European despotism, that torch blazed in the faces of the Spaniards and lit them to their bloody graves.

It blazed again, ere the battle of Palo Alto. We will journey into the wilderness and behold its light. In the wilderness of Chaparral and prairie, which extends from the shores of the Rio Grande, there are many desert wilds, scarcely ever trodden by the foot of the white man. Stunted trees, lacing their gnarled limbs together, with their trunks joined in one, by thickly grown vines, form an impenetrable barrier, between those deserts and the step of the civilized intruder. Even the Ranchero, that combination of the worst vices of civilization and barbarism, dare not profane these silent solitudes.

On the morning of the Eighth of May, 1846, we will journey for miles through these impenetrable thickets, and in the centre of the wild, behold a scene, which but a short distance removed from the cities of the white race, is yet stamped with all the traces of the people of Montezuma.[15]

In the centre of the wilderness, a space some two miles square, bloomed like a garden. Do you see its fields of tall green corn, waving yonder, near a wilderness of fig trees, rich with their tempting fruit? Here, the pomegranates hidden among large green leaves, meets your eye, and there, dangling from the vines, the grapes come quivering into light. Wherever you turn your gaze, all is bloom, verdure,[16] fruitfulness. There are birds of radiant plumage upon the trees, and flowers, that make you forget the rainbow scattered everywhere along the sod.

Do you distinctly see this garden in the wilderness, hemmed in on every side by the impassable chaparral?

Gaze in its centre, and you will behold a circle of huts, formed of reeds woven together, like basket work, cemented with clay, and defended from the sun and rain, by a roof of vines and blossoms.

The tall corn waves greenly about them, and the fig floats its perfume through their narrow doors, and the meek-eyed dove of the tropics, a gentle thing, looking like the holy spirit of home, murmurs its low music in the vines above the roof. Altogether, the quiet picture, blooming under the morning sun, in the wilderness, steels on us, like a dream from Heaven, a delicious leaf, cut freshly from the book of eternal beauty.

Here dwells one of those remnants of the Aztec people, which have been hidden in the desert, from the eye of the white man, for three hundred years. You see the dark-faced men, with long black hair, stand before the doors of their homes—the tawny children playing among the flowers—the brown Women, with large lustrous eyes, gathering the rich fruitage of tree and field.

But the object in the centre of the desert village, that mass of stone, piled up, rock on rock, until it swells far over the roof into the serene upper air?

Ascend those steps—toil slowly up the rugged stairway—stand upon the summit—gaze upon the village that blooms below!

But the fire, that burns upon the summit of this mound of rocks, that clear flame, burning beneath the shelter of a large flat stone, supported by two masses of granite?

16 "Verdure" is used here as a description of lush "[g]reen vegetation; plants or trees, or parts of these, in a green and flourishing state." *Oxford English Dictionary.*

This mound of rocks, is one of the last altars of the Aztec race; a Teo-calli of that faith of blood, which offered its victims in the days of old.

That fire, is the sacred flame, never once extinguished since the days of Montezuma.

Before that fire, crouching on the rock, sits an old man, with long black hair floating down his back, while a loose robe of coarse white cotton, enfolds his withered form.

The last priest of Montezuma!

From early childhood he has watched that fire, fed it with fragrant wood, and gazed upon its flames, as though it was a God. Before his day, his father watched it; when he is gone, his son, tall and straight as the desert palm, will assume the sacred duty. So from age to age, from father to son, burns on the flame of Montezuma!

Does not the image of this peaceful people, dwelling alone by their rude altar, in the wilderness, never trodden by the white man, gathering their bread and attire, from the maize and cotton of the field, their knowledge of God, from the traditions of their fathers, at once bewilder and enchain you?

The day wears on—they have come from the fields to partake of their simple meal—the old man still sits upon the mound, watching the sacred flame!

The day wears on! Hark! From the east a sound like thunder. It is the cannon of Palo Alto, the old man rises, listens, and thinks it thunder. He knows nothing of the wars or battles of the white race.

The day wears on. The sun is yonder in the west. The mound of rocks flings its shadow over the village. Still the sound of thunder to the east, thunder, deep and blooming, from a sky, without a cloud.

III. The Dead Woman of Palo Alto

The affrighted people of the Aztec village, throng to the altar, the strong-limbed men, the brown women with the lustrous eyes, the tawny children scattering flowers.

They seek to propitiate their God, by a sacrifice. That thunder from a cloudless sky terrifies their souls. A dove, one of those gentle doves of home, is the destined victim. Look! It flutters on the large flat stone above the flame, and murmurs its sad music, even as the hand of the priest is laid upon its glossy neck.

A prayer in the Mexican tongue, a wild and momentous hymn to the strange deity.

It is a picture to remember. That solitary mound rising above the hamlet in the wilderness, its huge shadow, blackening over the fields—that erect old man, upon the summit, the centre of a crowd of dark-skinned worshippers—the bird fluttering in his hand, the sacramental knife raised over his head.

At the moment a cry quivers from every lip, and every eye is turned toward the east.

There, stealing from the forest, comes the form of a woman, her dark hair floating over her snowy robes, while her large eyes roll from side to side, with a look of fear.

Her dress is torn by the briers; her hair tangled by the perfumed blossom rent from the wild vine; she totters on toward the altar—

It is the Lady INEZ, daughter of the stern Mexican General, wife of the gallant Virginian.

———

Within the same hour, a scene of deep interest took place on the field of PALO ALTO.

It was in the last hour of that fight—when the battle, which we will shortly look upon in all its details, was about to close—that a solitary Mexican officer, flying from the field, spurred his bay horse through the devious path of the chaparral.

Look yonder, and by the light of the solitary sun, you may behold his pursuer, a young American, mounted on a dark steed. With the uniform torn in ribands from his right arm, he brandishes his sword—it drops blood upon his broad chest—and dashes on.

He nears the Mexican, he is within twenty paces, when the flying soldier is about to leave the path, and seek the shadows of the chaparral. The American raises his pistol—fires! The bay-horse totters to and fro, and falls on his forefeet, precipitating his rider on the sod.

Beside his dying horse—whose life-blood wells from the fatal wound—that rider stands and confronts the enemy. The American starts in his saddle, and pulls his bridle-rein, throwing his dark horse, back on his haunches, as he beholds him.

For in that American officer stained from head to foot with blood, you recognize the pale face and full deep eyes of the VIRGINIAN, husband of the Lady Inez. Look upon that Mexican, his green uniform rent with sword thrusts, his white moustache, dyed with crimson drops, his bronzed face traversed by a fearful wound, and you behold *her father*.

Words of deep meaning were spoken there in that lonely chaparral.

"Yield, General!" cried the VIRGINIAN in Spanish. "You are faint with wounds. I will not fight with the father of my wife."

There was something terrible in the silent malignity which shone from the old man's eyes.

"You are mounted," he quietly said—"My horse is dying—" and then wiping the blood from his sword blade with his left hand, grasped the hilt with his right, and stood prepared for a deadly fight—"Come!" he cried in the settled tone of a mortal hatred—"You escaped from the prison of Mexico, but cannot escape *me!*"

It was interesting to notice the conduct of that young Virginian, whose blue uniform was in many places turned to red, by the blood of his foes. He quietly dismounted, flung the rein on the neck of his dark steed, wiped the battle sweat from his face, and then struck the point of his sword into the sod.

He then calmly advanced along the path, with the wall of the chaparral on either side. Stern and unrelenting, the old General awaited him.

"General you see me, unarmed, defenceless before you!" said the Virginian advancing—"Let me ask you once for all—why do you pursue me with this unrelenting hatred? I came to your Mexican home, a stranger from the far north, and was grateful for your generous hospitality. I met your daughter—we loved—were joined in marriage before the altar of your solemn cathedral. Why hurl me from your daughter's arms, into a prison, only reserved for the vilest outcast? Why, even as I rotted in the dungeon, did you drag my wife from the city, force her to accompany you in your march, and last night bid her prepare, for the miserable nuptials which were to take place to-day? Come—be friends with me—in this hour, when you are forced to leave the field, a fugitive, I will aid your flight!"

There was an earnestness in the young man's tone, that would have touched the hardest heart. Frankness was written on his pale face, and honor spoke in the gleam of his large hazel eye.

"Where is my daughter?" said the Mexican General, in a low voice, but still keeping his hand on the hilt of his sword.

"Last night, when I bore the message of Fort Brown, to our General—that message which called for help, in direst extremity—I left Inez in a *ranche* (farm house) some few hundred yards to the west of this place. When the battle is over,—I will join her again."

"Coward! You will never join her again! After I have laid you dead upon the sod, I myself will go and bear your message to my daughter."

With a ferocious look in his eye, the General dashed upon the unarmed man, making a thrust, with all the vigor of his right arm. To say the least, there was something cowardly in this movement, indeed, it looked very much like Assassination.

The Virginian darted aside, but the sword passed between his side and his left arm, transfixing a piece of his coat.

As quick as thought he turned, darted on the Mexican—who had been almost thrown on his face by the impetus of his ineffectual thrust—and clutched his throat with a grasp of iron.

"This your Mexican chivalry! To stab an unarmed man!"

He shook him fiercely in that tightening grasp—the General made an effort to shorten his grasp of the sword, and use it as a dagger, but the blade fell from his hand—he sank backward on the sod, with the knee of the Virginian on his breast.

He uttered an incoherent groan—his eyes began to start from their sockets.

The Virginian, touched with pity released his grasp, but seized the fallen sword.

"I hate you"—slowly said the Mexican General, raising himself on one hand, while his face grew deathly pale—"Not so much because you stole my daughter, as that you are one of the accursed race, whose destiny it is, to despoil our land, extinguish our name, annihilate our flag!"

He tore open the breast of his coat, and disclosed a mortal wound, which had been killing him, slowly, for hours.—

"If there is one word, that may express the hatred of a dying man, better than another, I fling it in your face and curse you with that breath, whose passing, leaves my lips cold forever!"

There was something so terrible in these last words of a dying man, uttered with rattling breath and a pale face, deformed by hideous contortions, that the American soldier shrunk from his touch, and gazed upon him in silent horror.

He never spoke again, save to murmur, in his Spanish tongue—"Water! Water!"

Reaching forth his arms, he grasped the blade of his sword which the Virginian held—kissed the hilt, and fell back, with a torrent of blood, streaming from his mouth.

The Virginian turned to search for water; the murmuring of a brooklet reached his ears; he left the dying man and rushed along the path. Turning to the east, he saw the lakelet, spreading calm and beautiful in the depths of the chaparral. Scarce a ray of sunlight, streamed over its dark and tranquil bosom.

Our young soldier bent down, with his helmet in his hand, its horsehair plume sweeping to the ground, and filled it with the cool water, when another sight palsied his hand, and turned his face to the color of ashes and clay.

Before him, in a nook formed by the foliage, on the soft, short grass, lay the dead body of a human being.

It was a woman, naked as Eve before she fell, with the blood streaming from her white bosom. As she lay there, her hair—so intensely dark, with a glossy richness almost every wave and curl—fell over her arms and clotted in some places with her blood, streamed in masses over the sod.

Not a vestage[17] of apparel was there, upon her form, to denote her rank, or enable the living to identify the beautiful dead.

17 "Vestage" is a nineteenth-century variant spelling of vestige. *Oxford English Dictionary*.

For she was very beautiful. Had you seen the matchless outline of her young limbs, chaste yet voluptuous, her bosom, just blossoming into bloom, her olive cheek, which pillowed the dark eyelashes, her lips, which death had not despoiled of their vermillion—you would have knelt by her, and gazed for hours upon the silent beauty of the murdered girl.

Murdered? By whom? Where the weapon? Where the traces of the wrong?

The leaves were above her, the lakelet stretched away from her feet, and the blood welled slowly from the wound in her heart.

The Virginian forgot the dying man, dashed his helmet away, and sank beside the dead girl.

"Inez!" and bending down, he earnestly perused those features, sealed forever in the sleep of death.

Meanwhile but a few paces distant, the Mexican General started into a sitting posture, with the blood pouring from his mouth, he rushed along the path, beheld for a moment the form of the dead woman—knew it, for a horrible agony writhed over his face—and then fell forward on his face—dead.

While his ashy face, was stamped with a despair that fast fevered into madness, the Virginian looked from the naked form to the dead soldier, and murmured—

"The Murderer and the Murdered!"

―――――

It was night in the wilderness; the groans of a thousand hearts, quivering in mental agony, palpitated through the chaparral, from the shores of the Rio Grande, to the bloody rivulet of Palo Alto.

III. The Dead Woman of Palo Alto

It was night and through the wall of woven thorns, a solitary horse, dashed like a shell, hurled from the blazing mortar—a solitary horse, his nostrils quivering as though they shot forth, jets of flame, his dark hide flecked with shots of foam, his bloody mane, waving over his eyes and about his arching neck. Those eyes seem to burn in the darkness, like the meteors of a swamp.

The Rider! Throat bare, brow uncovered, hair damp with sweat and clotted with blood, he shook his clenched hands on high, sank his spurs into the flanks of the horse and whirled away. Ha! Ha! how he shouted in horrible laughter, while the thorns tore his flesh, as though they were living things, poisonous with venom, and the gnarled boughs struck his breast, as though they were the arms of warriors fired with battle rage.

The chaparral darkened round him, a wall of prickly pear—the sod beneath was broken into pits and ravines—wherever he turned his burning eyes, was nothing but that impassible desert, upon whose wilderness of stunted trees, cold and dimly fell the night of the midnight stars.

He was Mad, the brave Virginian. You may talk of hearts, if you please, and of minds, steeled against the fiercest sorrow, however vulture-like the beak, with which it may drink our heart's blood, but show me the soul, that can gaze without madness, upon this horrible vision! A young, a virgin wife,—whose kiss was warm upon her husband's lips this morning—found at the setting of the sun, in the lonely chaparral, the blood oozing slowly from her mangled breast, found a naked and dishonored thing, the peerless beauty of her uncovered form, only making her death more horrible to look upon!

For hours the young soldier, has thundered madly through the wild, not caring whither his horse's footsteps turned, only so that they bore him

18 "Chaunt" is a less common British variant of chant.
19 "Travellers" is a nineteenth-century variant spelling of travelers. *Oxford English Dictionary.*

farther from the face of man, farther into the desert, the darkness and the night. Madly he dashed along, and yet all the while, with a consciousness of his horrible calamity pervading his whole being, like the forked lightning, quivering through the blackness of the thunder cloud.

At last after hours of mad wandering, he suffered the rein to fall on the neck of his steed, his hands sank listlessly by his side, his head drooped on his breast. The stupor had succeeded the frenzy of despair.

Slowly the horse wandered along, the Rider knew not, cared not whither, while the moments of that night of agony, throbbed slowly away.

Hark! The Virginian roused from his stupor, lifts his head in wonder. A low, deep monotonous chaunt[18] breaks on the night. Look! The impenetrable wall of chaparral, gives place to a field of corn, whose broad green leaves wave above the horse's head.

At once, the vision of a quiet group of homes in the wilderness, and the delicious perfume of fruits and flowers, rush on the senses of the bewildered man. By the light of the stars he gazes wildly around, and suffers the wounded, the bleeding steed to take his way.

Through the field of maize, by the wilderness of fig trees, among the vines that trail luxuriantly over the ground, the horse wanders on.

At last—what new wonder is this?

Far above the roofs of that desert-girdled home, a light shines like a star, and sheds a radiance, at once serene and vivid upon the air.

Is it a star, shining from the midnight sky? Or, one of those wild lights, which born of the atmosphere of the swamp, bewilder travellers[19] on their way, and lead them on to death?

His eye grows accustomed to the darkness. That light shines from the summit of a huge mound of rocks, and the forms of human things, intervene between the eye and its steady blaze.

Again that deep chaunt, swelling through the night, like a requiem over the dead!

The bewildered traveller rushes forward, springs from his steed and darts up the rocky steps of the mound, his eye glaring madly all the while, his chesnut hair, hanging in bloody flakes, about his feverish brow.

A strange fancy has taken firm hold of his brain. He imagines himself in one of the last retreats of the Aztec people, in that rude mound, he sees a TEOCALLI, a bloody altar of the far gone time; that flame is the fire of Montezuma; those forms, grouped between him and the light, the figures of the sacrificial priests gloating over their victim's writhing form.

That victim—oh! the horrible frenzy made his blood run cold, hot as it was with the fever of madness—his own wife, the lady Inez, whom he had left a murdered and dishonored thing, in the shadow of the lonely chaparral.

He ascended the mound of rocks, and stood with gasping breath upon the Summit. A sight too wondrous for belief or words, met his silent gaze.

They were Indian forms grouped upon the summit of the rock, men, with stout arms and broad chests, women with olive cheeks and deeply lustrous eyes, children with long black hair, about their tawny faces. Indians did we say? No! To the bewildered traveller's eye, they looked more like the Aztec people of three hundred and twenty six years ago. They stood in a circle, their backs to his face, their visages bathed in the red light, which sheltered by a huge flat stone, shone through the night afar.

Slowly, on tip-toe the traveller drew nigh.

In the midst of the silent group, stood an old man, attired in a loose robe of coarse cotton, gazing upon the object which held every eye enchained.

Nearer drew the traveller, his heart choking his utterance, or he would have groaned.

What struck him with surprise, was the universal expression which reigned upon every face. Whether old man, or stout-armed Son of the forest, or round limbed woman, or dark haired child, all wore one look. It was pity, it was sympathy, it was love, yes, as the angels love! It was religion!

Upon their rude faces, that look sat enthroned like a gem in the dust, like one serene ray, in a night of universal cloud.

Hush every breath, as the maddened traveller, worried into a fiercer agony, draws near, looks over their shoulders, feels the flame upon his face, beholds the object which enchains every eye.

That chaunt, swelling low and deep from every lip, drowned the echo of his step.

The sight that he saw—a bleeding victim, disfigured by the knife! No!

A sleeping Woman, wrapped in a white robe, with her smiling face—warm cheeks, red lips, large lashes, and all—framed in her darkly flowing hair!

And the sleeping Woman, smiling in her calm repose, while the tawny people, bent over her, as though she had dropped among them, from God, was the Lady Inez, the wife whom we left a murdered thing in the darkness of the chaparral.

Softly she slumbered, the light of the eternal fire upon her face, the blossoms gathered by little children's hands, wound among the tresses of her beautiful hair.

It was a dream. Choking down the agony of his soul, he darted forward, knelt and gazed upon her.

With one cry, the Indians shrank back, from that contrast—his frenzied face, her smiling countenance!

It was her Ghost. He knew it. Afraid to touch the hand, which lay with its white fingers unclosed, upon the rock, he gazed in the stern silence of despair, upon that image of slumbering womanhood.

At last those lids were unclosed, those dark eyes met the light of his own, the white robe, falling back, revealed the white shoulders and the bosom of snow. The traveller darted forward—there was a form palpitating upon his breast, a hand pillowed on his shoulder, masses of dark hair waving about his face.

"My Husband!"

Was it a Ghost?

That throb from the virgin bosom, kindling a heaven in his veins—ah! such electric fire, never quivered from the breast of spirit or Ghost before!

And while the fire of Montezuma burned through the dark night, the chaunt swelled on the air once more, and the Aztec people—I see them, now, upon the lonely mound, their faces bathed in red light, while all beyond is darkness—grouped wandering round the central figures, the Husband on his knees, with his beautiful wife upon his breast, her dark hair, waving over his shoulder.

Where is the thread to this mystery of the wilderness?

At the setting of the sun, you show us the dead body of the Lady Inez, laid naked and dishonored in the chaparral of Palo Alto, and at midnight, we behold the Lady Inez, calmly slumbering, on the mound of the wilderness, her smiling face, lighted by the eternal fire of Montezuma?

—Here is all that ever was known of the dark history.

It was in the last hour of Palo Alto, when the cannon of Taylor, flamed their lightning into the Mexican camp, that the beams of the declining sun, stealing through the battle clouds, shone on the trappings and tinsel of a gorgeous canopy, which towered in the heart of the dark chaparral.

Around this tent, the banquet fires were blazing, you see them smoking and flaming beneath the luscious viands, intended for the feast of victory. When Arista has conquered Taylor, and bound him in chains, he will come hither in royal state, and drink his iced wine, and feast on his luxurious banquet, while the tri-colored flag of Mexico waves in triumph over his head.[20]

But unfortunately old Zachary is hard to conquer. Even as we look upon the gaudy tents, with its ornaments glittering like diamonds in the light, we hear the rush of Taylor's legions to the north, and the tramp of the flying Mexicans to the south.

The lacqueys have left their banquet fire; the sentinels their place by the tent. For a few moments, while the tide of battle rages all around—look! how the smoke rolls yonder, up against the setting sun—the camp of Arista is silent as the grave.

In a moment the thunder of battle will envelope this place, in smoke and flames, but ere that moment comes, we will behold a sad, a touching scene.

Enter the tent of Arista. Pass through the gilded curtains, and behold the scene which spreads before you.

On the rich carpet, amid piles of scattered trunks, masses of charts and papers, heaps of plate, solid silver and gold, behold the kneeling form of a young, a beautiful girl. Attired in a garment of richest dyes, which half-revealing the warm bosom, girdles her slender waist, and terminates at her knees, displaying the sculptured proportions of her voluptuous limbs, she kneels amid the scene of splendid havoc, clasps her hands and raises her large dark eyes!

---

[20] Arista met Taylor in battle only two times throughout the war, the Battle of Palo Alto and Resaca de la Palma. After his defeat at Resaca de la Palma, Arista was removed from command.

While her bosom beats tumultuously into view, she prays, yes, in the Spanish and the Mexican tongue, prays to the God of the Christian and the God of Montezuma.

There is one portion of her costume, which imparts to her face and form, a beauty almost divine.

A veil of fine lace, like a wreath of transparent mist, as white as snow, flows from her forehead to her feet, with her long dark hair, and her bare arms, gleaming through its bewitching folds. Jewels worth many a solid piece of gold, sink and swell upon her breast, pearls which remind you of a pure virgin's tears, gleam in circlets from her brow.

While the battle rages afar, she prays, not for herself but for her lover!

Is it the Lady Inez, whom we behold?

The same form: the same red ripeness on the lip, and voluptuous swell in the outline of the form; dark flowing hair, and large full eyes, all the same; it is the Lady Inez! And yet we know, that at this very moment, the Lady Inez, is far away, in the tangled mazes of the wilderness!

Listen! Amid the roar of the battle, thundering afar, we hear a footstep, and presently the form of a young soldier, remarkable for his manly beauty, appears at the doorway of the tent. Scarce twenty years old, a dark mustache on lip, his bold features, relieved by long curls of jet-black hair, he silently advances, while we behold his handsome uniform, torn in fragments and spotted with blood.

He stands behind her, contemplating her form with a mingled look—pity and passion! Silently he unsheaths his dagger, poises it above her head, turning his face away, prepares to strike—

"The Battle," he cries in Spanish, "is lost and I will not leave you, to the mercy of the foe!"

She lifts her eyes, and beholds at once her lover and the trembling dagger. Her cheek does not blench, but her bosom all at once, falls into pulseless quietude.

"Kill, for I am thine, Francisco!" she says, raising her eyes, so lustrously beautiful to his face. "Who lifted the beggar girl from the hut of the Lepero to the couch of the lord? Who wound these pearls upon her forehead, and bade these jewels gleam upon her bosom? Who shared with her, the love of her noble heart? Francisco! And to who should the life of Mahitili belong, but to Francisco?"

She spake in the strange Mexican tongue, which, the same as fell from the lips of Montezuma, may be heard at this day in the mountains of Mexico.

"But the battle is lost, Mahitili," shrieked her lover, quivering in agony—

"For myself I care not; I will not fly; to die upon the lost field is all that is left for me. But you Mahitili—you my own love, whom I gathered from the huts of poverty, and wound to my heart—you, who have not hesitated to watch by my side, in the peril of pestilence, nor to follow my footsteps into the crash of battle! When I am dead what will be your fate?"

Calmly she rose, and placed her small fingers on the blade of his dagger.

"We will die together!" she said, enfolding him in her arms, until her snowy veil, was stained with the blood which dyed his uniform.

"To die, at this hour, of all other hours! To die, when I have just discovered that you are no child of poverty and shame, but the lost daughter of our brave General * * * *! The twin-sister of his proud and lovely child, with the blood of Montezuma, coursing through your veins! Nay stare not so wildly—it is true as the Virgin's purity! From a dying soldier on the battle field, I heard the truth, and received from his hands, the undeniable proofs! Kill you now—I cannot—we will fly!"

He seized her to his arms, but the robber form of a Ranchero, with his wide sombrero, and tawny face occupied the doorway of the tent. His dark eyes shone with the lust of plunder; one hand upon his rifle, one upon his knife, he silently confronted the youthful pair.

"Here is gold—" cries Francisco—"Secure for me, one of those riderless steeds, now running wild in the smoke of battle."

The Ranchero clutches the purse, hurries it in his bosom and disappears. They wait there, in Arista's tent, trembling with suspense and watching for the return of the Ranchero. Mahitili nestling close to Francisco's heart, like a bird to its nest, in the hour of storm, her white veil and raven hair, encircling his form, as with a robe of strange texture and beauty.

He does not return, the tawny Ranchero; the battle swells nearer the tent. Hark! That crash—a cannon ball whizzes through the silken curtaining, not an inch above their heads.

"Kneel, Mahitili! Kneel and pray to the Virgin until I return! I will secure a horse or die!"

He is gone, but scarcely has his form passed through the curtain folds, when the Ranchero stands before the tent, holding a noble black horse by the bridle rein. On his glossy hide smokes the blood and foam of battle.

"Come!" exclaims the Ranchero, in barbarous Spanish. "He waits for you, yonder in the chaparral!"

Without a suspicion, she bounds to the saddle, while the Ranchero huddles the goblet and other vessels of silver and gold scattered along the carpet, into a capacious sack, tied to his girdle. Mahitili does not behold this movement. Her eyes have no gaze but for yonder cloud, which gathering volume, every moment, comes darkening over the chaparral, near and nearer the tent of Arista.[21]

21 After the Battle of Resaca de la Palma, "the men found a great booty in General Arista's tent. Though the silver and valuable luxuries automatically became the property of the U.S. government, piles of his writing paper fell into individual hands, and many a proud note was written home on sheets of it." Eisenhower, *So Far from God,* 84.

The Ranchero, that half-savage, with the stalwart form, and bronzed face, leaps in the saddle, and girding the trembling girl to his breast, bounds away.

Away, into the narrow path, leading far up the darkness of the chaparral. Deeper the shadows gather them in, fainter and more faint, the sun beams tremble over the dark horse, the Ranchero, and his voluptuous burden.

"Francisco?" she cried at last, quivering with an unknown fear. They had turned a bend of the path, and a dark lakelet, scare enlivened by a ray, spread before them. "My Lover?"

The Ranchero surveyed with one gloating look, the warm beauty of her face, and the luxuriant swell of her bosom—

"He is here!" he said, and Mahitili felt the blood grow cold, from her heart to her fingers.

———

Not fifteen minutes passed, and on that sod, beside the dark lakelet, the MEXICAN GENERAL, with the blood pouring from his mouth, the VIRGINIAN with his heart turning to ice in his bosom, beheld the naked body of a murdered and dishonored woman.

There was the print of horse's hoofs toward the lakelet, and a goblet of sculptured gold, gleamed from the mire by its waters.

———

Francisco? Look yonder by the light of the moon, and behold a young form, stretched stifly on the prairie, his face buried in the sod, his arms extended, the fingers clutching the bloody grass, while the head of a dead steed rests upon his back!

He found the horse for which he sought, it seems, and—died with him. Perchance in the very act of mounting, for the same cannon ball, which pierced the flanks of the steed, crushed the young soldier's chest into mangled flesh and bones.

And as we look upon them, the jackal crawls from the bushes, and snuffs the air, turning from the dead warrior to the dead steed, and from dead steed to the warrior, as if hesitating where to commence his horrible meal.

How came the Bride of the Virginian, the guest of the rude Aztec people?

Alarmed by the thunder of the battle, she had strayed from the *Ranche* where her husband left her, lost her way, and wandered deeper into the chaparral until the hidden village bloomed upon her eyes. The old priest, the hardy people, the brown women, all hailed her, with her white attire, and beautiful form, as a good spirit sent from God; even the little children clung to her robe, and looked up fearfully into her large eyes.

Now, at the dead of night behold her, standing on that mound of rocks, her husbands arm about her form, while the sacred flame bathes their faces, and reveals the group of wondering Indians.

As we gaze, the old Priest—who received from his father the tradition and prophecy, and who will leave both to his son, as a holy heritage—bends down and lights a torch at the flame of Montezuma—

"There is doom for the Spaniard in the air!" he chants as he waves the torch—"Even as he crushed the children of Anahuac in the days of the old, so will a new race from the north, crush his people, in the dust and blood of battle!

"The Murder done by the Spaniard, returns to him again; and the blood that he once shed, rises from the ground, which will not hide it, and becomes a torrent to overflow his rule, his people, and his altars!

"Montezuma, from the shadows of ages, hear the cry of thy children! Arise! Gaze from the unclosed Halls of Death, upon the Spaniard's, ruin, and tell the ghosts to shout, as he dashes to darkness in a whirl pool of blood:

"Montezuma, and all ye ghosts, sing your song of gladness now, and let the days of your sorrow be past! Even, above the ocean of blood, which flows from thy mouth, over the land of Anahuac, behold the Dove of Peace, bearing her green leaves and white blossoms to the children of the soil!"

IV

Palo Alto[1]

An old man, dressed in a brown coat, and mounted on a grey horse, was riding through the chaparral, as the noonday sun shone over the wilderness of prickly pear, darkening on either side, while far behind, in all the windings of the narrow path, two thousand swords and bayonets, rose dazzling into light.

Look yonder, and behold Zachary Taylor and his Men, on their march to the field of Palo Alto!

A broad brimmed hat of grey felt, shaded his ample brow. There was no sword by his side, but he carried a spy glass in his right hand. The old grey steed which bore him onward, was none of your fiery chargers, shooting jets of flame from the quivering nostril and the dilating eye.

An ancient and favorite horse, dear to the warrior's heart, for he had borne him, through many a bloody fight, through the everglades and hammocks of Florida.[2]

The head of the old man is slightly drooped, one hand placed within the folds of his vest, while the other grasps the spy glass. As he rides leisurely onward, you might take him for some substantial Pennsylvanian Farmer, mounted on a favorite nag, but gaze beneath the shadow of his broad-brimmed hat, and you behold a Hero's soul, stamped upon his face. A bronzed face, with the under lip slightly projecting, as the upper is pressed against the teeth, the brows drawn downward, the eye dilating until it seems to burn!

Chapter IV

1. The Battle of Palo Alto took place on May 8, 1846. For further detail see T.B. Thorpe, *Our Army on the Rio Grande* (Philadelphia: Carey and Hart, 1846) and John S.D. Eisenhower, *So Far from God: The U.S. War with Mexico, 1846–1848* (Norman: University of Oklahoma Press, 2000).

2. "The everglades and hammocks of Florida" is a reference to Taylor's service in the Second Seminole War (1835–1842), where he won a major victory in the Battle of Okeechoee on December 25, 1837. J. Reese Fry, *A Life of Gen. Zachary Taylor; Comprising a Narrative of Events Connected with His Professional Career, Derived from Public Documents and Private Correspondence* (Philadelphia: Grigg, Elliot & Co., 1848), 58–59.

The old man is thinking of Fort Brown, and of the few miles that intervene between him and the brave three hundred; terrible miles, swarming with six thousand Mexicans.

As he rides leisurely there,—alone, with his own thoughts—you see, gleaming far ahead, the arms of the advance ground. Some few paces behind, the staff officers, come riding in their chivalric array. Far in the distance, winding with every turn and sweep of the road, the brave thousand soldiers, with sword and bayonet blazing over their heads, come flashing on. There, you behold the cannon, flashing back the sunlight from each brazen tube, there the bold war-horses, moving on with a monotonous tramp, and in the rear, the train of two hundred waggons[3] formed in a solid square, announce that the hour of battle is near.

And near that train we behold a sight, which for a moment winds us from the glitter of arms—merely, a poor woman toiling painfully along, with a babe in her arms. Her husband is in the ranks; she knows there will be a battle soon, and as she comes along, with the hot sun pouring on her face, her tears fall slowly, and trickle down the face of her sleeping babe.

It is a sight of absorbing interest that we behold. Two thousand men, fainting under the hot sun, and tortured by thirst, which the brackish water of the prairie only maddens, and yet panting onward to the conflict with six thousand foes.

The blood which flowed in the Revolution, is about to flow in battle again, for there waves the plume of RINGGOLD, the descendant of John Cadwallader; here you behold the stern, heroic face of TWIGGS, the Son of the Hero of Georgia; and in that young man, CHADBOURNE, with the soldierly bearing, and eagle eye, you recognise the grand-son of Revolutionary LINCOLN.[4]

---

3   "Waggons" is a variant of wagons. *Oxford English Dictionary*.

4   General John Twiggs (1750–1816) served in the Revolutionary War and was the father of Colonel David E. Twiggs (1790–1862), commanding officer of the 2nd Dragoons. Col. Twiggs was promoted to brigadier general as a result of his service at the Battles of Palo Alto and Resaca de la Palma. 2nd Lieutenant Theodore Lincoln Chadbourne (1822–1846) served in the 8th Infantry and died the day after the Battle of Palo Alto at the Battle of Resaca de la Palma on May 9, 1846. His maternal grandfather was Benjamin Lincoln who served as a major-general in the Revolutionary War and later as Secretary of War under the Articles of Confederation. Amos Blanchard, *American Military Biography: Containing the Lives and Characters of the Officers of the Revolution, who Were Most Distinguished in Achieving Our National Independence* (Cincinnati: E. Walters, 1830), 184, 189; J. Harris Chappell, *Georgia History Stories* (New York: Silver, Burdett and Company, 1905), 172; David B. Mattern, *Benjamin Lincoln and the American Revolution* (Columbia, SC: University of South Carolina Press, 1995), 1–3, 36; *Pictorial History of Remarkable Events in America in Four Parts* (New York: F.J. Dow & Co, 1850), 48–49; William Hugh Robarts, *Mexican War Veterans: a complete roster of the regular and volunteer troops in the war between the United States and Mexico, from 1846 to 1848* (Washington, D.C.: Bretano's, 1887), 23–24; Thorpe, *Our Army on the Rio Grande*, 195, 223, 295; Eisenhower, *So Far from God*, 97, 104.

The chivalry of the army glows before you, from the bearded face of May, and you behold the backwoodsman of the olden time; created in the sinewing form of Captain Walker. And palpitating with the hunger of battle, the brave two thousand thunder through the defile, their martial array,—relieved on either side by the chaparral—resembling an immense serpent, as it winds brilliantly along.

Meanwhile the old man Taylor, mounted on his grey steed, rides alone, the shadows growing deeper over his anxious face.

Hark! A murmur quivers like an electric shock along the line, as a solitary horseman, separating from the advance guard, thunders along, to the side of Taylor,

"General, the Mexicans await us, in order of battle, on the prairie of Palo Alto!"

You should have seen the old man's eye flash!

"We must reach Fort Brown!" he said, in a composed tone, as the rumor of battle quivered along the line.

Then came the moment of feverish interest.

Emerging in two narrow columns from the chaparral, our brave army beheld, extending before them, the level prairie, three miles in extent, bounded on all sides by the prickly pear of the desert, over whose impenetrable wall rose the wiry timber, which gave its name to the immortal field, Palo Alto.

It was a glorious place for a battle field. No hillocks to obstruct the view, no ravines for ambuscade,[5] no massive trees, to conceal the tube of the deadly rifles, smooth as a floor, green with the rank prairie grass, in some places, blooming in others with flowers of delicately contrasted beauty, it seemed the very place for a battle, the convenient and appropriate theatre for a scene of wholesale murder.

5   According to a contemporary source, "ambuscade" is an ambush, or "a private station in which troops lie concealed with a view to attack their enemy by surprise." Noah Webster, *An American Dictionary of the English Language* (New York: Harper & Brothers, 1844), 31.

Indeed, the bronzed warrior, Zachary, in pursuing along the road some days ago, pointed with his sheathed sword, to the prairie and exclaimed quietly—"Not a finer place in the world for a good fight!"

Behold the battle field at the moment, when the Americans emerge upon its level plain. Stand here, in the chaparral, our faces to the east and gaze with hushed breath upon the scene.

A wide plain, here rank with grass, there perfumed with flowers, the road winding through its centre, and gleaming with small lakes of cool, fresh water, that break upon your eye, like mirrors of silver framed in emerald.

How beautifully the lakelets flings back the smile of the cloudless sky! In ten minutes they will throw back sullenly, the reflection of a bloody and darkening heaven.

Yonder, in the centre of the prairie, from the tall rank grass, gleams a dazzling line, a mile and a half in length, a line composed of swords, lances, bayonets, and marking by its extent, the firm position and battle resolve of six thousand Mexicans.

They stand there in imposing array, the sunlight quivering tremblingly on the points of lance and bayonet, the cannon glooming death from every dark muzzle. Behind their ranks the prairie extends, then the chaparral and the wiry timber of Palo Alto.

In this moment of breathless silence, do you hear distinctly the low murmur of the half-dried rivulet?

It is upon this array of six thousand veteran troops, that the two thousand Americans gaze, as they emerge into the plain. Zachary Taylor—you see him yonder, the bronzed-faced warrior in the brown coat, mounted on the old gray horse—gazes with a brightening eye on the array. It must be confessed that the details are very beautiful.

Far on the right, advanced some distance in front of the Mexican line, a regiment of lancers,[6] in brilliant uniforms, mounted on strong-limbed battle steeds, awaited in gorgeous array, the signal word of fight. Above their heads, glittering against the sky, a forest of lancers, with a red flag, waving from each deadly point of steel.

The artillery next enchains your eye; then the infantry, an iron mass, composed of muscular forms, musquets and bayonets, all linked in one; then the cavalry again, and so on, through the whole extent of that brave army, alternate bodies of cavalry, infantry, artillery, or in other words, first, men, horses, lances and swords; then men and cannon, then men with fire and steel, girded to their hearts.

Yonder in the rear of the centre of the line, with his uniform burdened with ornaments, you see Arista, his white teeth, gleaming below his mustache, as with a smile, he sees rough Taylor come. Around him, glitters a brilliant staff, and in front, the tri-color of Mexico rushes into the sky.

Taylor beholds it all. "It is certainly, my object to reach Fort Brown," he says in his quiet way, "And therefore, the sooner we get about it, the better."

The word of command passes his lips. Look! The army break into companies, they stack their arms, and calmly marching to the brink of those small lakes, assuage their burning thirst, with copious draughts of fresh water.—Drink brave men, and fill your canteens with the clear liquid, for ere ten minutes are gone, that water, will be red with blood!

As we gaze, they march from the lakes into the prairie once more; refreshed by hearty draughts, they spring to their arms, with elastic steps and blazing eyes, while one thunder shout, swells into the sky, as bared to the light, the Banner of the Stars, streams over the field of Palo Alto.

[6] Cavalry, who carried lances instead of swords, were of particular use when charging an enemy's line. *Oxford English Dictionary*; Thorpe, *Our Army on the Rio Grande*, 77; Webster, *An American Dictionary*, 484.

7   Lippard here correctly identified the infantry, cavalry, and artillery detachments, their assigned positions on the battlefield, and their officers.

Lieutenant Colonel James S. McIntosh (1784–1847) was wounded in the Battle of Resaca de la Palma and was promoted to colonel following this battle. However, he was wounded again, more severely, in the Battle of Molino del Rey and died soon thereafter.

Captain Lewis N. Morris (1800–1846) was promoted to major following the Battle of Resaca de la Palma, though he died in the Battle of Monterrey (September 21–24, 1846).

Major George W. Allen (d. 1848) served with General Taylor in the Second Seminole War (1835–1842). He was promoted to lieutenant colonel for his service in the Battles of Palo Alto and Resaca de la Palma. Allen died in Veracruz in 1848.

Lieutenant Colonel John Garland (1793–1861) was promoted to colonel following the Battle of Resaca de la Palma. He eventually received the rank of brigadier general and was wounded severely, but not fatally, in the capture of Mexico City.

Captain Croghan Ker, along with Captain May, commanded the two squadrons of dragoons assigned to support the 3rd Brigade on the right side of the field. Ker's squadron was likely split in two so that a portion of his dragoons could protect the supply train. Ker was also the leader of one of the scouting parties sent to verify rumors of Mexican troop movements. He and his men encountered nothing, while Captain Thornton, the leader of the other party, was ambushed, which the U.S. considered an act of war.

Lieutenant Colonel Thomas Childs (1796–1853) received several promotions for his conduct during the war, which culminated with a promotion to brigadier general for refusing to surrender the city of Puebla

That Banner speaks to two thousand hearts, and speaks of far-off friends—of Home—of Glory—of WASHINGTON. Again that deafening cheer, and more rapidly goes on, the determined preparation for battle.

At last the battle is formed:*[7] history never recorded a more beautiful array.

The American line, presents three striking points; RINGGOLD's artillery on the right; CHURCHILL's[8] two eighteen pounders[9] in the centre; DUNCAN's[10] artillery on the extreme left—Three silent volcanoes with the lava of death, boiling in their breasts!

Around these three points, shone the glittering array of bayonets. Each cannon was relieved by the steady mass of infantry. It was to be, so old Taylor said, a fight with cannon, a deadly combat of whirling horses, brass and iron, of blazing muzzles and hissing balls; the infantry and cavalry, had scarce a duty to perform, save to stand still, defend the cannon, see the battle, and feel the madness of the fight blazing in their veins.

At last the word was given to advance!

At Two o'clock, the very hour, when Washington, under as clear a sky, came to do battle at BRANDYWINE, did Zachary Taylor, give the word and see his army slowly, steadily advance, over the prairie of PALO ALTO.

---

* Viewed merely with the eyes of military men, it was a splendid plan of battle. The RIGHT, was formed in this manner: The *Fifth* infantry with Lieut. Col. Mc.Intosh; Ringgold with his artillery; the *Third* infantry under command of Capt. L.N. Morris; Lieut. Churchill, with two eighteen pounders, of the *Third* artillery; *Fourth* infantry, commanded by Major G.W. Allen; The THIRD BRIGADE, composed of the *Third* and *Fourth* Regiments, commanded by Lieut. Col. Garland, and two squadrons of dragoons, under command of Captain Ker and May. The entire wing was under the orders of Colonel TWIGGS.

The LEFT wing: a battalion of artillery, commanded by Lieut. Col. Childs; Duncan's light artillery; eighth infantry, Capt. Montgomery; the whole forming the First Brigade, under Lieut. Col. Belknap. Captain Cressman and Myers, were entrusted with the train, which was packed near the water.

Any man who has seen a battle, knows that the shout of carnage, is not half so terrible, as the awful silence before the first fire. Then, as a man hears the beating of his heart, and when the crushed grass, beneath his feet, seems to echo his tread with a sound like thunder—so brooding, so intense is the calm before the storm—the Soldier sees Eternity yawning beneath him, over which he hangs suspended by a single hair.

Slowly, steadily over the prairie, men and horses and steel and banners moved on. More clearly they began to distinguish the Mexican banner, to see the hues of their uniforms, to note their cannon-muzzles yawning Death into their faces. The suspense was horrible—many a brave veteran felt his heart in his throat, and grasped his musket, with a hand clammy with cold dews.

At this moment, behold a deep worthy of the age of chivalry!

A single horseman, separates from the American army, and like a thunderbolt from a cloud, whirls away, over the plain. Both armies mark the athletic beauty of his form, his horse with arching neck and distended nostrils, his white plume, waving over a young face, remarkable for its expression of cool courage. He dashes over the plain—the Americans hold their breath, in suspense, the Mexicans in wonder.

Is he mad? Rising in the stirrups, in view of thousands, he approaches within one hundred and fifty yards of the Mexicans, calmly dismounts, flings his arm on his horse's neck, and taking from his pocket a spy glass, calmly surveys their terrible array.

Dotting the sod, between the two armies, that solitary soldier and his horse, form an object of interest for eight thousand men.

He can count their lances, their swords—tell the number of cannon which they display—and as if astonished by the calm composure of the audacious soldier, the Mexicans do not fire. One levelled musket, and he

when Santa Anna laid a "half-hearted siege" for 28 days.

Lieutenant William G. Belknap (1794–1851) was commander of the 1st Brigade, including the 8th Infantry, which under his command captured General Rómulo Díaz de la Vega (1800–1877) during the battle of Resaca de la Palma. By the end of the war, he had achieved the rank of brigadier general.

Captain George H. Crosman (1799–1882), here and elsewhere incorrectly noted as "Cressman," and Captain Abraham C. Myers (1811–1889) were charged with protecting the supply train during the Battle of Palo Alto, with support from Ker's dragoons. Both men were promoted to the rank of major for their service at Palo Alto and Resaca de la Palma.

Eisenhower, *So Far from God*, 65, 347–349; Charles Gardner, *A Dictionary of All Officers, Who Have Been Commissioned, or Have Been Appointed and Served, in the Army of the United States* (New York: G.P. Putnam and Company, 1853), 38, 112, 133, 334; *Niles' National Register*, ed. Jeremiah Hughes, LXX (Baltimore: Jeremiah Hughes, 1846), 386; Robarts, *Mexican War Veterans*, 6, 11, 18–21, 204, 210; *S. Doc. No. 388,* 29th Cong., 1st Sess. (1846); Justin H. Smith, *The War with Mexico*, vol. 1 (New York: The MacMillan Company, 1919), 181–182; Thorpe, *Our Army on the Rio Grande*, 38–40, 42–43, 75, 204, 210.

8   1st Lieutenant William H. Churchill (1819–1847) served with the 3rd Artillery Regiment. Following his service in the Battles of Palo Alto and Resaca de la Palma, he was promoted to captain. *Niles' National Register*, 386; Robarts, *Mexican War Veterans*, 15–16.

9   An "eighteen pounder" is "a gun throwing a shot that weighs eighteen pounds." *Oxford English Dictionary*.

10 Captain James Duncan (1811–1849) served in the 2nd Regiment of Artillery and was

promoted throughout the war, reaching the rank of colonel. Duncan died soon after the war. *Niles' National Register,* 386; Robarts, *Mexican War Veterans,* 14–15; *S. Doc. No. 388.*

11 Lippard's text rendered this word as "reconnoisance," which was likely a manuscript or typesetting error. The spelling error has been corrected, but the single quotation marks used in the original have been retained.

12 Lieutenant Jacob E. Blake (1812–1846) was a topographical engineer. He and Captain Lloyd Tilghman were sent to spy on the Mexican forces and report back concerning their position and strength. Blake died on May 9, just before the Battle of Resaca de Palma commenced, when he was shot by his own pistol as he removed his holster and, according to Lippard, "flung" it on the ground. Gardner, *A Dictionary of All Officers,* 71, 448; Robarts, *Mexican War Veterans,* 9; *S. Doc. No. 388.*

13 "Tierra caliente" is Spanish for "hot land." Lippard's original text renders this phrase as "terra caliente," which could be due to Lippard's unfamiliarity with Spanish or a typesetting error.

14 Vera Cruz (Veracruz today) is a major port city on the Gulf of Mexico, to which General Scott laid siege in 1847 as part of his march to Mexico City. Orizaba is also a Mexican city, though by using the phrase "from the shadows of Orizaba," Lippard is likely referring to Pico de Orizaba, a dormant volcano and Mexico's highest mountain, located to the northwest of the city of the same name. Eisenhower, *So Far from God,* 253–258; J. Jacob Oswandel, *Notes on the Mexican War, 1846–47–48* (Philadelphia: 1885), 224, 408, 452, 632.

is dead! Presently you see, two Mexicans in their gaudy costume, dash from the army and approach him.

The young soldier sees them come, waits until he has completed his 'reconnaissance,'[11] mounts his steed and rides—not directly back to his army again—but down in front of their line, with cannon glooming and bayonets glittering, a wall of death before him, rides with his plume waving and the shout of his comrades, breaking in his ears!

Then, dashing like an arrow, across the plain, he approaches the General, and calmly tells him the numbers and exact condition of the foe. The old warrior smiles, and the army move silently on.

Little did the gallant soldier BLAKE,[12] in that moment of excitement, dream of the sad and singular fate which awaited him.

Seven hundred yards now intervene between the armies. Take care! Do not breathe a word! A single whisper may scare the slumbering Death into action, and send him rioting over the field.

At this moment, when the Armies glare in each other's faces, when Arista, with a smile surveys plain Zachary's rough costume, when the umbering wheels and monotonous hoofs alone are heard, tell me, what means this meet of opposing hosts on the plain of Palo Alto?

Here the Americans in blue—there the Mexicans in green—here, the tri-color of Anahuac, there the Banner of the Stars! Here, the veterans of Mexican battles, tawny heroes from the *tierra caliente,*[13] of Vera Cruz, and robust mountaineers, from the shadows of Orizaba,[14] the men, who butchered the Texans at Alamo, and the Rancheroes, who will butcher the wounded and strip the dead ere an hour is gone! There, an untried army of two thousand men, gathered from the hills and vallies of America, with here and there, a veteran from the fields of Poland, or a 'grey mustache' from the ranks of Napoleon!

What does it mean?

It means that the Sword of Washington, is about to blaze, in conquest and civilization over the land of Mexico. It means that one bloody battlefield will soon call to another, until a chorus of victories, join their cries and shout to the world, that the American People, are in arms for the freedom of a Continent. It means, that to-day, a Beginning to be made, to prepare the way for a glorious End. It means that Kings and Tyrants, their panders and satellites have no business on this Continent. It means, that the British had better look to Montreal, for the day comes when the Banner of the Stars will crown its towers, that they had better look to Quebec, for the hour is not far off, when the tramp of American legions will be heard upon its rock.

It means that a great Reform, is about to commence, a Reform, that will blaze for awhile in the distance, then envelope the borders of our Union, and last of all, burn up the evils which threaten our peace at home! So, whenever the sword of Washington waves in the air, let us follow its flashing with prayer, and shout Amen! as it strikes home.

For a brief moment, in that awful suspense, the opposing enemies regarded each other, and then—but hold! Did you ever see a summer storm girdle the horizon, with its fantastic clouds, and while you watched its sullen march up the sky, a flash of lightning shone, in the far north, and shot from peak to peak, dazzling away, until the heavens were wrapt in a belt of flame?

So on the Right of the Mexican army the contest began; the cannon flamed out, volumes of smoke, rushed into the sky, and a storm of ball and grape,[15] whirled over the American army, singing their battle-song! In an instant, that flame, that smoke, that crash, leapt along the whole Mexican line, and the thunder and lightning of the battle-field were born.

15 "Ball" refers to the lead balls fired by muskets. "Grape" refers to the clustering of metal ammunition balls placed in a canvas sack, often called "grape-shot." *Oxford English Dictionary*; Webster, *An American Dictionary*, 385.

Those columns of white smoke, mingled with belts of black rolled slowly upward, into the serene sky.

At the same moment from the centre of the American line, two separate volumes of fire, blazed from the eighteen pounders,—there was a cloud in the air—and two bloody lanes were hewn, by the hurricane of iron, right in the centre of the Mexican line; two lanes of mangled and dead.

The battle had indeed begun—the smoke of the Mexican cannon, and the smoke of the American battery, floated slowly into the sky, met in the serene air, and formed a bridge of cloud, above the heads of the contending armies.

Hark! The rumbling of wheels, the heavy sound of horses hoofs beating against the sod!

From the right of the line, Ringgold sweeps into the prairie, at the same moment, that Duncan crushes its tall grass to the left, and from either extremity of the army, blaze answers blaze, and cannon shouts to cannon. Every shot makes a lane of dead, every ball bears a head, or an arm away!

It is now that Ringgold is terrible. It is now that the fruits of long years of training are seen. It is now, that these men of his band, disciplined by him, into separate pieces of iron, forming one great machine of battle, display their firm hearts and steady eyes. Few persons, who beheld the erect soldier, attired in his elegant uniform, pacing along the fashionable street of his native city, can imagine, his appearance and demeanor now.

Reined beside the blazing battery, his white horse, fixed as a statue, to the sod, still quivers beneath him. Erect in the saddle, his muscular chest and arms, displayed by the close-fitting uniform, whose rich dark blue so well relieves his boldly featured countenance, he gives the word of command to his men, marks the effect of the shot, with his eye, and sees whole platoons of gay uniforms go down, in blood.

The revolutionary blood of John Cadwallader burns in his veins, and the fire of battle mounts his heart. Over his head whirls the fury of the Mexican hurricane—were those guns, aimed with half the precision of his own, his command would be blasted into the dust, ere a moment. But as it is, from the want of deadly skill, on the part of the Mexicans, their terrible missiles only hiss, in upper air.

As Ringgold, erect on his white horse, rises before us, a strong picture, boldly marked out, by the blaze of battle, you behold a single feature of the infernal revelry of war. The common soldier, by his side, attired in a blue round jacket, his broad chest, laid open to the light? You behold him, touch his cap, and stand motionless, in the act of listening to the words of Ringgold. His swarthy face is all attention, his honest brow, covered with sweat, assumes an appearance of thought. Look! Ringgold in the energy of the moment bends forward extending his hand—and at the very instant, the soldier is torn in two, by a combination of horrible missiles, which bear his mangled flesh away, whirling a bloody shower through the air. That thing beneath the horse's feet, with the head bent back, until it touches the heels, that mass of bloody flesh, in which face, feet and brains, alone are distinguishable, was only a moment past, a living man.

And from the space between the cannon wheels, where she had sheltered herself,—her babe slumbering in her arms amid the fierce roar of the battle—crawls forth the Woman, whom we saw following the army not long ago, was her husband. She placed the gory head upon her lap, and with her face bent down, said not a word, but wept in silence.—Ringgold turned his eyes away, and was not ashamed of tears!—A fine, matronly woman, not twenty-six years old, with the hue of vigorous health upon her cheeks, she had followed her husband, from the desolated fields of Ireland, across the ocean, then into the army and—*now!* And thus, with the bloody head upon her lap, she sat all day, while the fight whirled round her. At night, when there was nothing but a pale moon, shining over heaps of slaughter, she was still there,—upon her knee the gory head, upon her breast the slumbering babe. Day came again, the armies passed away, the battle whirled far to the south—the Woman, and the Dead Man and the Child were still together, there, upon the field of Palo Alto.

Yes, when the jackals prowled around her, when the vulture, attracted by the scent of the festering body, swept the air, not one foot above her head, she still kept the watch, moving her body, slowly to and fro, and singing a wild Irish song. It was until they came with spades to hide the hideous corruption of the field, that she could be torn from her loathsome burden. And as they huddled the miserable thing, into the hurried grave, she was seen, taking her desolate way, across the wilderness, her babe still clinging to her bosom, while that low-toned, monotonous lament broke over the dead silence of the deserted field.

To the battle once more!

While the cannon of RINGGOLD blaze on the right, there is a flash on the far left, and a roar from the centre of the line. Slowly the eighteen pounders, advance from the centre, scattering a terrible mass of balls, into the Mexican array. Steadily on the left, DUNCAN, pours the hurricane of iron, and sees, whole lines of men and horses, crushed into dust, ere the battle flash of the cannon, leaves his face. Sternly on the right, RINGGOLD, on his war-horse, pursues the work, whirling his bolts of flame, upon those gay lancers yonder, whose points of steel fluttering with crimson flags, cannot save them from the death, which rends their arms, crushes their skulls, and piles them up, in bleeding heaps along the sod.

The Infantry stood in silent masses, the blood boiling in their veins as they gazed upon the clouds of the fight, into whose whirlpool, they were not permitted to precipitate their legions.

Behold their stern array!

Shoulder to shoulder, their voiceless musquets in their grasp, they glare beneath their frontlets upon the battle, they mark the lanes of the Mexican dead, they force their breath between the clenched teeth, they rend the air, with shouts.

And every minute, there comes hissing into their ranks a shower of grape, that bears a human head away, over their living heads, and entangles their immovable ranks, with the howling wounded or glassy-eyed dead. Aye, glassy-eyed! Of all the horrible things in a battle, the most horrible, is to see the comrade by your side, crushed backward, by a ball, which unroofs his skull—only for a single moment he moves and all is still—only for a single moment, he rolls his glassy eyes upon your face, as if calling with that speechless agony for vengeance, and then there is no longer a man by your side, but a corse at your feet.

The battle now begins to wear its most infernal beauty! These lines of armed men, arrayed on the prairie, these volumes of flame, blazing from one living wall to another, this flag of three colors, and yonder banner of the stars, seen only through the intervals of rolling clouds, these piles of mangled and dead, with the infuriate and frenzied living trampling over their faces, these sturdy cannoniers,[16] stripping their bronzed forms to the waist, and hurling the hurricane into the faces of their foe, without a shout, the sky of God, over all, smiling through the windows of the smoke, upon the scene of Murder!—Ah, there is in every heart, the Instinct of Carnages and a scene like this, would make a Saint throw down his cross, and seize a sword!

16 "Cannoniers" is a variant of "cannoneers." *Oxford English Dictionary*; Webster, *An American Dictionary*, 120.

In the midst of the battle, on a gentle elevation, which commands the prairie, in every foot of its extent, you see Zachary Taylor, in his brown coat, mounted on his grey horse, his large eyes, rolling rapidly over the field. His broad chest swells, as though every impulse of the fight hung on his breath. You will understand that the scene before him is no child's play. Defeated, and what will be the fate of his men? Look yonder in the thicket, and see the bearded Ranchero, mangling the wounded, whom he has dragged from the field—whom he has stabbed, killed, stripped—mangling the dead body, and carving its features with this gory knife!

Defeated,—Zachary Taylor and his men, will be butchered in cold blood, their faces trampled into the sod of the prairie, mingled with gore.

Therefore, the old man,—styled, old, more in reverence to his rough, heroic genius, in veneration of his thirty-eight years of service, than in respect to his years—sits on his familiar grey steed, while his aids in their gallant military array, speed to and fro, and the Cannon Battle blazes steadily onward.

For two hours, from two o'clock until four, that terrible battle of cannon thundering against cannon, continued without one moment's interval in the steady work of death.

At this moment, we will cross the prairie, and hurry towards the centre of the Mexican army.

A magnificent cavalier, mounted on a charger as white as snow, with mane tossing to the battle breeze, is seen, the centre of a brilliant circle of mounted officers. Over his countenance, marked with the traces of courage, bronzed by long exposure to the fierce tropical sun, and distinguished by a bright red mustache, waves a cluster of snow white plumes. His green uniform, faced with buff, is heavy with ornaments of gold.

As his proud horse, arches his neck, and in fiery eagerness, to join the battle, curvets over the sod, it must be confessed, that the rider presents an appearance at once, impressive and chivalric.

It is General Arista, in the midst of his officers, watching the deadly cannonade.

Among that crowd, glittering in brilliant uniforms, let me ask you to single out one face, lowering in the brow and unmeaning in the lip; it is the visage of AMPUDIA,[17] who boasts of having boiled the head of a dead enemy* in a cauldron of oil. He is very gaily attired, and his bay horse is one of the finest in the world, yet it were well for him, to keep out of the range of the Texan rifles, for there is an old account to settle, and a record of blood to be blotted out

Around Arista, the scene is sad and touching.

The earth is crowded with mangled bodies. Here a leg, there an arm, yonder a head; it is horrible but it is true; the air quivers with death groans, and amid the deep boom of the cannonade, you hear the mangled Mexican howl to Jesus, to God, to the Virgin of Gaudalupe†[18] for pity!

"We can never stand this," exclaims Arista, as a cannon ball, passes beneath his horse's hoofs—"We must charge! away"—he shouts to an aid-de-camp—"And tell General Torrejon,[19] to lead his regiment of lancers against the Right of the enemy—we must take their artillery or be driven from the field."

The officer sped away, through the battle clouds, and presently the regiment of lancers, fifteen hundred strong, were seen moving forward, in compact order, their array looking very beautiful, very terrible, by the glare

---

* General Sentmanat—at Tobasco in 1844.
† The Patron Saint of Mexico.

---

17 General Pedro de Ampudia (1805–1865) was sent to reinforce and replace General Francisco Mejía at Matamoros. However, Ampudia was soon replaced by General Mariano Arista. This was, in part, due to his reputation for cruelty, earned for the execution of General Francisco Sentmanat, who was decapitated postmortem, so that the head could be boiled in oil and put on display. After his replacement by Arista, Ampudia began to sow "mistrust of Arista." Eventually, Ampudia was "reinstated as Mexico's general-in-chief, Army of the North." Eisenhower, *So Far from God,* 54, 63, 74, 86–87, 120.

18 Nuestra Señora de Guadalupe, "Our Lady of Guadalupe." The Virgin Mary was both a religious and nationalist symbol for Mexico. Independence fighter José Miguel Ramón Adaucto Fernández y Félix (1786–1843) renamed himself "Guadalupe Victoria," in her honor, and Santa Anna, on his way to San Luis Potosí, sought her blessing at her shrine. Smith, *The War with Mexico,* 223, 488.

19 General Anastasio Torrejón (1802–1861) was sent by General Arista with 1,600 cavalry to cross the Rio Grande upstream from Taylor's camp. Torrejón's cavalry ambushed an American scouting party, an act that the U.S. claimed as inciting the war. In the Battle of Palo Alto, Torrejón and his lancer cavalry were ordered to charge against the American artillery, which was under the command of Ringgold. The charge was repulsed. Eisenhower, *So Far from God,* 65, 79; Thorpe, *Our Army on the Rio Grande,* 42–43, 77.

of the cannon light, as with red pennons waving from their fifteen hundred points of steel, they began to gloom upon the band of Ringgold.

At their head—his helmet glittering in a single ray of sunlight—Torrejon waved his sword, and pointed toward the conspicuous form of the Cannon Hero.

Taylor saw their beautiful array and could not help admiring the imposing march, with which they rehearsed their funeral. A word passed from the old man's lips, an aid de camp whirled over the field.

In a moment, the Fifth infantry, formed in square, with their bayonets flashing back the light of fifteen hundred lances, silently awaited the approach of the formidable lancers. On their right, behold twenty mounted men, dressed in dark green frocks, with a young man, remarkable for his determined visage at their head. CAPTAIN WALKER, and a few of his iron-chested, death-eyed Texan rifles.

The Lancers come on! The brave RIDGELY,[20] with a portion of RINGGOLD's battery, prepares to give them a hospitable welcome. He unlimbers his pieces; in a moment, a hot feast of grape and canister, will smoke before their nostrils.

And in the midst of the Right Wing, erect on his white steed, his glowing cheek marking his intense interest, in the course of those lancers, you behold MAJOR RINGGOLD.

And all is silent as the Lancers come on. Terrible silence! Look yonder and see Zachary Taylor's grey eye fixed intently upon their approach—ha! ha! A shout,—he cannot keep it down—echoes from his lip, he raises his clenched hand and shouts again.

For all at once the infantry, have poured their fire into the lancer's faces; Ridgely has delivered his message of grape and cannister;[21] Captain Walker, with those twenty battle devils has poured the blaze of his rifles,

---

20 1st Lieutenant Randolph Ridgely (1814–1846) served under Major Samuel Ringgold in the Battle of Palo Alto, commanding the battery that repulsed Torrejón's cavalry charge. Following Ringgold's death, Ridgley took the command at the Battle of Resaca de la Palma. Ridgely died during the truce that followed the Battle of Monterrey as a result of a head injury sustained by falling off his horse. Eisenhower, *So Far from God*, 83, 154; Smith, *The War with Mexico*, 172; Thorpe, *Our Army on the Rio Grande*, 77.

21 "Cannister" is a variant of "canister," a type of munition consisting of small iron balls placed inside a metal cylinder and fired from an artillery gun. *Oxford English Dictionary*.

into their foremost ranks, and now, with twenty upraised knives, charges them home.

There is much smoke; there are horrible groans. The smoke clears away, and you behold the foremost lancers, mown down, horses and men together, into one bloody mass. Again they form, again the Americans wait until they can count the buttons on their coats, and the iron shower, rained hissing from cannon and rifle and musket, beats a hundred faces into dust.

Hark? that hurrah! You see Walker alone, with his brave twenty charging a detachment of the lancers, at least one hundred strong. At first it looks like a cloud of men, horses and steel, but presently you see the rifleman's plain uniform, come out, in strong contrast, with the gaudy lancer's trappings—you mark the flash of the bowie knife[22] and see the answering stream of blood.

It would have done old Daniel Morgan[23] good, to see this young Walker. A very unpretending man in appearance, with a sun-burnt face, a form altogether full of iron sinews, and yet not remarkable for gigantic height; an arm that strikes suddenly and strikes home. In fact the modern Lee of the American army, fighting always, on his own account, and flashing out, in individual deeds of glory.

"Again, my brave comrades" shouted Torrejon, as his horse reared among heaps of dead—"Charge! Turn their flanks—and the train is ours!"

Advancing over the bodies of their own dead, the Lancers raised once more their glittering front into light, but the FIFTH infantry, a solid wall of bayonets received them. But on they pressed, the contest deepened, lances and bayonets were locked together, when the veteran Colonel TWIGGS, his stern visage, manifesting in each lineament, the fever of the hour, uttered

22 A "bowie knife" is a long, double-edged knife named after James "Jim" Bowie, a frontiersman who commanded the Texan force at the Battle of the Alamo. *Oxford English Dictionary.* See Robert F Scott, "Who Invented the Bowie Knife?" *Western Folklore* 8, no. 3 (1949): 195–201.

23 General Daniel Morgan (1736–1802) was a Revolutionary War general known for both his tactical skills and the guerrilla tactics employed by his soldiers. See Don Higginbotham, *Daniel Morgan: Revolutionary Rifleman* (Chapel Hill: University of North Carolina Press, 1961).

the word of command, and in a moment, another band* marched to the extreme right, their arms glittering in the battle light.

It was too much for the Lancers.

It is true, they thrice outnumbered the American troops, it is true, they were the flower of Mexican chivalry, but when they saw that wall of bayonets joined to another glittering line, they fell back over the faces of their dead.

At first in good order, squadron by squadron, but this gallant Ridgely cannot see them depart without a warm farewell; again his batteries blaze, and yonder in the Mexican ranks—horse and man, go thundering to the sod together. Even as he directs the fire, the flanks of his horse are torn in bloody fragments by a cannon ball—they fall to the earth, the horse, writhing over his prostrate master. It is a fearful moment: Ridgely is lost! But no! He rises, wipes the blood from his face, and beholds a frightened horse, plunging before the muzzle of a cannon.

He darts forward, seizes the bridle rein, and in the full blaze of contending fires, he wheels the maddened horse aside.

Look yonder—a glorious sight! The brilliant uniforms of the lancers seen through the aperture of that colossal cloud, their steel points, and red pennons, breaking together, like waves upon a rocky coast.

And Ringgold—where is he?

Unconscious of the fearful destiny, that awaits him, he pours his fire once more, and by its light, sees whole companies splintered into fragments. Still, with that sternly compressed lip and eagle eye, he watched the effect of each discharge, nor hesitated, when he saw glimpses of the clear sky, through the lanes which he made in the Mexican ranks.

---

* The THIRD infantry.

At this moment, the eye of old Zachary, beheld a glorious sight to the far left.

It was the battery of Duncan, blazing amid the bayonets of the eighth regiment, and the horses of Captain Ker's dragoons. These horses and bayonets encircle the battery; you see its steady hurricane, pour in unremitting fury upon the Mexican ranks.

Note the effect of a single discharge: a band of men, arrayed yonder, present their beautiful horses, their splendid costume, to the aim of Duncan's. There is a blaze—a report—a mass of white smoke! Now look for your chivalric Mexicans, and look until your tired eye sickens with the sight of blood. By the light of the sun streaming through the battle blaze, and looking like the eye of a mad debauchee, behold the earth littered with horses and men, woven through each other, in all the horrible shapes of pain.

But the battery has no heart—it only seems to know that the Mexicans are yonder, that they are in the way of old Zachary, and then swearing its awful thunder oath, it cuts them down.

Yet, do not think that the Mexican cannonade spends all its fury in air! No! Could the mothers, the sailors, the wives, scattered through the American Union, at this hour, thinking fondly of their beloved ones, at this moment, behold them, they would see the tall rank grass, waving over their mangled forms, undulating to each pulse of pain, while the cannon shot, cannot altogether drown the cry of agony.

Even as our hearts writhe within us, at the horrible chorus of groans, which fills the air, the cannon of Duncan communicates its blaze, to the tall prairie grass, which dried and blasted, waves before their muzzles, and withers into flame. Such a glorious flame! Over the plain, across the space between the armies, like a flash of lightning it hisses along, burning the cold faces of the dead to cinder, and crowding the prairie with a mass of fire, that blazes far overhead, in a thousand points of light.

Then a dense smoke rolls up between the armies, shutting them from each others view, and like the curtain of the theatre, closing the first act of the glorious drama of PALO ALTO.

And amid those clouds of smoke, which hide the foemen from each other's sight, and all at once, silence the voices of battle—all but the groans—you may see the bronzed visage of Zachary, lightened by a smile, and gleaming gladly from the large grey eyes.

Far to the south,—aye, through the dense folds of smoke you hear it—comes a murmuring yet welcome sound. *The Mexicans are retreating from the field, to form a new line of battle under the cover of the smoky pall!* With two thousand untried men, Taylor has beaten back six thousand of the bravest veterans of Mexico. Taylor and his heroes have done it: Taylor and Duncan, and Twiggs, and Ridgely and Churchill and Ringgold, have forced the tri-color to give way before the Banner of the Stars.

There is a pause in the dim of battle, a mighty breathing time in the work of blood. While the Mexicans form their new line, beyond this gloomy pall, let us take the ground which they occupied, not ten minutes since.

Let the Banners of the regiments advance! Then Churchill's two eighteen pounders move forward drawn by twenty yoke of oxen, complacent beasts, who put their hoofs on dead men's faces, and crop the tall rank grass, as they walk peacefully along.

But the wounded—yes! God pity them, we must bear them gently to the rear, and keep stout hearts within us, for here are sights to wring the soul of the strong man, and shame his scarred cheek with womanish tears!

To the rear with the wounded—yes, American and Mexican, with brows bleeding and limbs crushed, with the breath rattling through the pierced lungs, and the mouth choked with blood—bear them to the rear? Rather face the burst of Ringgold's cannon, than witness sights like these,—who would not? For the dead we do not care.

Care; no! They may lie upon their faces, biting mouthfuls of bloody dust, they may rest upon their backs glaring with stony eyes, upon that cloud, which covers them, like a pall, they may be torn in pieces, here a grisly head, and there an arm.—They who have wives or mothers, or sisters, weeping for them, even now in a faraway land—but what care we? Pain, want, the world itself, to them, are now but empty names, for they are dead.

But the wounded, oh, have you the heart to gaze upon them, as they pass by, in the arms of sturdy living men?

A young soldier, with his coat thrown open, and the gash from the throat to the waist laid bare. A very boy, pale and clammy in the delicate features, his arms and legs dangling over the ground, as they bear him away. He faced the battle, with a quickening pulse and boyish shout, but now, in his delirium, he only mutters certain childish words about his Sister and his Home!

Then a strong man is borne along, his skull laid open by a chain-shot. Howling, mad with pain, he blasphemes his God, and reaches forth his arms to choke the wounded Mexican, who, shrieking in ludicrous English for "Water!" is carried by his side.

But now, the Soldiers to whom this sad duty is entrusted, approach a form, hidden in the tall grass—an old man—

Yet, ere we gaze upon him, and hear words which will fill our eyes, and make our hearts beat quicker, let me tell you a Legend of two worlds.

---

24 The Palace of Fontainebleau, in France, was one of the palaces built and reserved for French monarchs. Napoleon, as emperor, made regular use of the palace. It was here, in April, 1814, that Napoleon signed the Treaty of Fontainebleau, abdicated his throne, and agreed to go into exile. In this scene Lippard is alluding to the legend that Napoleon attempted suicide. While "Comrade Joseph" is surely Lippard's literary invention, Napoleon's attempted suicide does have some historical standing as described by Lippard. Baron Agathon Jean François Fain, *The Manuscript of 1814: A History of Events which Led to the Abdication of Napoleon* (London: Henry Colburn and Co., 1823), 258–259; General Count Montholon, *History of the Captivity of Napoleon at St. Helena*, vols. 1–4 (Philadelphia: Carey and Hart, 1847), 133–135; Harold Nicolson, *The Congress of Vienna, a Study in Allied Unity: 1812–1822* (New York: Viking Books, 1961), 96, 287; Harold T. Parker, "Napoleon Reconsidered: an Invitation to Inquiry and Reflection," *French Historical Studies* 15, no. 1 (1987): 155; Louis Tarsot and Maurice Charlot, *The Palace at Fontainebleau* (Paris: Henri Laurens, 1900), 1, 64, 67–68; J.M. Thompson, "Napoleon's Journey to Elba in 1814. Part I. By Land," *The American Historical Review* 55, no. 1 (1949): 4.

There was a night, when a solitary lamp burned in the Imperial Palace of Fontainebleu.[24] The gardens around were dark; the halls within desolate; the fountains hushed. The Palace wore the aspect of a Tomb. It seemed as though a cloud of mourning hung over its wide roofs and towers: mourning for the crimes and miseries of France. The sceptre was about departing from her hands, the laurel from her brows.

Along this corridor of the deserted palace, before a narrow doorway, stalks the sentinel, his stealthy tread scarce arousing the ghost of an echo. All is dark around him, yet as he approaches the deep-embayed window, at the end of the corridor, you see the costume of a soldier clothing his broad chest, the musquet of a veteran in his grasp. And as he walks along, looking earnestly toward the narrow door—now pausing to listen—he utters a subdued groan, and the tears stream down his rugged cheeks.

Within that door burns the solitary lamp of Fontainebleu. It is a small door, and yet it leads into a spacious chamber, furnished with all the luxury of Imperial grandeur. The hangings are of rich purple, spotted with golden bees; the carpet glows with the dyes of oriental art; the bed is worthy to be pressed by a young and beautiful woman, that woman the Bride of an Emperor.

Its curtains of deep azure are gathered on the summit, in the beak of a golden eagle—the Eagle of France.

Near the bed stands a small desk, on which the light is placed. Beside the desk, the carpet is littered with maps and charts, and the gleam of a half-sheathed sword arrests your eye.

As you wander through the room, wondering at this magnificence, which the faint light invests with a graveyard gloom, starting at the echo of yon step, which makes you shudder, you know not why, there is a movement among the curtains of the bed, and from its shadows a half-naked man struggles painfully into the light.

With the curtains surmounting him like a frame, he sits on the edge of the bed, a loose dressing gown falling about his limbs. One hand dropped by his side, grasps a phial;[25] the other, in a gesture expressive of physical exhaustion, rests languidly on the desk.

His head is downcast; the light falls on a forehead remarkable for its massive outline, and reveals his large eyes, with ghastly blue circles underneath. His cheeks are sallow, his lips white—the entire appearance of that face, indicates a great soul sinking in the apathy of despair, a vigorous body withering into hopeless torpor.

He sits there, on the edge of the imperial couch, grasping the phial in his right hand, while his head sinks nearer to his breast. Not a word passes his lips—a sense of desolation seems to enclose him, and press down upon him, as the coffin lid shuts in the corse.

That man is called NAPOLEON.

Do not start and wonder, for only a few days since, a battle was fought called WATERLOO.[26]

Alone in his deserted palace, alone, while the Idiots of Royalty, the Bourbons,[27] are coming back to Paris and to this Fontainebleu, on barbarian bayonets,—alone with the despair of his great heart—this Man has taken poison, but he cannot die.

For, as I said a moment ago, his Name is NAPOLEON. His mighty life demands a sublime death-bed. An Island-Rock[28] in the midst of an Ocean, can alone afford a couch for his dying hour.

He has taken poison but cannot die, for Destiny does not forget her child.

25 A "phial" was a "small glass vessel used for holding liquor." Webster, *An American Dictionary*, 607. This particular phial contains poison.
26 The Battle of Waterloo (June 18, 1815) was Napoleon Bonaparte's final battle. His army was defeated by a combined force of the British and Prussian armies, under the command of Arthur Wellesley, Duke of Wellington, and Prussian armies. As a result of his defeat, Napoleon was forced to abdicate for a second time on June 22, 1815 before being exiled to St. Helena, Alison, *History of Europe*, 659–664.
27 The House of Bourbon was the ruling dynasty of France from 1589 to 1799 and then again from 1814 to 1830. The fifteen-year gap in their reign was due to the French Revolution. Napoleon ruled France as emperor during ten of those fifteen years. See J.H. Shennan, *The Bourbons: The History of a Dynasty* (London: Hambledon Continuum, 2007).
28 "Island-Rock" is a reference to the island of St. Helena, where Napoleon was exiled after he abdicated his throne following his defeat at Waterloo. This island was chosen due to its remote location that made it impossible for Napoleon to return from exile, as he had done previously from Elba Island.

A few days ago, he pressed this couch, with a young and beautiful woman by his side, a lovely child smiling upon his face, his own image, hallowed by the outlines of infancy. Only a few days, and he walked these halls an Emperor, with crowds of liveried Lords—the parasites whom the justice of the Revolution had spared, the Generals who had won their titles on the battlefield—Lords, I say, and Dukes and Princes, doing him the commonest offices of menial service.

Where is the wife now? The child? Where the long lines of liveried Princes, who did honor to the Emperor? Where the Generals and Marshals of France, who had flashed into Kings at his word?

The wife—what better could we expect from royal blood, cankered by the scrofula of a thousand years—has fled, taking with her the Child of Napoleon. The Princes in livery, are even now, making their peace with the Russian Barbarian,[29] and doing homage to that immortal British Mistake, who *did not lose* the battle of Waterloo, that immense fog of history, My Lord Wellington.[30]

And NAPPOLEON is left alone, to die, with the poison phial in his hand!

As wrapped in the apathy of despair, he crouches on the edge of the imperial bed, he hears the sentinel's footstep, and starts to his feet. That sound is strange to him—it speaks of the Camp, which after all, was Napoleon's only Throne. He rises, opens the door, calls.

The Sentinel enters; you see him by the dim light, a man of some forty years, with Aboukir, Moscow, Austerlitz, written on his bronzed face. His dark green uniform is miserably worn, and hideously patched with blood. A thick dark moustache covers his upper lip, and hides its tremor.

You see him, tall and erect, stand before the Fallen Destiny, that man in the dressing gown, with the marks of poison on his god-like face.

---

29 Alexander I (1777–1825), Emperor of Russia, allied with several other European powers to defeat Napoleon. Alexander, who had years prior been on friendly terms with Napoleon, convinced some of Napoleon's most loyal supporters to betray him and was successful in preventing Napoleon's son from inheriting the throne upon his father's abdication. Archibald Alison, *History of Europe from the Commencement of the French Revolution to the Restoration of the Bourbons in MDCCCXV*, vol. XIII (London: William Blackwood and Sons, 1860), 199; Fain, *The Manuscript of 1814*, 234–238, 242–244; Alphonse de Lamartine, *The History of the Restoration of Monarchy in France*, vol. II (London: Vizetelly and Company, 1852), 191, 196.

30 "My Lord Wellington" is a reference to the Duke of Wellington (1769–1852), who fought against Napoleon at the Battle of Waterloo and had been criticized for errors during the battle despite his victory. For further information, see Jac Weller, *Wellington at Waterloo* (South Yorkshire: Frontline Books, 1992), 181–186.

"Who bade you watch here?"—his voice is harsh, abrupt.

"My heart, Sire!" says the soldier, whose twenty years of service, have left him where he began—in the ranks.

There was something in the voice of the soldier, that went straight to Napoleon's heart.

"Your heart? Nonsense! All have deserted me—why not you?"

"It is not true, Sire," and the Soldier rose powerfully erect—"All have not deserted you! These lords, these princes, these dukes—*Sacré!*[31] They could not desert you, for they were never with you. But the People, Sir, the People were with you, always with you—they are with you now! Look you, Sire—these tears! I—weep—I, who never wept when I saw Moscow's flame upon your face,—nor shed one tear when Waterloo flung its clouds upon your brow—I weep now! To see you thus, when at a word from your lips, forty thousand men, who watch around this palace, would tear the hearts from their bodies, to serve you! Come, Sire, say the word, and we'll raise the Eagle again!"[32]

The head of Napoleon sunk upon his breast. The broken appeal of that soldier stirred his leaden apathy into tears.

"Your name?"

"I have fought so long in the ranks, by a name which my comrades gave me, that I have almost forgotten the name which my father bore, which I took with me from my native village twenty years ago. Call me *Comrade Joseph,* Sire!"

"In the ranks?" cried Napoleon—"With your years of service! What! No Cross, no badge of honor? No token of merit? No reward?"

"Wrong, Sire, again! After Austerlitz, as I lay mangled near your horse's feet, you pointed to me, and muttered, '*Poor fellow! He has fought bravely!*' I have been rewarded."

31 Sacré, as an interjection, is a "profane imprecation." *Oxford English Dictionary.*
32 "Raise the Eagle" is a reference to the bronze eagles held aloft when Napoleon's soldiers charged the enemy's lines during the Napoleonic Wars.

33 A "sou" is a historical unit of French coinage that was of low value. *Oxford English Dictionary*.

34 The "Légion d'Honneur" was established by Napoleon as the highest honor a Frenchman could earn in service to his country. It remains the highest honor in France. Edgar Munhall, "Portraits of Napoleon," *Yale French Studies* no. 26 (1960): 6.

35 Empress Marie-Louise (1791–1849) was forced to leave Paris with her son after Emperor Francis of Austria laid siege to the city. Marie-Louise refused to support Napoleon's return from exile and received the duchies of Parma, Piacenza, and Guastalla following Napoleon's defeat at Waterloo. Fain, *The Manuscript of 1814,* 185, 213, 234, 244, 256–257, 260–266; Deborah Jay, "The Forgotten Archduchess," *History Today* 66, no. 2 (February 2016): 72.

He brought his musquet down upon the rich carpet, with a sound like thunder, by way of adding emphasis to his words. It is not to be concealed, that this speech affected Napoleon deeply. Turning away, the fallen Emperor opened a secret drawer of his desk.

"Come hither, Comrade Joseph—all whom I ever made rich by princely gifts, have deserted me. You—to whom I never gave so much as a *sou,*[33] you, whose services of twenty years have been passed unrewarded by, you are true, when all the world is false. Joseph, I have no Cross to give—for the Legion of Honor[34] is dead. Joseph, speak! Will you accept a name from me—"

"Sire—" the Soldier gasped, with choking utterance.

"Take from the fallen Emperor, the name of Joseph Austerlitz! Here is a picture—my picture—wear it next your heart, Joseph, and treat it better than its last possessor—" he bowed his head and veiled his face from the light—"*My Empress, Maria Louisa,*[35] *left it, when she fled from me!*"

And at midnight, in the silent palace of Fontainebleu, did the fallen Man of Destiny hang round the veteran soldier's neck, that golden chain, to which was attached his own picture, with its god-like forehead, and large, eloquent eyes.

On the field of Palo Alto, amid the tall rank grass, behold an aged man, whose hair and mustache white as the driven snow, contrast strongly with his bronzed and battle-worn face. His blue uniform, thrown open across the breast, reveals the death-wound; you see his blue eyes roll from side to side, and hear the air rattling in his mangled chest.

His stiffening fingers grasp his short artillerist sword, as with his face to the sky, or rather toward the cloud of prairie smoke, he bites his lips, and chokes down the involuntary groan of pain.

"Comrade," exclaim the soldiers, whose place it is to bear the wounded to the rear, "We are sorry to see you in this condition—" and the sight of the old man's head, baptized with the snows of seventy years, held them spell-bound to the spot.

He raised himself on one arm—venerable sight! His broad chest was bared; they could see, written in that scar near the throat, the word Moscow.

The bronzed face, marked on each cheek, and over the brow, with the traces of long healed wounds, spoke eloquently of Aboukir, Marengo,[36] Austerlitz and Waterloo.

Perchance some memory of these glorious names, was busy at his heart, perchance the thought of France, came up to him in this moment of agony, but he merely said—

"Go on comrades! It is but an old man lost!"—And fell back dead.

Near his wound a golden chain sparkled into light, and beneath that wound, rising with the last pulsation of his heart, appeared the portrait of NAPOLEON.

Thus, on the sod of the battle-field, miry with blood, are drawn many pictures of wild and contrasted interest.

Near the corse of the soldier of Napoleon, a child of Poland breathes his last, and yonder, an old man, in plain farmer's costume, sits amid the long grass, holding on his knee, a boy not more than nineteen years old, whose pale cheek, and closed lids, and smiling lips, announce a long and peaceful sleep.

36 The Battle of Marengo (June 14, 1800) was fought between the France and Austria in northern Italy. For more information, see Herbert Howland Sargent, *The Campaign of Marengo* (Chicago: A.C. McClurg and Company, 1901).

It needs no words, to indicate the tie which binds these two together. An old farmer of Texas, who left his plough for the rifle, and took with him, to battle, his only son!

His only son! The old man wipes his brow with the back of his hand, and looks upon that serene face, smiling upon him, in its calm slumber. His sunburnt face is unruffled by an emotion, still you may distinguish an almost imperceptible twitching of the nether lip, while the veins of his bared throat swell, until they resemble cords of steel.

His only son. Dying, not with convulsive howls of pain, but calmly as an infant goes to sleep. The agitation of the old man, finds vent at last in these rude words, spoken hurriedly, without a tear, yet with husky utterance:

"Your Mother, boy, what'll I say to her, when I go home, and see her standing in the door and askin' for—you? She'll ask whar you ar', and what can I say?"

And unable to hold the agony that was clasping him, the old man wrapped his huge arm about the dead boy and wept terribly; as only a strong man can weep.

―――――――

It was now four o'clock. The sun was sinking in the west: his disc, like an immense globe of fire, glared through the darkening cloud of battle smoke. The Americans have advanced, yes, through the fire and smoke of the burning prairie, you may see on the very spot, when an hour ago, floated the tri-color of Mexico, now waving proudly the Banner of the Stars.

Calmly reining his old grey horse, in the very centre of the late battle-field, stout-hearted Zachary prepares for the second fight of Palo Alto. A sad, a terrible prospect meets his eye beneath his horse's feet—the earth harrowed by cannon balls, and miry with blood. But around him—ah, that is the sight to stir the old man's heart, even through the gathering shadows, the bayonets gleam like shattered rays of light.

On his right, he beholds Ringgold's cannon, backed by the hearts and steel of the heroic Fourth. Beyond the cannon you behold the Fifth Regiment, their bayonets glittering on the extreme right of the newly formed line. Far on the left the unwearied Duncan repairs the wounds, which his battery has endured, and brings forth fresh stores of powder and ball, for the last fight of Palo Alto.

Churchill is not idle, you may be sure; he is teaching his terrible eighteen pounders, how to speak in the coming battle.

To the south, the prospect stirs the General's blood. Through those vast curtains of prairie smoke, now descending upon the fiery sod like a pall, and now undulating like mists about the mountain top, he sees the long line of Mexican arms, glitter far over the plain, into the shadows of the chaparral.

"Arista has chosen his last position!" said the General, with one of his quiet smiles.

Flutter, Banner of the Stars, flutter beautifully, and fling forth your belts of scarlet and snow, for all that is left of the two thousand men, looks up to you with hope, as the trumpet of battle shrieks along the breeze!

And from the Mexican line—look! That volume of flame, streaming through the smoke of the burning prairie—hark! That hurricane of iron balls!

Around the cannon of Ringgold, the fury of the Mexican battle descends, in a whirlwind of cannister and grape. Arista smiles, as from afar he surveys the effect of his fire: for every discharge flings a shower of blood into the faces of living men, and from the solid ranks, picks out brave forms and crushes them into the grave, dug by the cannon ball at their feet.

37 Lieutenant Colonel Matthew M. Payne served as the inspector-general, aide to General Taylor, and commanding officer of the 4th Regiment of Artillery. He was severely wounded at the Battle of Resaca de la Palma and received the rank of colonel for his service. Lippard's assertion that Payne found Ringgold after Ringgold was wounded is corroborated by T.B. Thorpe's account. Gardner, *A Dictionary of All Officers,* 352, 520; Robarts, *Mexican War Veterans,* 16; *S. Doc. No. 388*; Thorpe, *Our Army on the Rio Grande,* 81, 99, 110.

Behold the gallant Fourth; hear the howl of pain, as bayonet after bayonet sinks to rise in its owner's hands no more.

It was in the heat of this terrible fire, that a scene took place, which for its strong lights and dark shadows, has no parallel in history. Let us behold the picture, framed as it is, in the smoke of the burning prairie.

We stand on this space of sward, burnt and blackened by the heat of battle. Before us glooms the terrible eighteen pounders, which all day long, have thundered their message of death into the Mexican ranks.

Around those cannon extends a circle of manly chests and glittering steel. You see them, there, the heroes of the day, standing amid the dead bodies of their comrades. Three figures in the picture, standing out from all others, rivet our eyes.

CHURCHILL, standing erect, near his cannon, his face begrimed with powder and stained with blood. By his side PAYNE,[37] the Inspector General, a man of gallant presence, whose uniform, as yet unstained with blood, glitters gaily in the light, as bending down he 'sights' one of the remorseless eighteen pounders, and prepares to hurl its hurricane of iron into the Mexican army.

In the open space, near the cannon, behold the prominent figure of the picture—a warrior, mounted on a white horse, his head thrown proudly erect on his shoulders, as with a gleaming eye, he gazes upon the battle. It is a beautiful horse, with neck arched, and mane fluttering to the breeze.

That manly form, enveloped in the blue costume, relieved by ornaments of gold, that stern face, surmounted by the helmet, over which descends the shower of waving plumes, that broad chest, heaving with the fever of the fight—it is a magnificent picture of manhood in its prime.

At this moment you behold Churchill standing erect, Payne bending over the cannon, the soldier on the white horse lifts his helmet, and a ray of sunlight warms his pale, high forehead.

Then the eighteen pounders yell forth their battle cry, and the soldier on the white horse, is enveloped in a cloud of smoke. At the same moment, the thunder of the Mexican cannon is heard, you see that cloud of smoke, mingled with a cloud of dust, roused by a shower of iron balls.

The smoke is there, rolling slowly—not toward the sky—but downward, until it shuts the soldiers and the cannon from your view.

A moment passes, and from the bosom of that smoke, shrieks a yell, which makes your blood run cold.

And from that cloud, writhes into view, the figure of a mangled horse—the beautiful steed which we beheld only a moment ago—his limbs quivering, his eye horribly dilating, his flanks gored through and through by a cannon ball.

The saddle is red with blood, and the pistols splintered from the holsters, fall in fragments by the side of the dying horse.

But the rider—the man of the noble form, and white forehead, gleaming in the sun?

You hear, from the bosom of that cloud, a low, and almost unutterable groan, and then from its folds, there rushes a rude soldier, his form bared to the waist, darkened by powder, while his rough features are stamped with an expression of horrible agony.

"Colonel," he shrieks rushing toward the gallant Payne,—"Look there!"

He points to the sod, and every soldier in the group, utters a cry of horror.

There, beside the writhing horse, you behold the soldier, who but a moment ago, towered in all the pride of manhood. Horribly wounded;

38 In a letter dated May 11, 1846, J.M. Foltz, a United States Navy Surgeon, reported that Major Ringgold was mounted on his horse when a shot "struck him at right angles, hitting him in the right thigh, passing through the holsters and upper part of the shoulders of his horse, and then striking the left thigh, in the same line in which it first struck him.... An immense amount of muscles and integuments were carried away from both thighs," J.M. Foltz, "Major Ringgold Camp Isabel, Near the Mouth of the Rio Del Norte, 11th May, 1846," *Loom: A Voice from the National Fair* 1, no. 6 (May 28, 1846): 4; *Niles' National Register*, 201; Eisenhower, *So Far from God*, 80; *S. Doc. No. 388*.

39 Patrick Kelly was widely celebrated for his decision to remain with Ringgold, despite the expiration of his term of service the night prior. Though Lippard doesn't record it, Kelly lost an arm in the battle. *The Brooklyn Daily Eagle*, December 18, 1846, 2; "Congress," *Racine Advocate*, January 6, 1847, 3; *Richmond Enquirer*, December 18, 1846, 4, *Acts and Resolutions Passed by the Second Session of the Twenty-Ninth Congress of the United States* (Washington D.C.: C. Alexander, 1847), 19.

with the bones of each leg laid bare, from the knee to the thigh, he rests his head upon his hand, while a serene smile steals over his stern visage.

"Leave me," he calmly says to Payne, to Churchill, to the soldiers who clustered round him. "There is work for you yonder! You must drive the Mexicans before you, and save our comrades at Fort Brown!"

He reached forth his arm, and laid it upon the neck of his steed, which quivered in its death agony by his side. Then, with that calm smile stealing over his features, as they glowed in the red light of the cannon flash, he took the chain from his neck, and with it the gold watch—

"Give it," he said and his voice trembled for a moment, as the memories of home, came crowding round his warrior heart—"Give it to my sister. It will serve to remind her of Palo Alto and—"

As if afraid to trust his tongue with further words, he said no more, but laid his head upon the neck of his steed, while his wounds poured their torrents of blood along the sod.

As for the officers who stood round him, they could not speak. In the description of the varied scenes of a battle, we meet with many that rend the heart, but to hear told, but this, before the eyes of Churchill and Payne, was the most heart-rending, the most touching of all.

RINGGOLD dying on the neck of his dead steed.[38]

Payne near his head, clasping his hands, as his full heart gushed to his eyes. Churchill by his side, on his knees, veiling his face in his hands, unable to gaze upon the sight. In the background the line of soldiers, all awed into silence, by the spectacle before them. In front of all, a rugged fellow, his form bared to the waist, stained with powder, as he lifts his brawny arms to his face and shrieks the name of Ringgold, with deep sobs.—As long as the name of the hero remains, would live the name of that brave teamster KELLY,[39] who although his time expired the night before the battle, preferred to remain by his commander's side, and die with him, or worse than all the horrors of battle,—see him die.—

In the midst of the awe-stricken spectators, curtained by the battle clouds, the dying man was stretched upon the neck of his horse. The cannon balls rent the earth every moment, but the steed lay still, and the dying man did not stir. Ever and anon, as the clouds above rolled away, the full light of the setting sun poured upon his pale forehead, and lighted his face as with a glory.

And while the revolutionary blood of John Cadwallader, pouring from the veins of Ringgold, crimsons the battle-field, who shall dare pierce the shadows of that far off home, and gaze upon the Sister's face,—illumined by the same sunset that glows over the face of the dying man—as wrapt in a day-dream, she sees her absent brother, mounted on his own gallant steed—sees him, come from the wars, the laurel upon his white forehead, the glow of victory upon his battle worn cheek! Dream on sister of the hero, dream on, Sister of Ringgold; not many weeks will pass, before the watch and chain, placed in your hands, and stained with his dying blood, will make your heart swell with agony too deep for tears, as you think of the corse, which sleeps upon the sands near the Ocean Wave!

And at the very hour, when the Sister of Ringgold, thinks of the absent brother in another home of our land, a wife sitting in the silence of her chamber, rests her pale, beautiful cheek, upon her white hand, while the dark eyes, fire with tender light as she pictures the form of a brave soldier, now far away on the field of battle. How he will return, how she will hear his footstep in the hall, how she will spring forward to the threshold, and bury her head upon his bosom—she thinks of it all!

At this hour, amid the mist of Palo Alto, not one hundred yards from the spot where Ringgold fell, that husband writhes upon the dust, his limbs quivering in the blood, which pours from his wound, and swells in little pools, where the horse's hoofs have broken the sod. A horrible, a ghastly wound! The whole lower jaw torn off by a cannon ball, that manly face, in a single moment, wrecked into deformity!

Days pass; the wife hears that her husband has been wounded in the fight of Palo Alto.

At once she leaves her home, and hurries, like a dove through the cloud, to the distant battle field. Over the mountains, and across the rivers, on ship-board, she hastens to his side, hungering to behold him, to pillow his head upon her breast once more. But a strange chance separates them, or—can we doubt it? Providence wished to spare her yet awhile, the full cup of agony.

While the mangled husband is borne to New Orleans, the wife is on the gulf, hurrying toward the field of Palo Alto. She retraces her way, and pinioned by her love, resumes her Pilgrimage, a holier pilgrimage than was ever made by the devotee to the gilded shrine, for it was the pilgrimage of a faithful wife to the couch of a wounded husband.

At last, she beholds him. Well may the heart of the Painter grow sick, as his pencil delineates that scene of all the scenes the most heartrending. A door was opened; the wife stood quivering on the threshold. "Enter"—they said—"Your husband is here!"

She entered, trembling all the while. Through the closed curtains, a soft light stole round the place. It was very quiet, very dim, aye, filled with shadows, broken by threads of sunshine and breathlessly still.

"My husband here?"—And with that volume of her woman's faith, glowing over her cheek and gleaming through her tears, she advanced, gathering her hands to her breast, for the swelling heart, seemed choking the life within her.

"Where is he?" she said, standing on tip-toe, in the centre of that darkened room, and look! as with her arms outspread, her pale face turned from yonder sofa, and turned toward the light she listens.

Where is he? Ah, that groan, scarcely audible, sounding like a sigh from the dying, as their lips are muffled by the cold hand of death.

She turns and gazes into the shadows of the chamber. The sofa stands in that recess, and by degrees, the form of a man clad in undress military costume, breaks on her eye.

But that cloth upon the face, that thing white as snow, falling over the brow, and covering the features, as the shroud covers the heart of the dead? What does it mean? A white hand is extended—"My Wife!" exclaims a choking voice from beneath the folds of the cloth, and two arms are stretched forth, to clasp her home to the husband's heart.

Then looking tremblingly up, she beholds the white cloth hanging about the face of her husband, and with her heart bursting in a flood of tears, learns at a glance the fearful truth. She may not look upon the husband's face. Those features which once won her love, with their chivalric manhood, are now a mass of ruins. The husband seems to *feel* that her eyes are upon his veiled face, and utters one long and prolonged groan of anguish, as he clutches her to his heart.

The last scene of this sad history! Beneath the smile of the morning sky, on the deck of a steamboat, which dashes the waters of the Missouri from its prow, two figures, rivet the eyes of a weeping crowd: a dying husband resting on the breast of a faithful wife, who even in this dread hour, may not see those features which she loved so well, for upon the brow and the shattered face still rests the white cloth, fluttering to the last impulse of the warrior's breath.*⁴⁰

Gazing from the centre of his new line of battle, Arista marked with undisguised complacency, the fire of his artillery, poured in all its concentrated fury upon the Right Wing of the American army. As the battle-light lit up his swarthy face, he turned his eyes to the sun—shining like a thing of evil omen, through the dark clouds—and exclaimed, "It shall not set before I have crushed these Americans on the field, and made them feel the Invaders fate in the chaparral!"

His fire had wreaked all its fury upon the right wing. He now resolved to carry the field by one brilliant effort. Yonder on the left of the American line, beyond the smoke of the burning prairie, you behold the train of the little army, a prize which Arista swears shall be his own, before the setting of the sun.

At once, the glittering officers of his staff were seen hurrying over the field. The point of attack had been the right, it was now to be suddenly changed, and the left of the American line was to feel the last desperate blow, stricken by the Mexican host.

The orders of Arista produced an effect like magic. His right wing, infantry and cavalry, in magnificent array, advanced with one impulse, toward the unprotected left of the American army. It was a sight that would have stirred your blood, to see them come on. Men, horses, lances and bayonets, locked together, like an immense engine of battle murder, moved suddenly to the attack. You see their horses moving proudly on, you hear

---

* The brave Captain PAGE, wounded at Palo Alto, died on the 13th of July, 1846, on board the steamer Missouri, while on his way to Jefferson barracks.

---

40 Captain John Page (1795–1846) was hit in the lower jaw with a cannonball. He and Ringgold were the only two officers who died as a result of injuries sustained in the battle of Palo Alto. Eisenhower, *So Far from God,* 80; S. Doc. No. 388.

the dead, sullen tramp of the infantry, you see the tri-color wave, and far along the field the points of their lances gleam like torches, and their red flags flutter against the southern sky.

Arista's white horse is seen rearing proudly, as his rider, already feels the throb of victory pulsate in his veins. He has caught that rough old Zachary at last. He knows not that Ringgold has fallen, nor that Page lies a mangled wreck upon the ground, but he has seen the effect of his deadly fire upon the right wing.*[41] He knows, that with all his dead and dying, counted twice over, he still twice outnumbers Zachary Taylor and his Men. To add to his joy, but a moment ago he saw that terrible DUNCAN, who, all day long had poured his hurricane of iron from the left, suddenly whirl along the American line, and with his horses, his men, his cannon, disappear in the clouds toward the right. He has gone to supply the place of Ringgold—it is evident that the train is the prize of Arista, that the left wing will be turned and hurled back upon the right, that Zachary Taylor and his men, will soon—aye, ere fifteen minutes have passed—be prisoners of war.

And in the Mexican dialect, a Prisoner of War, means a Man who is to be hurled into a dungeon, or shot like a dog, or cut to pieces with assassins' knives.

In this proud moment, as men and horses and steel—that solid mass of battle—moved toward the left wing, their joy broke forth, in the music of a full band. You see that immense column of advancing cavalry, under the command of Don Cayetano Montero,[42] one of those brave gentleman, splendid in his dress and musical in his name. In front of this column, attired in burning scarlet, the band of the army advance, their instruments stirring the blood of at least three thousand men, into madness, as they

---

* The gallant Lieut. Luther of Pennsylvania, was wounded in this fire.

41 Lieutenant Roland A. Luther (1815–1853), of the 2nd Artillery, was wounded in the Battle of Palo Alto. Gardner, *A Dictionary of All Officers*, 287; Robarts, *Mexican War Veterans*, 15; *S. Doc. No. 378,* 29th Cong., 1st Sess. (1846); *S. Doc. No. 388*; Thorpe, *Our Army on the Rio Grande,* 81.

42 Colonel don Cayetano Montero was the commanding officer of the 7th Cavalry (lancers). He was ordered by General Arista to charge the American artillery. The charge was not successful. George C. Furber, *The Twelve Months Volunteer; or, Journal of a Private, in the Tennessee Regiment of Cavalry, in the Campaign, in Mexico, 1846-7* (Cincinnati: J.A. & U.P. James, 1850), 38; Thorpe, *Our Army on the Rio Grande,* 87, 158.

blaze in the light like pieces of burnished gold. O, sweetly, O, sadly, O, terribly that music rose into heaven, with every varied note of joy and woe, as though it spoke of blood and tears, of Mexican mothers robbed of their sons, and of American soldiers, who soon would bite the sod, with their clenched teeth, and feel the hoofs of the horses trampling over their breasts.

That man is to be pitied, who has not felt his blood dance, at the music of a battle band. Even in the streets of the every-day city, it makes your veins swell with frenzy. But when it comes from a band, who walk calmly on, in front of an advancing army,—Death before and Death behind them—when in the intervals of the drum's thunder and the trumpet's peal, you hear the moan of pain, the short, quick cry of the dying, then this music of a battle band, makes the blood run riot. You hunger for the battle, and grow thirsty for human blood.

They advance in their beautiful order, secure in the confidence of victory, and seem to have forgotten one essential fact. There is a brave old warrior in yonder ranks, whose name is Zachary Taylor.

As they come on, a dark mass is seen moving through the clouds of prairie smoke. Like a dark shadow within the cloud, it moves from the right to the left of the American line, it grows larger and wider, spreading forth through the smoke, like the pinions of an immense bird.

As one man, the Mexicans halt, falling back, rank on rank with a sudden recoil, and a crash like the smothered thunder of a volcano. For that Cloud, moving rapidly through the prairie smoke, begins to resolve itself into shape. It begins to grow into form. From its bosom, uprearing into the battle light, the heads of horses start into view. A rumbling sound from that cloud, a murmur as of wheels passing over a burnt and cindered sod, and then the brazen cannon flash into light. Then, amid the flashing of dragoon scimiters[43] and the circling light of bayonets, appears the face of

---

43 "Scimiter" is a variant of "scimitar," meaning "a short single-edged sword with a curved blade that typically broadens before the point." *Oxford English Dictionary*.

DUNCAN, black with powder, stained with blood, and terrible to behold, for it says to the whole line of Mexico,—We are here—here to receive you! We have seen Ringgold in his blood, and Taylor on his grey steed! Ringgold tells us, with his dying voice, that there is work for us ahead—Taylor bids us to end this battle, and we have come to do it!

Arista saw them come and ground his teeth. But they did not give him breathing time, those men of iron. Dashing from the cloud, they arrayed their cannon in battle order, and fired. At the moment, when the sturdy cannoniers lifted the match, you might hear the full chorus of the Mexican band, and admire their beautiful array—their uniform blushing scarlet, their burnished instruments flashing in the lurid light.

That cannon shout drowned their music forever. They were arrayed in the very front, and received the battle blast in all its fury. Crushed to the earth—not in mere poetical phrase—literally hewn away by the hail of canister and shell, they strewed the ground, shattered trumpets and mangled heads, broken drums and torn bodies, mingled in one bloody pool. It was the most horrible scene of the whole battle.

For a moment, the Mexican array quivered in every platoon, as with one electric horror of that sight. Then with their shouts of revenge, with their banners waving and their lances poised and bayonets fixed, they moved forward—no music sounded this time—gradually accelerating their pace, until an irresistible impulse seem to hurl them in one mass upon the foe.

But DUNCAN was there to receive them. As they came on, he showered once more his iron hail. Here a shell, hurled blazing from his cannon's throat, alighted amid a circle of brave lancers, and scattered man and horse into fragments of flesh and pools of blood. Yonder, the infantry come charging with fixed bayonets; their green uniform and swarthy faces tinted with red battle light. They near the guns, with a shout they pour to the last charge, when a cloud of smoke rushes into their faces; and when it clears away, you see them no more.

It was a fearful sight to see the wreck accomplished by Duncan's cannon. Back, over the mangled forms and shattered instruments of their own musicians, he hurled the formidable lancers, back, over the faces of their slaughtered infantry, back, with that iron shower tearing their pennons, splintering their spears, cutting lanes into their woven ranks, he hurled the chivalry of Mexico, until the shadows of the chaparral alone, saved the wreck of their glittering array.

—Taylor, viewing the scene from the saddle of his steed, turned to an officer and coolly said, "*the day is won.*"—

—Arista beheld it with an expression of overwhelming chagrin, and looked for Ampudia to head another charge, but that brave man, who had boiled a human head from mere vivacity, was gone. Perchance, the visage of Captain Walker, that unassuming young man, who always received the Mexicans with Kentuckian warmth, scared the hero of the boiling cauldron from the field?—

Again, mustering his forces for a last, a forlorn charge, Don Cayetano De Montero came from the chaparral, with his lancers formed once more in battle order. They moved to the attack with admirable regularity. The battery of Duncan had, in the meantime, advanced one hundred yards, the cannon wheels forcing a path through Mexican dead. De Montero came on, but in the same moment, the setting sun shone over his spears, the prairie cloud buried them in smoke, and then the hurricane of shell and canister crushed through their ranks again.

By that mingled light, the setting sun shining its level rays through the intervals of the clouds, and the cannon blaze, casting its red glare toward the sky, until the smoke rolled to and fro in wreaths of crimson, you might see the last picture of this battle day.

The wreck of six thousand brave men in full retreat, over a space of prairie three miles in extent, their scattered legions seen through the folds of the curtaining clouds.

Squadron crowding back on squadron, one column communicating its panic to another in the rear, until the battle became a rout, the cannonade a chase. In one place, a battalion of retreating horse crushes down a mass of foot-soldiers, and over their mangled bodies, scours away from that terrible blaze of Duncan's cannon. In another, two bands of horse and foot, stricken with the panic, and flying in an opposite direction from the field, became entangled and rocked to and fro like an immense wave, their arms glittering like spray. Not a moment passed before their contest was over. A wide lane splintered through their ranks by the cannon balls, and paved with the faces of the dead, divided them into two bodies again, who fled from each other's sight, as though a Plague stalked between them.

It was at this moment, when for the space of two miles, the prairie was littered with Mexican corses, with fallen banners and broken arms, that a scene took place, in every way worthy of this day of chivalry and blood.

Arista reined his white horse on the edge of the chaparral, and beheld his broken army, in all the panic of a retreat. Upon their frightened ranks rolled the full volume of Duncan's batteries. A space of earth, some hundred yards in extent, was illumined by the setting sun, shining through the clouds. Around that space all was dim and shadowy; it shone from the twilight of the field, like a broach of gold, set in a mantle of rich brown. Into this illuminated space, thundered the cannon of Duncan, pursuing a body of Mexicans, who, crowding upon each other, hurried wildly toward the chaparral. You see the cannon unlimbered, arrayed in battle order; the half-naked cannoniers are ready; in a moment, that band of Mexicans, at least five hundred in number, will be torn by the cannister, and blown to pieces by the shell.

At this moment, a solitary horseman breaks from the Mexican ranks, and holding a white flag above his head, speeds rapidly toward the foremost of the American cannon. He rides a beautiful dark bay, whose eye rolls with the madness of battle, as he sweeps with his master, right into the muzzles of the formidable battery.

It is a young man with the dark hair flying back from his brow, with the green uniform, thrown aside from his muscular throat, with the sunlight playing freely over himself and his bay steed. For a moment the cannoniers ceased, while a murmur of admiration ran along the American line. He came on a message of peace, that gallant youth, for fluttering over his head the white flag stood out against the sky.

Near and nearer; they can discern his features, see the wild light flashing in his eye. Not fifty yards from the muzzle of the foremost cannon, he thunders on. Look! He rises in his stirrups, he flings the white flag from his bosom, he tears from his breast another flag—the Tri-color of Mexico!

"Now!" he shouts in Spanish, his dark face convulsed with passion, the frenzy of despair, as he waved that flag and crashed on, to the very muzzle of the cannon—"Now! Let your cannon blaze—I am ready!"

The cannon spoke, and its smoke encircled him like a curtain. Every man held his breath as the cloud rolled away. The Mexican and his horse were gone, and the sod was covered with the fragments of gory flesh, mingled with the shreds of a tri-colored flag.

But the object of the gallant Boy, was gained. The last of the retreating Mexicans, had time to disappear in the chaparral, as the death rushed upon him. Many an eye was wet along the American line, as among the grass appeared that youthful face, smiling in death amid the ruins of his mangled body, while far away into the crimson cloud rolled the echoes of the Last Shot of Palo Alto.

Night came down on Palo Alto, and beside a grey steed stood an old man, leaning on his sheathed sword, his uncovered head bent upon his breast, as his large eyes, shone with unusual light. The monuments of the fight—corses, arms and wounded—were scattered around him. Above his head, hung that thin mist, pestilential with the smell of gunpowder, and through its veil shone the glad light of the evening star. Officers and soldiers formed a circle round the old man, leaning on his sword. All crimsoned with the traces of the fight, all darkened by the stain of powder, they stood in silence, their heads uncovered in respect to that old man. He drew his sheathed sword along the sod, with an involuntary gesture. His heart was too full for words. That day, deeds had been done, which history would never be tired of telling, deeds that would make her say in one breath, Washington and Taylor.

Therefore the old man stood in silence, his heart too full for words, while with his head drooped, he mechanically made circles with the end of his sword on the cindered sod.

At last he spoke—

"I think," he said, as the evening star, like a good omen, shone over his brow—"I think *that we will reach Fort Brown.*"

It was then that the fullness of the soldiers' hearts, found vent in words. Even as the soldiers of Napoleon hailed their young leader, standing amid the trophies of battle, by the name of the Little Corporal, so on the field of Palo Alto, the heroes of that day baptized Zachary Taylor with a name, warm from their hearts. A common soldier, feeling his heart swell with emotions that he could not speak, pointed to the old man, and blundered forth his admiration in three words, which leapt from lip to lip, until they grew into a thunder shout—

"Rough and Ready!"

Night came down upon the beleaguered Fort, and the town of Matamoras. Crowding to the shore, the people had heard that terrible cannonade, continued for two hours, and in the Fort, the voice of Taylor's guns, came like the trumpet peal of hope. All day long the shower of shot and shell had rained its fury on the little band, but now, crowding to the ramparts they raised their voices in a thunder shout.

A wounded soldier, who had rent his way through the Mexican lines, came tottering toward the Fort, shouting as the blood poured from his wounds—"Taylor is coming! Do not give it up now! The old man is on his way, and will be here!"

Then a shout went up again, which reached the ears of the veteran Brown, who resting in his rude couch, racked by pain, lifted up his head and exclaimed—"I knew that he would come!"

And by the light of the setting sun, and by the first gleam of the Evening star, masses of Mexican cavalry and infantry might be seen crossing the Rio Grande, above and below the Fort, their arms flashing vengeance for the disgrace of their flag.

It was a beautiful thing to see them glitter by thousands on the river, while the damsels of Matamoras waved them farewell with their white scarfs. It was a grand spectacle, their compact masses of horse, fresh as their riders, and as eager for battle, march in battle array, from the river to the shadows of the chaparral. They were hurrying to the aid of Arista—to-morrow, a new wall of cannon, horses, men and steel, woven together, as with bands of iron, would intervene between old Zachary and Fort Brown. Beautiful it was, I say, to see the going forth of this army—

But the coming back?

The heart grows cold to think of it.—Angel of death, hovering over those legions, with the light of the evening star, upon your livid brow, tell us, have you the heart to enter Matamoras now, and gaze upon those children, who will be fatherless to-morrow, upon those wives who to-morrow will look for their husbands, and find them floating with cold faces, on the river's wave, or seek for them in vain, among the heaps of battle dead?

The going forth is beautiful. To see these flags flutter so bravely from the lances, like the foliage of those trees of death, to hear the bugles speak out,—but the morrow? The coming back? Hark! through the darkened air, did you not hear a sound, like the closing of a thousand coffin lids?

Through the midnight darkness, which has descended upon the battlefield, the glare of torches breaks suddenly, like meteors glimmering over the abyss of a swamp. Those torches light the surgeons on their way, as they pass from the wounded to the dead, and bend over the mangled skulls and broken arms—the horrible summing up of the great game of war.

There is a groan in yonder thicket. It is the cry of the wounded wretch, as the knife of the Ranchero sinks into his heart.

A torch remarkable for its glaring light shone in the centre of the field.

Its beams lighted the faces of battle worn soldiers, who with their apparel rent, their faces stained with blood, took counsel with their General on the—morrow!

In the midst of that band, he stood erect, a plain and unpretending man, his faded brown coat torn in many places by the balls of the enemy, his brow uncovered, and his right hand resting on the hilt of his sheathed sword.

On his left, distinguished by his portly form, his massive features, and hair white as snow, you might see Colonel Twiggs, who like his General had seen long years of battle toil.

By his side, stood erect, a white haired man, the veteran M'Intosh. Near him seated on a trunk, his tired head resting in his hands, the brave Ridgely, who had done his part in the terror and glory of that Day. Duncan was there, covered with the memorials of his last charge, with Churchill by his side, and the other heroes grouped around. Above their heads, the tent canopy, moved to every impulse of the breeze, and triumphantly in the light of the midnight stars of Palo Alto, waved the Banner of the Stars.

"Shall we go on?"

A question to make men bow their heads and think.

By to-morrow's dawn at least nine thousand men, will build a wall of flame and steel in our path. Defeat is Massacre. Victory against such tremendous odds, a Miracle. At this very hour, in the American Union at least one hundred thousand hearts, are palpitating in fearful anxiety for us, afraid that every moment may bring the news of the utter slaughter of Taylor and his Men.

Shall we go on?

As the question throbs from heart to heart, the cries of dying men are heard, mingled with the jackal's howl.

Duncan speaks, Twiggs pours forth his few emphatic words; Ridgely eloquent with the fever of to day's strife and the hope of to-morrow's glory, looks in the old man's face, and cries with impassioned fervor—"Go on!"

May and Walker say nothing, but clutch their swords.

But there are other voices there. Glory we have won to day, but *to-morrow!*—let us not trifle with fate. Entrenched upon this field, we can wait for reinforcements. Our countrymen will hear of our peril and our glory, and their hearts and rifles will rush to the rescue.

As if from the excitement of the moment, Zachary Taylor draws his sword, half way from its sheath.

Hark! that sound—every heart beats, and those soldiers who stand erect, grasp their swords, and those who are seated, spring to their feet. It is the signal gun of Fort Brown.

"Go on!"—the words in a deep whisper, pass from lip to lip, and every eye is fixed on Taylor's face.

The old man quietly dropped his sword to the sheath:

"To morrow night I will be at Fort Brown if I live."

At this moment a sublime sight was seen. Far along the eastern horizon over the dark chaparral, a wall of clouds, black as death, without a ray of light, to break its monotony of gloom, towers into the upper sky.

Save that wall of blackness, the sky is clear, glittering over its awful dome, with the serene midnight of the stars. But look! As we gaze upon that mass of dark cloud, raising like a Fort of Death, above the gloomy horizon, along its border, runs a quivering thread of light. It widens, it glows, until the cloud resembles an immense castle, illumined on its battlements, with the rays of innumerable torches.

And then, beautiful and serene over the top of the cloud, bursts into sight the Moon, shining her clear calm light over the tents and the banners, over the cannon and the tired soldiers, bivouacking beneath their muzzles, over the encircling chaparral, and the blasted field, over the dying and dead of Palo Alto.

V

Resaca de la Palma

Halting on the edge of the chaparral. The rein thrown carelessly on the neck of his grey horse, Zachary Taylor looked back, and surveyed the field of Palo Alto.

If the view had been ghastly by moonlight, it was horrible in the calm clear light of that cloudless day. The Mexicans had fled through the mazes of the southern chaparral. From that wall of prickly pear,—look to the south of Taylor and you will see it—flashed the bayonets of the American army. Certain companies of the heroic band were searching the wilderness for traces of the foe, while the main body of the army halted on the southern verge of the prairie, the chaparral darkening behind their cannon and bayonets.

It was at the moment, that General Taylor, reining his steed, amid the tall rank grass, near the wagons of the train, surveyed the field of Palo Alto. A clear, bracing morning, with the song of birds in the air, and beautiful prairie flowers blooming beneath his feet.

The wide field lay calmly beneath the smile of the morning sun. Like an immense scar, the cinders of the prairie fire, blackened the centre of the plain. Here and there, men with spades in their hands, moved to and fro—they were digging rude graves for their dead.

But the horses, mangled in masses, and stretched far over the plain, the dead men, piled in heaps, their broken limbs, and cold faces, distinctly seen by the light of the morning sun, still remained, amid the grass and flowers, silent memorials of yesterday's Harvest of Death.

Chapter V

Even the old General could not repress a shudder, as he gazed upon the terrible evidence of Duncan's last fire—a line of dead men and horses, darkening far away to the left.

At this moment, when in presence of the entire army, Taylor read the alphabet of blood, upon the battle-field, was selected by Fate—by Providence—by God—for a scene of painful and singular interest.

A young soldier, mounted on a black horse, and covered with the traces of the fight,—the powder stain and the crimson drops of human hearts—rode from the chaparral and dismounted near the General. He flung the reins on the neck of his steed, and stood for a moment, regarding that sad prospect of the battle field. As his dilating eye shone with deep, with bitter thoughts, from the shadow of his downcast brow, his muscular figure, attired in a plain blue frock coat, with a plain row of gold buttons, presented a striking image of chivalric manhood.

Worn down, with the battle toil of the last twenty-four hours, with the incessant hurrying to and fro, the severe duty that left no time for food or slumber, the brave fellow, had ridden to the rear, to take some refreshment, and an hour's repose.

The eye of the General wandered from the battle-field, to the form of the young soldier, and an expression of admiration lighted up his bronzed face. It was the gallant Lieutenant, who the day before, in that breathless moment, before the first fire, had ridden into the muzzles of Mexican cannon, and with cool composure reconnoitered their array—The Hero, BLAKE.

Taylor looks upon him, as he is in the act of receiving a cup of water from the hands of a soldier, and turns his eyes to the field again. Scarce a moment passes, and then his gaze seeks the hero's face once more. Where does he behold him?

Writhing on the sod, in all the agony of a mortal wound, his body rent upward by a pistol ball!

Yes, as he took the cup of water, he flung his holsters on the ground. One of the pistols exploded, even as it struck the ground, and laid him quivering on the sod, beside its smoking tube.

"Alas!" cried the brave fellow, writhing in his death agony—"Alas! That I did not fall in the battle of yesterday!"

For a few hours he lingered, and then was clay. As he yielded his spirit, the thunder of the cannonade, echoing from the south, sung his death-hymn.—There came a day, when Philadelphia put on mourning for her son, and brought his dead body home, amid the tribute of a People's tears.—

While Zachary Taylor gazed upon his prostrate form, the moment after he fell, there came from the south, the clear, deep crack of a rifle, that sound spoke to the old man's heart. It was the first shot of the Twin-Sister of Palo Alto—RESACA DE LA PALMA.

Presently there appeared on the verge of the chaparral, the form of a sunburnt soldier, dressed in a green ranger's frock, and mounted on a steed that flung the foam from his flanks, as he whirled his rider along to General Taylor's side.

It was Captain WALKER, bearing to the old commander, the first intelligence of Arista and his army.

Away through the wilderness, along the road that leads to Fort Brown, until we behold the Mexican army.

Forth from his splendid tent, erected in the depths of chaparral, issued Arista, his form blazing with stars and orders, while his dark face, varied by the well-known red moustache, manifested not so much chagrin for yesterday's defeat, as hope for the triumph of to-day.

The white horse splendidly caparisoned, the saddle glittering like one mass of silver, awaits his master. Bounding into the saddle, he dashes through the paths of the chaparral, and surveys his formidable army. It must be confessed that he had every reason for that feeling of pride, which gave such a glow to his face, such fire in his eyes. Behind him was seen the glittering circle of his staff officers, all handsomely mounted and gaily appareled. Ampudia, with his sinister look and lowering brow, alone seemed to detract from the chivalry of that warrior's band. There, too, bestriding an elegant brown charger, whose glossy skin shone like velvet in the morning light, was seen the graceful LA VEGA, slender in form, rich olive in complexion, luxuriant in his dark hair, and silken beard, the very ideal of a Castilian cavalier of old.

Wherever Arista looked, to the right or the left, forward or in the rear, the prickly pear bore a dazzling fruit, looking very much like the sharp steel of the lance, the deadly point of the bayonet. Horses, too, in solid legions, backed by brave riders, who, refreshed by food and slumber, were eager to retrieve the fortunes of yesterday. And as Arista passed, a half suppressed shout was heard, and the full bands clanged out their battle music.

This was the manner in which the Mexicans were prepared for battle. Behold their death-like, yes, we must confess it, their terrible array.

Across the road, leading to Fort Brown, a ravine extends near a hundred feet wide, and four feet high. In the rainy season, the ravine becomes a torrent, it overflows the road, and dashes away to the Rio Grande. Even now in its depths sparkle lakelets of clear deep water, and on its southern bank, the chaparral forms an impenetrable wall.

The ravine is called RESACA DE LA PALMA.

Along this ravine, and on either side of the road, the Mexicans extend, nine thousand strong, a crescent of cannon and horses, men and steel.

One line is hidden behind yonder bank, another shrouds its cannon, its horses, its men, beneath the shadows of the southern chaparral.

In the centre of each line the battery glooms: yonder, to the right of the first line, you see another group of these death engines.

From an open space, near the road, Arista gazed upon the battle array, and turns with a smile to his general. That smile means much, it means that the American flag today will bow before the flag of Mexico, in the depths of that ravine, whose banks shall swell with a torrent, not of water, but of blood.

For, as you may see, old Zachary Taylor, in order to reach Fort Brown, must pass along the road, cut away with his seventeen hundred men, through the breasts of some nine thousand Mexicans, who have chosen their position at leisure, and whose cannon commands the road on either side.

And there, eager to meet the old war-horse, who foiled them yesterday, stands arrayed in battle order, the bravest band of the whole army, iron men, hardened by the tropical sun, and the battle blaze, the heroes of a hundred civil conflicts, the veteran Battalion of Tampico. Above their heads waves their beautiful banner, embroidered by the hands of beautiful women, and sanctified by the prayers of nuns, bearing beneath the eagle and serpent, the simple legend: BATTALON—GUARDA COSTA—DE TAMPICO.

Gazing on his army, Arista sent his commands to the menials of his camp, to bring forth his choicest plate, to bury his wines in ice, and to light the fires, in order to prepare the Festival of victory, by the setting of the sun.

It was four o'clock, when, with a cloudless sky above, and the chaparral far and wide, thronged with Mexican legions, the battle began its bloody career.

It was four o'clock, when Arista saw advancing from the opposite thickets, a bluff old warrior, dressed in a brown coat, with a grey steed beneath him. The sun shone clearly upon the old warrior as he came on, and Arista knew that the hour was near.

Hark! The tramp as of a thousand warriors thundering through the northern chaparral, and as you listen, it grows near and nearer—to the right, to the left, and yonder in the front of the ravine, the bayonets come dazzling into the sun.

There rides Captain Walker at the head of his Texian band, there Ridgely glorious with the mantle of the fallen Ringgold, comes with his cannon to battle, while in the front, those bayonets, bursting like lightning from the bushes move rapidly toward the ravine.

Sixteen hundred men advance against nine thousand—it is a moment of breathless suspense.[1]

All at once, as hushing your breath, with fear of the tremendous results of this fight, you watch tremblingly for its commencement, all at once, the Third, Fourth and Fifth regiments rush on, their bayonets forming a crescent of dazzling steel, above their heads.

They line the bank of the ravine, and in a moment the copper hail rushes through their ranks, and the white cloud of battle shuts them in. From the northern bank of the Resaca de la Palma, from the southern wall of the chaparral, pours the storm of the Mexican cannon, while Ridgely is rushing to the encounter, and Duncan unlimbering his pieces, answers roar with roar, and lights the field with his blaze.

From the verge of the ravine pours the steady fire of our musquetry our men come crowding to the attack, they spring upon the Mexican bayonets, they enter the bed of the Ravine, and the chaparral, which not five minutes

---

[1] Taylor's army consisted of approximately 2,000 soldiers; Arista's, 3,000. Daniel Walker Howe, *What Hath God Wrought: The Transformation of America, 1815–1848* (Oxford: Oxford University Press, 2007), 745.

ago, was quiet as the tomb, now blazes and howls like a volcano bursting suddenly from the waters of a waveless sea.

Through the folds of smoke, you may see Ridgely's men, their bronzed forms bared to the waist, plying their deadly task. Around his battery sweep the bayonets of the Fifth infantry, with the grey-haired M'Intosh in their midst—yonder, on the edge of the ravine, Duncan, with his cannon ready for the conflict, pauses in his fire, unable to distinguish friend from foe, in the whirlpool of the fight, which swells and rages through the deadly pass.

His grey eye blazing with the excitement of the battle, Zachary Taylor sat quietly on his grey steed, with the cannon balls of the enemy tearing the earth all around him, and felt the moment for a decisive blow had come.

Amid the smoke and flame that rolled and blazed above the deadly ravine, he clearly saw the whirlpool of the fight.

On to the front bank, pressed the American infantry, pouring the blaze of musquetry into the faces of the Mexicans, and then, hurling their solid force into the ravine, as one man, they charged them home. On either side their bayonets were seen glittering above the battle clouds. From the rear ridge the most formidable battery in the second line of the Mexican array, swept the air with a shower of poisonous copper balls. Ridgely's blaze made answer, and Duncan, arranging his pieces in battle order, sent his cannon shout thundering through the darkening cloud.

Beneath this pall of smoke and flame, this canopy of whirling balls, the American infantry hurling themselves into the ravine, drove back the foe. Charging them with bayonets, cutting them down with their short swords, they fought for every inch of ground, and fought everywhere, on the earth that rocked with the cannon thunder, in the lagoons that blushed with blood, beneath the banks, where the dying and the dead began to swell in ghastly heaps. It was, indeed, a bloody contest. Here the veterans of Mexico, recoiling one moment, only to roll back again in all the terror of blaze and bayonet—there, the Americans advancing without a shout, never heeding for a moment, their comrades, who with arms torn off and heads unroofed, sank in mangled masses, at every step, but holding on their way, every bayonet charging against the bayonet of an enemy, every eye glaring steadily into the face of a foe.

Amid the scene, like wrecks on the waves of a stormy sea, tossed to and fro, the tri-color of Mexico and the Banner of the Stars.

Still from the rear ridge, swept the concentrated fury of the Mexican batteries, their flame and copper hail curtaining the troops below, as again and again they rushed to the charge.

Taylor saw it all, and knew the moment for the blow had come—the blow which was to decide the battle, and hurl the Mexican army back into the Rio Grande.

You may see him bending over the neck of his steed, his battle-worn face glowing redly in each flash, as his eye roves from point to point, and at a glance, takes in the panorama of blood.

At this moment, he sent to the rear for an officer of the dragoons, and awaited his appearance in undisguised suspense.

There was a day, when an old man with white hair, sat alone in the small chamber of a National Mansion, his spare but muscular figure resting on an arm chair, his hands clasped, and his deep blue eyes gazing through the window upon the cloudless winter sky. The brow of the old man, furrowed with wrinkles, his hair rising in straight masses, white as the driven snow, his sunken cheeks traversed by marked lines, and thin lips, fixedly compressed, all announced a long and stormy life. All the marks of an Iron Will were written upon his face.

His name, I need not tell you, was Andrew Jackson, and he sat alone in the White House.

A visitor entered without being announced, and stood before the President in the form of a boy of nineteen, clad in a coarse round jacket and trousers, and covered from head to foot with mud. As he stood before the President, cap in hand, the dark hair falling in damp clusters about his white forehead, the old man could not help surveying at a rapid glance, the muscular beauty of his figure, the broad chest, the sinewy arms, the head placed proudly on the firm shoulders.

"Your business?"—said the old man, in his short, abrupt way.

"There is a Lieutenancy vacant in the Dragoons. Will you give it to me?"

And dashing back the dark hair which fell over his face, the Boy, as if frightened at his boldness, bowed low before the President.

The old man could not restrain that smile. It wreathed his firm lip, and shone from his clear eyes.

"You enter my chamber unannounced, covered from head to foot with mud—you tell me, that a Lieutenancy is vacant, and ask me to give it to you.—*Who are you?*"

"Charles May!"—The Boy did not bow this time, but with his right hand on his hip, stood like a wild young Indian, erect, in the presence of the President.

"What claims have you to a commission?"—again the Hero surveyed him, and again he faintly smiled.

"Such as you see!" exclaimed the boy, as his dark eyes shone with that dare-devil light, while his young form swelled in every muscle, as with the conscious pride of his manly strength and beauty. "Would you—" he bent forward, sweeping aside his curls once more, while a smile began to break over his lips—"Would you like to see me ride? My horse is at the door. You see, I came post haste for this commission."

Silently the old man followed the Boy, and together they went forth from the White House. It was a clear, cold winter's day; the wind tossed the President's white hairs, and the leafless trees stood boldly out against the deep blue sky. Before the portals of the White House, with the rein thrown loosely on his neck, stood a magnificent horse, his dark hide smoking with foam. He uttered a shrill neigh as his Boy-Master sprang with a bound into the saddle, and in a flash was gone, skimming like a swallow down the road, his mane and tail streaming in the breeze.

The old man looked after them, the Horse and his Rider, and knew not which to admire most, the athletic beauty of the boy, or the tempestuous vigor of the horse.

Thrice they threaded the avenues in front of the White House, and at last stood panting before the President, the boy leaning over the neck of his steed, as he coolly exclaimed—"Well—how do you like me?"

"Do you think you could kill an Indian?" the President said, taking him by the hand, as he leapt from his horse.

"Aye—and eat him afterwards!" cried the boy, ringing out his fierce laugh, as he read his fate in the old man's eyes.

"You had better come in and get your Commission"; and the Hero of New Orleans led the way into the White House.

―――――――

There came a night, when an old man—President no longer—sat in the silent chamber of his Hermitage home, a picture of age, trembling on the verge of Eternity. The light that stood upon his table, revealed his shrunken form, resting against the pillows which cushioned his arm chair, and the death-like pallour of his venerable face. In that face, with its white hair and massive forehead, everything seemed already dead, except the eyes. Their deep grey-blue shone with the fire of New Orleans, as the old man, with his long white fingers, grasped a letter post-marked "Washington."

"They ask me to designate the man who shall lead our army, in case the annexation of Texas brings on a war with Mexico—" his voice, deep-toned and thrilling, even in that hour of decrepitude and decay, rung through the silence of the chamber. "There is only one man who can do it, and his name is Zachary Taylor."[2]

It was a dark hour, when this Boy and this General, both appointed at the suggestion or by the voice of the Man of the Hermitage, met in the battle of Resaca de la Palma.

By the blaze of cannon, and beneath the canopy of battle smoke, we will behold the meeting.

"Captain May, you must take that battery!"

As the old man, uttered these words, he pointed far across the ravine with his sword. It was like the glare of a volcano-the steady blaze of that battery, pouring from the darkness of the chaparral.

Before him, summoned by his command, from the rear, rose the form of a splendid soldier, whose hair waving in long masses, swept his broad shoulders, while his beard, fell over his muscular chest. Hair and beard as dark as midnight, framed a determined face, surmounted by a small cap, glittering with a single golden tassel. The young warrior, bestrode a magnificent charger, broad in the chest, small in the head, delicate in each

2 This anecdote is likely one of Lippard's "legends."

slender limb, and with the nostrils quivering as though they shot forth, jets of flame. That steed was black as death.

Without a word, the soldier turned to his men.

Eighty-four forms, with throats and breasts bare, eighty-four battle horses, eighty-four sabres, that rose in the clutch of naked arms, and flashed their lightning over eighty-four faces, knit in every feature with battle-fire.

"Men, follow!" shouted the young Commander, who had been created a soldier by the hand of Jackson, as his tall form, rose in the stirrups, and the battle breeze played with his long black hair.

There was no response in words, but you should have seen those horses quiver beneath the spur, and spring and launch away! Down upon the sod, with one terrible beat, came the sound of their hoofs, while through the air, rose in glittering circles, those battle scimitars.

Four yards in front, rode May, himself and his horse, the object of a thousand eyes, so certain was the death, that gloomed before him, proudly in his warrior beauty, he backed that steed, his hair, floating beneath his cap, in massy curls upon the wind.

He turns his head; his men see his face, knit in the lip, and woven in the brow—they feel the fire of his eyes—they hear, not men forward! but *Men, follow*; and away, like, like a huge battle engine, composed of eighty-four men and horses, woven together by swords—away and on they dash.

They near the ravine; old Taylor follows them, with hushed breath, aye, clutching his sword hilt, he sees the golden tassel of May, gleaming in the cannon flash.

They are on the verge of the ravine, May still in the front, his charger, flinging the earth, from beneath him, with colossal leaps, when from among the cannon, starts up, a half-clad figure, red with blood and begrimed with powder.

It is Ridgely, who today has sworn, to wear the Mantle of Ringgold, and to wear it well! At once his eyes, catch the light now blazing in the eyes of May, springing to the cannon, he shouts—

"One moment, my comrade! And I will draw their fire!"

The word is not passed from his lips, when his cannon speak out, to the battery across the ravine. His flash, his smoke, have not gone, when hark! Did you hear that storm of copper balls, clatter against his cannon,— did you see it dig the earth, beneath the hoofs of May's squadron.

"Men, follow!"—Do you see that face, gleaming with battle fire, that scimiter, cutting its glittering circle in the air? Those men, can hold their shouts no longer. Rending the air with cries—hark! The whole army echo them—they strike their spurs, and worried into madness, their horses whirl on, and thunder away, to the deadly ravine.

The old man, Taylor said after the battle, that he never felt his heart beat, as it did then.

For it was a glorious sight to see, that young man, MAY, at the head of his squadron, dashing across the ravine, four yards in advance of his foremost man, while long and dark behind him, was stretched the solid line of warriors and their steeds.

Through the windows of the clouds some gleams of sunlight fall— they light the golden tassel on the cap, they glitter on the upraised sword, they illumine the dark horse, and his rider, with their warm glow, they reveal the battery, you see it, above the farther bank of the ravine, frowning death from every muzzle.

Near and nearer, up and on! Never heed the Death before you, though it is certain. Never mind the leap, though it is terrible. But up the bank and over the cannon—hurrah! At this dread moment, just as his horse rises for the charge, MAY turns and sees the sword of the brave INGE[3] on his

3   Zebulon M.P. Inge (1815–1846) also served in the Second Seminole War (1835–1842). Cullum, *Biographical Register,* 729.

right, turns again and reads his own soul written in the fire of SACKETT's eye.[4]

To his Men once more he turns, his hair floating back behind him, he points to the cannon, to the steep bank and the certain death, and as though inviting them, one and all, to his Bridal Feast, he says—

"COME!"

They did come. It would have made your blood dance to see it. As one man, they whirled up the bank, following May's sword as they would a banner, and striking madly home as they heard—through the roar of battle they heard it—that word of frenzy—"COME!"

As one mass of bared chests, leaping horses, and dazzling scimitars, they charged upon the bank; the cannon's fire rushed into their faces—INGE, even as his shout rang on the air, was laid a mangled thing beneath his steed, his throat torn open by a cannon shot, Sackett was buried beneath his horse, and seven dragoons fell at the battery's muzzles, their blood and brains whirling into their comrades' eyes.

Still May is yonder, above the cloud, his horse rioting over heaps of dead, as with his sabre, circling round his flowing hair, he cuts his way through the living wall, and says to his comrades—Come!

All around him, friend and foe, their swords locked together—yonder the blaze of musquetry showering the iron hail upon his band—beneath his horse's feet the deadly cannon and the ghastly corse, still that young soldier riots on, for Taylor has said, Silence that battery, and he will do it.

The Mexicans are driven from their guns; their cannon are silenced, and May's heroic band, scattering among the mazes of the chaparral, are entangled in a wall of bayonets. Once more the combat deepens, and dyes the sod in blood. Hedged in by that wall of steel, May gathers eight of his men, and hews his way back toward the captured battery. As his charger

---

[4] General Delos Bennet Sacket (1822–1885) fought at Palo Alto and Resaca de la Palma as the 2nd lieutenant of the 2nd Dragoons and later served in the American Civil War. Clayton R. Newell and Charles R. Sharde, *Of Duty Well and Faithfully Done: A History of the Regular Army in the Civil War* (Lincoln: University of Nebraska Press, 2011), 334.

rears, his sword circles above his head, and sinks blow after blow into the foemen's throats. To the left a shout is heard; the Americans, led on by Graham and Pleasanton[5] and Winship, have silenced the battery there, while the whole fury of the Mexican army, seems concentrated to crush May and his band.

As he went through their locked ranks, so he comes back. Everywhere his men know him by his hair, waving in dark masses, his golden tinselled cap, his sword,—they know it too, and wherever it falls, hear the gurgling groan of mortal agony.

Back to the captured cannon he cuts his way, and on the brink of the ravine beholds a sight that fires his blood.

A solitary Mexican stands there, reaching forth his arms, in all the frenzy of a brave man's despair, he entreats his countrymen to turn, to man the battery once more, and hurl its fury on the foe. They shrink back appalled, before that dark horse, and its rider, May! The Mexican, a gallant young man, whose handsome features can scarce be distinguished on account of the blood which covers them, while his rent uniform bears testimony to his deeds, in that day's carnage, clenches his hand, as he flings his curse in the face of his flying countrymen, and then, lighted match in hand, springs to the cannon.

A moment and its fire will scatter ten American soldiers into the dust.

Even as the brave Mexican bends near the cannon, the dark charger, with one tremendous leap is there, and the sword of May is circling over his head.

"Yield!" shouted the voice, which only a few moments ago, when rushing to death, said—"Come!"

The Mexican beheld the gallant form before him, and handed Captain May his sword.

---

5 William M. Graham previously served in the Seminole Wars and was killed during the Battle of Molino del Rey on September 8, 1847. George W. Cullum, *Biographical Register of the Officers and Graduates of the U.S. Military Academy at West Point, N.Y.* (Boston: Houghton Mifflin, 1891), 157. Alfred Pleasanton (1824–1897) was a member of the 2nd Dragoons and later fought for the Union Army in the American Civil War. "Hero's Obscure Ending," *The Weekly Wisconsin,* February 20, 1897.

"General La Vega is a prisoner!" he said, and stood with folded arms, amid the corses of his mangled soldiers.

You may see May deliver his prisoner into the charge of the brave Lieutenant Stephens, who—when Inge fell—dashed bravely on.

Then would you look for May once more, gaze through that wall of bayonets, beneath that gloomy cloud, and behold him crashing into the whirlpool of the fight, his long hair, his sweeping beard, and sword that never for an instant stays its lightning career, making him look like the embodied Demon of this battle day.

In the roar of the battle behold this picture. Where May dashed like a thunderbolt from his side, General Taylor, in his familiar brown coat, still remains. Near him, gazing on the battle with interest keen as his own, the stout form, the stern visage of his brother soldier Twiggs. They have followed with flashing eyes, the course of May, they have seen him charge, and seen his men and horses hurled back in their blood, while still he thundered on. At this moment, the brave LA VEGA is led into the presence of Taylor, his arms folded over his breast, his eyes fixed upon the ground.

As the noble-hearted General expresses his sorrow, that the captive's fate has fallen on one so brave, as, in obedience to the command of Twiggs, the soldiers, arranged in battle order, salute the Prisoner with presented arms, there comes rushing to the scene the form of May, mounted on his well-known charger.

"General, you told me to silence that battery. I have done it!'

—He placed in the hands of Zachary Taylor, the sword of the brave La Vega.

Again the contest thickens in the ravine, and once more the brave Mexicans come swarming to the rescue. Around their batteries they gather fighting in sullen silence about their voiceless guns, and through the white smoke you behold gleaming into light the bayonets of the Fifth Regiment. Scarcely have they rushed with one impulse and one shout, upon the batteries, when Colonel Belknap at the head of the Eighth, is seen moving along the road—he comes, waving the Banner of the Stars in his hand—a whispered word to the men about him, and up the bank, and into the ranks of the Tampico veterans—hand to hand, foot to foot, eye blazing in eye, they engage in the deadly conflict.[6]

These men of Tampico are no cowards. They receive the Americans with the bayonet, and fighting over their silenced guns, stab them one by one, with the knife. A shout—a blaze! Colonel Belknap is down, the staff of his standard broken by a ball; a cry of vengeance thunders through the battle air.

Then occurs the most deadly contest of the day. Amid the clouds of smoke, even where the battle whirlpool rages in its fiery vortex, you may see the plume of PAYNE, who yesterday saw Ringgold die. There, the golden tassel, the long hair and terrible scimitar of May, the white hairs of M'Intosh, the bloody face of CHADBOURNE, rising for a moment, and then sinking to shout the battle cry no more.

It is a terrible wall of bayonet and flame, which brightens and burns from every nook of the chaparral, but the Americans are not to be turned back in their steady course. Every Regiment is doing immortal deeds for the Banner—the Third, the Fourth, the Fifth, the Eighth—they are all there, in the ravine, among the bloody lakes and up the deadly bank.

Morris and Allen, Hays and Woods, Buchanan and Barbour, Lincoln and Jourdan, you may see them in every part of the scene, their swords

6 Lippard accurately places Colonel William Goldsmith Belknap (1794–1851) of the 8th Infantry in this battle. John S.D. Eisenhower, *So Far from God: The U.S. War with Mexico, 1846–1848* (Norman: University of Oklahoma Press, 1989), 83.

rising as with one impulse, while their men follow them into the very jaws of death. And suddenly a cloud rolls over the chaparral, and like a shroud enfolds the scene of murder.

Hark! Shouts from the bosom of the cloud—hark! The deadly clang of bayonet against bayonet, the death cry and the wild hurrah, mingle in one fiendish chorus. Men are dying everywhere—you see their ghastly faces in the waters of the lagoon, spouting blood into its bloody pool, beneath the silent cannon, as their skulls crushed into the sod, you hear their gurgling cry; amid the thickets of the chaparral, you count their butchered corses.

Sixteen hundred men, you will remember, are doing battle with nine thousand. Not on a level plain, as yesterday, but in the pass of a dark ravine, amid the assassin-ambuscades of a tangled chaparral, through lakelets knee deep, yes, breast high, every wave burdened with the bodies of the dead!

In a whirlpool of carnage like this, it is difficult to forget the roar, the smoke, the blaze, and gaze calmly upon the individual deeds of chivalry and murder. Yet, dipping our pencil in the blood of human hearts, and lighted in our task by the glare of battle, we will crouch here in the chaparral, and try to paint them all.

———

Taylor is on his horse, too near the ravine, his face lights every instant by the glare, the sod every moment, dashing against the flanks of the old grey, as the cannon balls, plough the grass into furrows. The soldiers beg the old man, not to peril his life, the officers surround him, and would turn his steed aside, from the fury of the battle.

What is it the old man says?

"Look there!" with a quiet wave of his sword. And toward the right a battalion of Americans, on the borders of the ravine, not two hundred strong, are threatened by a solid mass of horse and foot, who come thundering over the pass. Beautifully they rush to battle, their lances fluttering with crimson flags, their sharp steel glittering in deadly lines. It is a terrible sight, and the American battalion, quivers, it moves, not to the ravine, but backward, with a tremulous impulse. For, a contest with such an overwhelming force, cannot be called a fight; it is a Murder, a Massacre.

"Look there!" says the old man Zachary, and bounding from the encircling officers, he spurs his grey steed forward, and in a moment, plunges into the centre of the battalion's square.

"I am here, in the centre of your square!"

That old man, on his grey horse, with his form covered with a plain brown coat, presents a sight, at once heroic and sublime. Around him two hundred bayonets—yonder, not thirty yards in front, the advancing mass of Mexicans, horse and foot, at least one thousand strong.

"I am here in the centre of the square!" he says, and every foot is rooted to the sod.

No other words are needed. Silently they receive the terror of the Mexican charge. Bayonet to bayonet, the breast of man offered to the war-horse chest, they receive them, as they come up the bank, without one hurrah. But that fire, did you see that sudden flash, light up the entire Mexican array? That smoke, did you see its pall, gather them in?

Now, they shout, now plunging down the bank, they charge the Mexicans home, and precipitate the silent butchery of the bayonet, upon their splendid array. Again that shout—the Mexicans quiver, every horse recoiling on the horse behind him, every rank, falling back, on the next line, until men and horses, whirl together, like a thousand waves, meeting in one centre. Not a moment to recover themselves, not a pause for thought—again that wild hurrah!

Old Zachary, left alone on the verge of the bank, laughs quietly to himself, as he sees, beneath the curtain of clouds, that glorious sight—the Mexican array, shattered in its centre, broken on each wing, give way and scatter in mad disorder, along the battle ravine.

Paint for me, that picture, some Painter, whose heart glows into his canvass, at the memory of heroic deeds—a bluff old warrior, mounted on his old grey steed, bending forward, with extended hand, and brightening eye, as gazing into the shadows of the ravine below, he sees two hundred soldiers, burst like wounded tigers on a thousand, and at one charge level their solid ranks into dust.

Beyond the ravine, the battle went on, in horrible fury.

A picture from its scenes of carnage!

Do you see that wall of darkening chaparral, with horses and men, appearing at every interval, and lances shining from the thorns, as though they grew there?

It lies beyond the ravine, beyond the silenced batteries. At the head of the Fifth Regiment, a white-haired man, with his bared arm, grasping a sharp sword, spurs the Roan war-horse, and plunges into the ravine.

He is the first of the band; beautiful and bright the bayonets of his Regiment, sparkle through the shadows behind him. As he plunges, a murderous fire rushes into his face—it shrieks away over the regiment—but he is gone from the eyes of his men, gone through the chaparral, into covert not ten yards square. The instant, he plunges into the shadow, he feels his horse, the noble roan, quiver, and with a howl he goes down.

Springing from beneath his dead horse, the solitary warrior, darts to his feet, and finds himself alone in the covert, and at a glance, beholds it lined by foes with bayonet and lances, in their muscular arms.

It was worth ten year's life, to see how the solitary warrior met his foes.

A tall old man, with firm, even severe features, his wrinkled cheeks, whitened by his beard, his hair the color of snow, he set his lips firmly together, and placing one foot on his dead horse, looked into their faces, with a grey eye, that burned like a flame. His coat, had been torn from his form, and his broad chest, with the shirt thrown open, heaved in long deep respirations.

Even the Mexicans could not repress a yell of admiration! Alone, in that covert, with not an arm to aid him, the grey-bearded warrior, stood, with his foot on his dead horse, his bared arm grasping the sword that flashed its light into twenty tawny faces.

As one man, they rushed upon him. It was a sickening sight. Here, a lancer, bending over the neck of his horse, his lance in rest, and the point levelled at the old man's heart; by his side, a soldier, with the sharp bayonet, glittering near the throat of his victim; all around, a circle of deadly knives, glittering in the clutch of bony arms.

The American warrior, merely said, between his clenched teeth—"Come on!" and with his solitary sword, received their charge. For a moment he beats them back, for a moment splintering this lance, and unfixing that bayonet, he presses his dead steed with a firm foot, and maintains his position against twenty men.

But then occurs a scene to make the curse quiver from the lips of a saint!

They rush upon him, a cloud of lances, knives, bayonets. He is down, upon his dead steed, battling still, against his crowding foes.

Do you see that grim figure, bending over him, as with one blow he hurls his bayonet into the old man's throat? That piece of cold steel, enters his mouth, and appears behind his ear!

Still, balding over his dead horse, the old warrior fights for his life. He seizes the very musket, to which the bayonet is attached, and with his sword, shortened like a dagger, plunges it upward, into the chest of his foe. At the same moment, the blood gushes from his own mouth, and from the mouth of the writhing Mexican.

Covered with the red stream, he rises once more, tears the bayonet from his mouth, and shaking his bared arm, before his bloody face, says to them all—

"Come on! Cowards as you are, you shall see how an old soldier can die!"

A heroic picture! The battle flame beyond the covert, glares through this wall of prickly pear, and flashes upon his white hairs and bloody face, in bluish light. So tall, so firm, so erect upon his dead horse he stands, while round him, as if spell-bound by the sight, darkens the circle of his foes. O, had one drop of heroic blood, throbbed in their veins, they would have spared him then!

Ask mercy from the tigress robbed of her young, or even from the British soldier, drunk with ale and blood, but not from the Mexican Ranchero!

They hurled themselves upon him, their lances, bayonets and knives, forming a woven circle of steel around his bloody face—for a moment he battled against such formidable odds, and then upon his dead horse, he fell once more. One bayonet pierced his thigh, another pinned to the sod, his shattered arm. The blood from the wound on his throat, crimsoned his white hairs, and trickled in ghastly patches over his chest. Now look your last, upon that glimpse of God's beautiful sky, old man, and feel the ties of

Home about your heart once more, for there is Death, in every blade, that flashes above your gory head.

For a moment, change the scene. Beyond the ravine, on the way to Fort Brown, the narrow road, is broken by the waters of a lakelet or lagoon. Look, yonder toward the north, and see the cannon of Duncan come, with Ridgeley's glooming near, and the bayonets of Captain Smith's infantry, the swords of Captain Kerr's dragoons glittering on every side.

Ridgely and Duncan—heroes of Palo Alto—come crashing over the ravine, along the road, toward the lagoon. O, the wild excitement of the moment, when each hero, looks upon his grim cannon, and feels that they will speak, and speak thunder and lightning, ere you may count ten!

From the Fort Brown side of the lagoon, a deadly fire hurls its hail into the faces of the advancing soldiers.

Duncan, his form quivering with the hope of battle, turns and looks for an officer, who will support him with infantry, while he crashes over the lagoon, and tells the Mexicans how much he loves them, from the throats of his cannon.

Forth from the thicket, stalks with measured strides, a half-naked man, his shirt thrown open on his bloody chest, his white hairs clotted with crimson drops. For a moment he walks with that measured pace, but then his step becomes unsteady, he stands erect, his lips compressed, as he presses his hands to his throat.

Duncan is terrified, appalled at the sight. It is evident that the half-naked man before him, is suffering intolerable torture.

"Colonel," he shrieks, in a voice broken by emotion—"Can I be of any service to you?"

As the old man unclosed his lips, the blood gushed forth—

"Water!" he gasped, and then as the memory of that horrible encounter in the covert, crowded upon him, he exclaimed—"My Regiment? Where is it?"

The sun of Resaca de la Palma shone on no braver man, than this veteran, whom we now behold, baptized in blood—the white-haired Colonel M'Intosh.

For a while we leave the Battle.

We will speed through four miles of chaparral, and behold the river, the city and the fort. It is now two o'clock, and the sunlight reveals the devoted fortress. The cannonade from the city, from the battery yonder in the woods, still pours its fury upon the brave three hundred. So, from morning light, it has yelled its thunder, scattering its copper balls among the heroic band, who have resolved to wait for Taylor, and never give up the contest, while a pulse throbs.

From the shattered fort, still towers on high that staff, undulating with its precious ensign—the Banner of the Stars.

Amid the hail of copper and iron, the soldiers gather in the centre of the fort, around that bomb proof, formed by pieces of timber, supported on barrels and roofed with earth. In all that crowd of half-clad men, begrimed with the traces of one hundred and sixty hours incessant battle, there is not one eye unwet with tears. Captain Hawkins, that brave man who replied to Arista's summons to surrender, with the words—"I do not understand Spanish!" is on his knees, gazing upon the last hour of a dying man.

In the recess of the bomb-proof, where the hot atmosphere is almost choked into pestilence, behold a veteran soldier stretched on his back, his head supported by a knapsack, while the stump of his amputated leg, tells the story of his lingering agony. That heroic face, seamed by wrinkles is very calm. For the torture of pain has vanished at the coming on of the

Death sleep. He rolls his eyes with a softened glance, from face to face, and tells them all how good a thing it is to die in a brave cause. Even in a foreign land, under a hot sun, with cannon balls flinging dust into your face.

Then, these men of iron, who since last Sabbath morn, have laughed the fury of the enemy to scorn, and been merry with his rain of copper and iron, turn their sunburnt faces away. Some of them look upon the ground. Some brush their eyelids with their bony hands. One grim old war dog, seated on the ground, his rough face with its blunt features, worn by the perils of sixty years, clenches his huge fists, and sobs like a baby.

For the veteran Brown is dying and gliding so softly away, that not a twitch of the muscles disturbs the mild serenity of his face, not a groan heaves from his chest, to tell of the passing of his soul.

"Boys," he said, slightly raising himself upon his bent arm, "Taylor is coming."

And he laid his head upon his arm, and closed his eyes, composing himself for a peaceful sleep. Why does the breeze, warm with the fever of battle, play with his grey hairs, and toss them about his brow? Can it not feel, as these stout hearted soldiers feel, that the sleep which the veteran sleeps, is called—DEATH?

Two hours passed away, and the dead man lay on his rude death-bed, when a soldier, gazing to the north, bent his head to one side—listened for a moment—and rent the air with a shout. Two hundred throats at once swelled that shout into thunder.

Boom—boom—boom!

They heard it; from the north it sent its voice, that cannon of Ridgely, and to the tired soldier's ear, it seemed to say, "WE COME!"

Boom—boom—boom! Clang—clang—clang! Cannon and musquetry speaking together, and saying to the Spartans of Fort Brown—"WE COME!"

Then a silence like death, so terrible from the thunder which went before it, a silence that lay upon the chaparral like a spell.

Hurrah! They are charging upon them now. Silence! Now cold steel to cold steel, horse to horse, and man to man. Silence and suspense, the silence so dread, the suspense so horrible. Long the soldiers listened, quivering they gave to their ears every sound, when suddenly, from the north, there came a noise like the trampling of nine thousand men,—not so loud as cannon, nor so shrill as musquetry—but a subdued, half-hushed, brooding murmur. It grew, it spread far and wide over the chaparral, and it began to say, "Zachary Taylor Comes!"

To the Battlefield once more.

The tent of Arista rising proudly in the centre of this green space, with the chaparral darkening around. Its gaudy curtains wave gaily in the light, while on every side the banquet fires are blazing. The choice wines stand buried in pails of ice, the goblets gleam along the festival table, set in the deep shade behind the tent. But where are the menials charged with the preparation of the feast?

Where are the glittering throng of cavaliers, who this morning went forth to battle? Where the gloomy Ampudia, that terrible boiler of dead men's heads, or Arista, the general-in-chief, hardened by the perils of battle and tears of exile—where is he?

This magnificent tent, adorned with all the marks of luxury, standing in the midst of the deserted chaparral, is your only answer.

Hark! From yonder thicket the clamor of battle, and a band of Americans emerge from the prickly pear, and advance toward the silent tent. While the roar of the fight yells on every side, you may note the appearance of the leader of the band; a young man, whose well-proportioned form, is clad in the blue and silver of the Fourth Infantry. His florid face glows with enthusiasm, his eye sparkles with battle delight.

As he advances from the north, along this road, southward from the tent, a solitary Lancer rides slowly along, examining with cool scrutiny, the numbers and arms of the Americans. They fire—he gallops away unharmed. Again returns, and again rides laughingly away from their fire. A third time he comes back, and whirling along like an avalanche of horses, men and spears, comes the glittering lancer array.

As they come, the Americans pour their fire into their faces, and two dying men bite the dust. Then every form seeks the covert, and the lancers come dashing on. Only one man—it is their leader—stands unsheltered; his manly chest a mark for each deadly lance. They come charging on, a cloud of dust marks their career, their lances glittering above it, a long and dazzling line. With a shout they charge: one man, you see his uncovered brow glow in the sunlight, confronts their charge, and takes its battle bolt upon his breast. Once you see his arm raised, once he shouts, and then, falling on his face, is pinned by twenty lances to the sod.

The lancers whirl like a cloud before the wind, away, and you see only—the deserted tent, the dead man, and the darkening chaparral.

—So, on the field of Resaca de la Palma died the chivalric COCHRANE— while far away, by the waters of the Susquehanna, where its islands are most beautiful, its mountains most sublime, his young Wife watched for his return—with his face to the dust and his back to the sky, he yielded up his breath, and in his blood they found him, the young hero of the LAND OF PENN.

Look through yonder thicket, and see that face, distorted with all the agonies of despair!

A warrior reins his horse alone in the shadows of the chaparral, near Arista's tent. The white horse, the gorgeous battle array, the dark olive cheek and the red mustache, all tell you his rank and his name. It is Arista, listening to the carnage shouts of Resaca de la Palma. Leaning his clasped hands on the pommel of his saddle, he bites his nether-lip until the blood starts, and then dashes the cold dews from his brow.

It is not death he fears,—no, the sharpest steel or deadliest ball were welcome now as bridal kiss to him—but it is the disgrace, the dishonor, the loss of glory. The utter wreck and ruin of six thousand men, all veterans and heroes, by sixteen hundred Americans, led on by a rough old warrior, in a brown coat!

Around that solitary Chieftain roars the contest, near and nearer, Duncan's cannon shouting to Ridgely's, and May's sabre clattering a wild hurrah to Walker's sword. Bigger and blacker, the clouds came glooming over the waste, every nook and path of the chaparral became the scene of a bloody contest, and riding across the ravine, Zachary Taylor beheld his army in full chase after the retreating Mexicans, the dust rising beneath their feet, and the battle cloud rolling above their heads.

It was in this moment of his peril, that Arista hesitated, whether to advance or fly. It was his first impulse, to fling himself, with his white horse, upon the bayonets of the foe; but a hope, a wild, miserable hope burned in his eyes once more, and he suffered the gallant steed to take his own path, into the mazes of the chaparral.

But think not that the Mexicans fled without fighting. No! It is only the part of a hired British libeller, to deny courage to a chivalric foe: let no American be guilty of the baseness of such denial. The officers of the General's staff were gone—some of them prisoners, some corses, some fugitives—Ampudia, look for him yonder, his head thrown forward, his eyes rolling with fear, as he digs his spurs into the flanks of his flying steed. Yet still, there were Mexican men, common soldiers, who faced the foe, in this sad hour, and wrote their courage on the sod, with the last convulsive movement of their stiffening hands.

There was an old man, who came rushing from the chaparral into an open space, some thirty yards square, hedged in on every side by that wall of prickly pear.

His green uniform hanging about his broad chest in ribbands,[7] his dark beard and mustache silvered with the toil of sixty years, he tottered forward, while from the thicket crashed some twenty dragoons, in hot pursuit, every arm wielding its flashing scimitar.

Why pursue this old man, who, fainting from many wounds, still totters on, tracking his course with his blood?

Around his right arm he bears the last memorial of the veteran band, the Battalion of Tampico. It is their banner, embroidered by the hands of beautiful women, and sanctified by the prayers of white-robed nuns. He received it from the hands of a dying comrade, received it, as his warm blood spouted over his face, and swore, never, while one throb of life remained, to yield it into American hands.

Where is the Tampico battalion now, that went forth so steadily to the fight, not two hours ago? Where are its bronzed faces, its iron forms? Some are in the ravine, their cold faces washed by the bloody waters of the lagoon, some in the chaparral, splintered into fragments, some have flung away their arms, and rushed bare-chested upon the foe, in the frenzy of despair.

---

7   "Ribbands" is a variant of "ribands," meaning ribbons.

The Battalion is dead. This old war-dog, tottering on, with its banner wound about his arm, alone remains of all its proud array.

Planting his right foot firmly in the centre of the glade—all hope of flight is vain—he clutches his short sword with a grasp like death, and glares, like a maddened bull, in the faces of his pursuers.

These dragoons, brave fellows, who have done noble work in to-day's fight, and who always doff their helmets when they see courage, even in a foe, rein in their steeds with one impulse, at the sight.

One of their number dismounts, flings the rein on the horse's neck, and sword in hand advances. You see his short yet robust form, manifesting in the bared sinews of the right arm, an almost superhuman strength. His blunt face, with heavy features, short, stiff hair, and keen grey eyes, announces the tenacious courage of a bull-dog.

"Look yer, stranger," he exclaims—"You're faint with blood, and had better yield—the old man's won the day, and there haint no further use for that flag—"

His comrades, with their steeds recoiling on their haunches, and their battle-worn faces bent forward, await the result of this scene, with deep suspense.

But, look! The stout old veteran is dying; his eyes are half-closed; he totters to and fro, still with the Tampico banner wound about his arm.

The American dragoon, touched with pity, springs forward to catch him as he falls, and at the same moment, feels the short sword of the old man driven to the hilt in his breast.

Then, with a wild yell, that veteran crashes into the thicket and is gone. The dying dragoon breathes in gasps; he clutches the earth by handfuls, and rolling slowly on his face stiffens into clay.

You should have seen the expression of horror which sank like a shadow, upon every face. For a moment not a word was spoken. Only an instant ago, that tottering old man, with his eye swimming as if by dissolution, and that muscular dragoon, advancing with a look of rude pity, to his aid. Now!

There was a dead man on the sod. The place of the veteran was vacant: you hear him yonder, crashing through the thicket.

It is in vain to attempt the mazes of that barrier of thorns on horseback. A moment's hurried consultation is held; a young dragoon springs from his steed, and plunges into the chaparral. His comrades behold his tall form, his swarthy face, with prominent features, shadowed by short curling black hair, behold him for a moment only, and he is gone.

On, crashing through that wilderness of thorns, cutting his way with his sword, or crawling on hands and knees, guided by the echo of the old soldier's tread, he hurries, his heart palpitating with the fever of revenge. Hark! He nears his foe—these footsteps sound heavy and sullen—the old man is fainting from loss of blood—soon he will fall, and from his dying clutch the victor will rend the Banner of the iron band.

At last they stand face to face. In a nook of the chaparral, where the torrents, now dried up and vanished from the burnt soil, have formed a deep gully, the young Dragoon beholds the old soldier, leaning against the bank of clay, the banner wound firmly around his right arm, with the hand still clutching the fatal short sword.

It is a sad and pitiable sight. So weak with his wounds, so near his death hour, his head sinking on one shoulder, his bent knees, bending beneath his massive frame, he glares into the face of the Dragoon, with those glassy eyes fired with deadly hatred.

The Banner was given to him by dying hands, and he will keep it in his death hour!

"Yield!" shouted the Dragoon, advancing with a firm tread, his sword grasped by a vigorous arm, while his well-knit figure towered erect, and the battle flush crimsoned his face from the chin to the curling dark hair.

The old man with a great effort raises himself, and with his sword before his chest, his back against the bank, stands on his defence.

For a moment they regard one another silently, those glassy eyes, fading into eternal darkness, glaring upon the fiery eyes of youth and vigor. The Dragoon drops his sword—

"You murdered my comrade—aye, murdered him, as he sprang for'rad to help you, but I cannot kill you. You'll die in a few minutes, and the Banner will be mine!"

He silently contemplates his expiring foe.

But the old soldier—what means that long deep heaving of the bloody chest? That convulsive movement of the arms? That swelling of the veins in the throat? He is preparing all the strength within him, for a desperate effort, yes, with a bound like a wounded panther, he darts upon the young Dragoon, and pinions his throat with those iron fingers, with the death-grip of a desperate man!

To force the American back on his knees, to crush the sinews of his throat, until his eyes started from their sockets, to press his own knees on his chest,—it was done like a flash. The American's stiffening fingers dropped his sword—gurgling as in this death agony, a thick and choking groan, he sank back on the sod. His eyes started from their sockets. His face was discolored by streaks of blue and red; livid as the visage of a poisoned man.

A moment longer, and that death grip will finish the career of the gallant Dragoon. Glaring with his dilating eye, into the victim's face, he growls a hoarse oath, tightens his clutch, and—

Did you see that form, leap into air, the face ghastly, the eyes rolling in death, the chest heaving with a fiendish howl? It is a horrible spectacle! He stands for a moment, rends the flag from his arm, gazes madly—almost fondly—upon it, as it quivers in his grasp, and falls upon it, with his face, crushing its folds into the grass.

He rests upon the flag; his face you cannot see, and yet on either side of his head, you see a widening pool of blood, that clots the fine embroidering of the Banner, and paints with crimson the words—BATALLON DE TAMPICO.

The American Dragoon arose, with the livid mark upon his face, the blood drops starting from his blood-shot eyes, and gazed with a look, wild with terror upon the sight before him—The dead Veteran, and his bloody Banner.

Zachary Taylor, spurring forward his favorite grey, beheld the fury of the battle roll along the narrow road—the wall of the chaparral on either side—swelling its waves of blood toward the Rio Grande.

"I will be at Fort Brown to night, if I live!"

And he was going there!

Would you behold his path?

Down the narrow road, hedged in by prickly pear, paved with corses, roaring with thunder, blazing with the lightning of cannon. Gaze there, and see the Mexicans go down at every shot, by ranks, by platoons, by columns.

It is no battle, but a hunt, a Massacre! You have read of the Indians firing a prairie, in a circle, and waiting patiently until the flame, roaring toward the centre, hems the frightened deer, panthers and buffaloes into a furnace of burning grass! Old Zachary has fired his prairie; the circle grows narrower every moment; that circle formed by Ridgely's cannon, by Duncan's battery, linked with the lines of Montgomery, grows narrower every instant, and crushes and hurls and burns the Mexicans toward the centre of death, the Rio Grande.

And now, Walker and May at the head of their deaths-men, wave their swords and seek the game, as it issues from the flames. The heart grows sick of the blood. The chaparral seems a great heart of carnage, palpitating a death at every throb.

Volumes would not tell the horrors of that flight. Happy the poor wretch who could creep into the chaparral, and bleed to death in darkness! Woe to the wretch who pursued the road to Fort Brown! The sword of May severed his throat, or the hail of Ridgely crushed him down, on the cannon of Duncan, thundered over his mangled corse.

Still in the midst of the scene, old Zachary spurred his grey steed, while the bullets riddled his brown coat, he pointed toward the Fort.

The setting sun, struggling with the black and red clouds that choked his beams, spread over the chaparral, a pale and livid light.

Boom, boom, boom! At Fort Brown, that sound was heard, and springing to the parapet, beside the flag staff, the soldiers beheld a strange, a meaning sight.

From the chaparral,—while that terrible murmur grew louder in its depths—burst a solitary horseman, dressed in the gorgeous costume of a Mexican officer, his brow bared, and his extended hand waving a sword in mad circles above his head. On, on, to the river, he rushed, his horse bleeding all the while; on, and on, shouting in Spanish—"It is lost! The Day to Mexico is lost!"

Hark! That cheer how it went up from Fort Brown, and startled Matamoras to its inmost home!

For the flying soldier was AMPUDIA, the murderer of Sentmanat; yes, into the river he plunged his horse, looking back over his shoulder in mad terror, as the people on the roofs and shore, heard his shout—Lost! All is lost!

In Fort Brown, every soldier held his breath. For look! From the northern chaparral, where the cloud darkens up against the sun, a mass of panic-stricken fugitives rush by hundreds and by thousands, filling the air with the cry of their terror.

They come, scattering their arms by the way. They come, trampling over those who fall fainting in their path. They come, the cavalry—those gay lancers—riding down, without remorse, their own infantry; they come, the chivalry of Mexico, transformed into a Mob, drunk with terror and blood.

The whirlpool rushes to the river, as to the centre of its fury. By two roads, it pours its frightened fugitives along; one above and one below the fort, one leading to the upper and one to the lower ferry. These roads are black and bloody, with the living and the dead.

Pouring in one steady stream, flinging their clothes upon the road, they dash from the chaparral toward the river, man and horse, maddened by the same fear. The wounded too, placed in sacks, borne by mules, rudely tossed to and fro, wring the air with incessant cries.

Now cheer again, brave defenders of Fort Brown! Cheer once more, and turn the blaze of the eighteen pounder toward the upper ferry. That blaze carries twenty deaths with it; in the ranks of the fugitives, twenty men, sink howling on the road.

By the shore behold this scene. A crowd of panic-stricken soldiers, have seized the raft; with mad cries and shouts, they push it from the shore, when like a whirlwind, a body of their own lancers rush upon them, urging their horses through the waves, and planting their hoofs upon the faces of their dismounted countrymen. For a moment, burdened with human agony, a mass of faces and bodies, writhing beneath the trampling horses, that raft quivers, rolls over the waves, agitated by its motion, and then, like a rock from a heighth, goes crashing down.

As it sinks, you see that solitary Priest, standing amid the crowd, in the centre of the raft, his uplifted hand, holding into light, the Cross of God. For a moment, it glitters, and then the raft is gone, a horrible yell rushes into heaven, and where a moment ago, was a mass of human faces, lancers' flags and war-horse forms, now is only the boiling river, heaving with the dying and the dead.

It was horrible to see them die, horrible to witness them clutching at each other's throats, ere they sank below, horrible to behold the Women, on the opposite bank, who tried to recognize a brother, or husband in that whirlpool of waves and blood.

Four days afterward, those bodies, festering in corruption, floated blackened and hideous, upon the waters of the Rio Grande. Upon the root of a tree, which protruded from the river bank, left bare by the receding wave, hung the corse of the Priest, his right hand clutching that hallowed Cross.

While the scenes of death, took place on the river, the eighteen pounder in the Fort, was hushed, and the heroic three hundred, crowding to the parapet, gazed in silence, upon that strange, wild panorama, which was stretched before their eyes. Brown lay cold in death, but Hawkins, leaning on his sword, his face manifesting strong emotion, looked to the north, and looked to see old Taylor come.

Soon, from the chaparral, shone the American bayonets, flinging back from their dazzling points the light of the setting sun, and then, from the darkness of the thicket, a volume of blaze, a cloud of white smoke, rushing forth together, told that Ridgely and Duncan were near.

Along the roads those bayonets extended, pressing the fugitives to death, while through their intervals the cannons moved on, shouting their thunder cry, as from the wood to the river, they mowed the Mexicans into heaps of mangled flesh.

It was then, amid this hurrying scene of slaughter, when the river burdened with corses, the town black on its roofs with affrighted thousands, the separate roads strewed with dying and dead, the Fort crowded on its ramparts with the Spartan band, glowed in all their strong contrasts with the beams of the setting sun, it was then, as the American banner, which had endured four thousand shots and still waved on, flung its belts of scarlet and snow against the evening sky, that riding amid the battle clouds toward the Fort, there came an old man, mounted on a grey steed, his brown coat thrown back from his chest, and his bronzed face beaming with a smile.

You should have heard the shout that went up from the Fort, as they saw old Taylor come!

Nine days ago, with two thousand men, he left the Fort—the country all around swarming with Mexicans by thousands—marched to the relief of Point Isabel; and now, he comes back, having hewn his way through the breasts and steel of two bloody battles; he comes back, his brows wreathed in laurels, and behold the sungleam of victory light with one glow, the river, the fortress and the corse of the veteran Brown.

Beside that corse, beneath the evening sky, he stood, while around, their deep silence unbroken by a word, grouped the heroes of the Fort. The body of the veteran bleeding from the shattered leg, even in death, his upturned face moulded in a look of ineffable calmness, so that his white lips seemed to say, You have come at last! The form of the warrior, his body bent forward, his clasped hands resting on his sheathed sword, as with downcast eyes, he surveyed that face, now cold in death forever. Such was the picture; but what language can portray the emotions which quivered in the warrior's breast at this still hour, as gazing on the soldier's mangled body, the full consciousness of the glory he had won, rushed like a torrent on his soul?

The scenes of his life passed like a vision before him.—The Child of a Revolutionary lineage—his father fought beside Washington in the Christmas Festival at Trenton—he stood once more, a mere boy of Eighteen, in the presence of Jefferson, and received from his hands, his Lieutenant's commission.

The scenes of deadly and bloody Indian wars—on the prairies of the north and among the everglades of Florida—his long and laborious life, long without fame, and laborious without glory, suddenly ripening into fame and glory, on these fields of Palo Alto and Resaca de la Palma, before whose light the brightest names of age would bow their laurelled heads—all glided before him, like the historic panorama of some long past age. Standing beside the corse of Brown, with the evidences of his success around him, waving in the Banner above his head, and glaring upon him from the cold face of the dead soldier, he still might scarce believe himself, plain Zachary Taylor, at once the Victor and the Hero.

Chosen by Almighty God, in the strong maturity of his grey hairs, as the Instrument of great events, called forth in his vigorous old age, to become the hero of glorious battles, can we doubt that in this moment of silent thought, Zachary Taylor recognized with awe, that awful hand which beckoned him onward, through the cloud of the Future, and felt himself the Child of Destiny, the Champion of a People, the Man of an Age?

Felt that in his hand was placed for deeds of high responsibility, the SWORD OF WASHINGTON, and saw it flash over the battle-fields of a redeemed Continent!

O, Tricksters of Council and Cabinet, who, while you fill the nation with your petty broils, and swindle adroitly into your own hands, the Money of a People, still with pursed lips and expanded eyelids, talk with righteous horror of '*a Military Chieftain,*' making that phrase portentous as the bug-a-boo[8] of an Idiot's dream, come here to the Rio Grande, in this silent evening hour, and learn some wisdom from this heroic old man!

Does God rule the world? Does he sleep? Do men arise and fall, do wars go on, and lands grow rich in peace, without His awful and direct interposition? Deny this, and you stand before that God, guilty of a cold-blooded, practical atheism, compared to which, the Satanic sneer of Voltaire is Love and Charity. Admit it, and you must answer another question—

Why was Zachary Taylor permitted to remain in comparative obscurity, for the space of thirty-eight years, and then elevated suddenly into the Hero of Palo Alto, Resaca de la Palma, Monterey and Buena Vista?

Did Almighty God raise this man for nothing?

Did *he* raise this man merely for a uniformed show, a glittering pageant, a nine days wonder, and an hour's hurrah? Gaze upon the plain old man's brown coat, and unpretending manner, and have your answer!

Or, did Almighty God, in the time of peril, when those gamblers in fraud, those grey-beards in falsehood, termed politicians, have usurped the control of the Nation, from the Ward House to the Capitol, and transformed the Capitol itself into one immense gambling saloon, where the honor of the country and the safety of the people are played away every winter, by pot-house demagogues—in this time of peril, when the Power of this great Union is centralized, not in a Royal Pageant, but in the tool of a Convention, or the parasite of a Party—when the statesmanship of the country has become so thoroughly rotten, that any act of perjury, any abortion of infamy, is deemed a virtue, if mantled by the word—"*politics*"—did

8   "Bug-a-boo" in this context means nonsense.

9   Lippard's footnote in this chapter is largely a commentary on the politics of antebellum America.

Lippard refers to Andrew Jackson and Henry Clay, two of the most prominent politicians of the day, as "party men," meaning "[o]ne of a party; *usually* a factious man." Noah Webster, *An American Dictionary of the English Language* (New York: Harper & Brothers, 1848), 719. His mention of Southern nullification references Jackson's success in preventing South Carolina from seceding over the tariff of 1832. According to David S. Reynolds, "Resolving the nullification crisis was one of the greatest achievements of Jackson's presidency. He established the principle that America was not a compact body of loosely bound *states* but an enduring union of people." David S. Reynolds, *Waking Giant: America in the Age of Jackson* (New York: Harper Collins, 2008), 100–102.

The high protective tariff that Henry Clay advocated was likely the Tariff of Abominations, and the "Compromise" mentioned was the Compromise Tariff of 1833 that ended the Nullification Crisis when passed on March 1, 1833. Ibid., 74; Howe, *What Hath God Wrought*, 408.

Henry Clay (1777–1852) did indeed have a career that, at the time, had spanned forty years, as he was first elected to national office as a senator in 1806. Zachariah Frederick Smith, "Henry Clay (1777–1852)," *Register of Kentucky State Historical Society* 10, no. 28 (1912): 17. The "Harrisburg Convention" refers to the first national Whig convention held in Harrisburg, Pennsylvania in December, 1839, where Clay lost the party's nomination for president to William Henry Harrison despite having arrived with "most of the southern delegates and a significant minority of northern ones behind him." New rules requiring states to vote as blocs aided in precluding him from

the same God, who guided Washington on to Peace, through seven years of blood, raise this man, Zachary Taylor, in his old age, to win glorious battles in a far-distant clime, as much by his moral power as by his bayonets, so that covered with the confidence of every honest man in the land, he might come to the Capitol, and with one sturdy blow, split the forehead of the Demon, Faction, and crush its worshippers into the kennel which gave them birth?*[9]

---

* Last winter, on the floor of the Senate, a grave Senator declared in his place, that did the People know the rotteness of the government at Washington, the pestilence of the corruption, which infected its every department—White House, Senate and Representative Hall—they would assemble, in mass, and precipitate the 'President, Senate, Congressmen, heads of departments all together, into the Potomac.'

No one in the Senate dare give the Senator the lie.

The truly great men of the Nation, the Andrew Jackson's, and Henry Clay's have never been, in the technical meaning of the phrase, *party men*. Their proudest triumphs have been above all party. Jackson, a *Democrat*, when he would save the Union, from Southern nullification, called to his and the *Federal* principle. Henry Clay, a *high protective* tariff advocate, when he would restore peace to a convulsed Nation, also held his country, dearer than his party, for he urged and carried a *Compromise*. Both these men, have been repeatedly betrayed by Faction. When Jackson commenced his war in the Infamy of Chartered Despotism, his party friends fell away by thousands. The *People* sustained him. When Clay, by the force of his Genius, had upheld his brilliant career as a statesman for forty years, the party which claimed him, sacrificed him, without remorse, in a Harrisburg Convention.—His fame, at this time, comes not from the leaders of a party, but from the honest sentiment of a People.

The people who are divided into two parties, are one in feeling: alike Democratic to the core. There is no real difference between honest men of either party. They hold the same opinions, modified by locality. The difference between them, is precisely such, as would exist between any two bands of honest men, who might be arrayed against each other, by hypocrites and robbers. In the North, among both parties, in 1844, the Tariff sentiment prevailed, as in the South, among both parties, the Free Trade doctrine was a common opinion. This cannot be denied—And yet the people, divided into these parties, were in North and South, arrayed against each other, on the ground of "*Principle*." Principle, by the last political dictionary, meaneth loaves, and fishes and places. To hear these pot-house heroes, within their tavern breaths, reel to the pools, shouting—"Principle!" is it not enough to make the heart grow sick?

To make the matter plain, let us take the last cases of political honesty, as manifested in two papers, published in a well-known city, one Democratic, one Whig; holy names, which are prostituted, every day, at the head of their columns.

—Zachary Taylor is a Military Chieftain! Whose voice spoke there? Some superannuated trickster of politics, who has grown grey in the shackels of party, and without one noble deed to relieve the dotage of a miserably spent life, snarls forth his envy, when a Man in reality, great, crosses his little shadow.

A Military Chieftain? In what does he differ from Arista, Ampudia, and all the mere Military Chieftains of Mexico? Why did he, with only sixteen hundred, conquer nine thousand brave men, at Palo Alto and Resaca de la Palma, headed by Chieftains like these? In a word, we have the difference—in a word, the reason of his conquest—his chieftainship is centred, not in balls or bayonets, but in the hearts of his soldiers. The Mexican, even as he plunged into the battle's front, had no confidence in his leaders. While he poured forth his blood, they were flying from the field. What soldier could fight, with a consciousness like this, paralyzing his arm? But the Americans fought directly under the eye of Zachary—whatever might be their fate, he was there to share it—and therefore, sixteen hundred men hurled nine thousand before them, while in their centre, rode *that plain man, in a brown coat, with his spy-glass and old grey horse; his bronzed face lighted by his speaking battle eye, shining its fire into every heart.*

The so-called Democratic paper, admired the course of Taylor, applauded the moral power, the giant intellect, displayed in his battles, in the fatherly care of his soldiers, in his magnanimous treatment of the foe, and yet, solemnly, and with the unctuous tears of office, in its eyes, doubted his—*principles.*

The Whig paper—gravely called so—edited by two or three political Jonahs, cast up from the whales' bellies of as many factions, derided the war, and for the space of one year, day after day, and columns after columns, called it a '*black, bloody, infernal butchery*' in fact, preached that kind of treason, which would have hung the Editors, in the days of a man called Washington, and left them on the gibbet, with the label, TRAITOR on each brow—This paper, after twelve months of elaborate sympathy with Santa Anna, came out, one fine morning, with the name of *Taylor* as its Candidate for President!—The old man received the news of this nomination, just after his battle of Buena Vista, and trampled it under foot, as Washington would have trampled a nomination from the lips of Benedict Arnold.

---

the nomination. See Howe, *What Hath God Wrought,* 571–572.

Lippard's utilization of the phrase "loaves and fishes" is a reference to the miracle spoken of in the Bible when Jesus fed 5,000 people with five loaves of bread and two fish, Matthew 14:13–21, *KJV*; Mark 6:31–44, *KJV*; Luke 9:12–17, *KJV*; John 6:1–14, *KJV*. His use of contemporary terminology necessitates definition. "Pot-house" means "a low drinking house," and "gibbet" means "a gallows; a post or machine in form of a gallows, on which notorious malefactors are hanged in chains and on which their bodies are suffered to remain." Webster, *An American Dictionary,* 448, 764.

Benedict Arnold (1741–1801) was a major general during the American Revolution notorious for his defection to the British. *American Military Biography: Containing the Lives and Characters of the Officers of the Revolution* (Cincinnati: Chronicle Office, 1830), 350–363. Lippard's reference here is consistent with his allusions throughout *Legends of Mexico* to the Revolutionary War and prominent figures of the war.

10 "Military Chieftain" is a reference to Santa Anna; "General of the People" is Taylor.
11 Lippard likely pulled inspiration from a speech given by Senator Thomas Corwin (1794–1865) of Ohio on February 11, 1847 to craft this quote. *Speech of Mr. Corwin of Ohio, on the Mexican war. Delivered in the Senate of the United States, February 11, 1847* (Cincinnati: Stevenson, Looker & Todd, 1847).

Never since the days of Washington, has a Commander so thoroughly possessed the hearts of his men.

Let us close this Battle Picture of Resaca de la Palma, with four sketches, delineating these respective characters, the Trickster-Statesman; the Politician; the Military Chieftain; and the General of the People.[10]

Let us fancy for a moment, that these scenes, take place, at the same hour, on the same day, within a circle of two thousand miles:

It is the Senate Hall of a great nation, crowded with solemn men, whose faces are seen, by the same light which glows upon the portrait of Washington. Amid that crowd of renowned men, a Senator arises, distinguished by his dark complexion, his brilliant eye, and deep, ringing voice. He has been sent hither by the people of a state, to speak for them, with that picture of Washington before his face. He fulfils his high responsibility in these words:

"This is a cruel, black, horrible, murderous war. Those soldiers whom we have sent to a foreign land, are assassins and robbers. Were I a Mexican, as I am an American, I would say to them, have you no graves in your own country, that you come here to die! Yes, I would welcome them all, these robbers and assassins with bloody hands and a hospitable grave.[11]

The Senator speaks his patriotic heart, in these words, and sitting down, looks the portrait of Washington in the face.

This is a politician; but only a fancy sketch, you will remember.

Gaze yonder through the glittering circles of the Havanna theatre, where a man of mature manhood, attired in a green and gold uniform, with the traces of battle manifested in his amputated limb, sits smiling quietly, his pale melancholy face and high forehead, the object of a thousand eyes. That man is a Military Chieftain, who has carved his way with sword, overturning the governments of his native land, at pleasure, with his iron-faced soldiers, and playing in his tumultuous life, these varied parts—President, Dictator, Exile. As he reclines in the crowded theatre, pausing for a moment, ere he leaves the dance and song, for the more intellectual amusement of the cock-pit, his native land is the scene of bloody battles, his country's flag the object of accumulated dishonor.

And at the very moment, when rising in the Havanna theatre, he draws a thousand eyes to his singularly impressive face, in the city of Washington, by the lamp of a cabinet council, you behold a man of somewhat portly form, his face dead-white in hue, his eyes clear azure, bending over a table, in the act of writing an important paper. It is one of the Rulers of the American People.[12] The paper which he writes, it must be confessed, is important in the last degree: for it is a Passport, which worded as it may be, still bears but one meaning—it commands the Captains of American ships-of-war, to permit Santa Anna to enter Vera Cruz, or in other words, solicits the Military Chieftain to leave the Havanna theatre, return to his native land, and fight old Zachary Taylor at Buena Vista.

—And yet, the man in the city of Washington, with the dead white face and porcelain blue eyes, is a Statesman.—You will remember, this is still but a fancy picture.—

Or, should you wish to gaze upon another Statesman, not a military chieftain, for such personages are dreadful to contemplate, but a Statesman of the highest order, gaze yonder, into the hallowed walls of Faneuil Hall, and behold that muscularly formed man, tower above the heads of thousands, the light shining upon his massive forehead, as with his thunder-tones, he utters words like these:

"What shall we say of this unconstitutional war with Mexico? Where will we find words to express our withering disapprobation of its measures

12 Lippard is likely referring to James Buchanan, Polk's Secretary of State.

and its men? Yet hold—it is an American habit, not to count the horrors of a war, the blood, the tears, the groans, the sighs,—but the Cost!"[13]

With his thunder tones, in Faneuil Hall, he uttered this sentiment, and spoke it boldly before the Portrait of John Hancock, and heard a thousand voices answer him with deep hurrahs. He spoke it, in the birth-place of the Revolution, where the Adamses had been, and in sight of the hill where Warren fell,[14] and did not feel that he was a blot upon that sacred soil, a living scorn upon the dead, a Traitor for all his burning eyes and snow-white hair. O, that stout John Adams could have started from his grave, and heard the pedlar's throats of Faneuil Hall shriek like a Puritan hallelujah, the word—"Cost!"

Yet this man is called a statesman, not military chieftain, ah, no! But as the pious folks of Puritan land have it, a Godlike statesman.

—Still it is only a fancy picture. Remember that!—

And while the politician on the floor of the Senate, prepares for American Soldiers, his bloody hands and hospitable grave, while Santa Anna enjoys his game cocks in Havanna[15] and the Statesman writes his passport in Washington, while the Godlike Statesman in Faneuil Hall, proclaimed to all the world, that it was an American habit, not to count the blood and tears of a war, but the Cost—here, beside the Rio Grande, with the evening star shining upon his bronzed face, behold the object of all their schemes, that plain old man, in the brown coat, covered with the blood and laurels of two victories, which all America had feared, would have been but Massacres to himself and his little band, here beside the dead body of his brother soldier, he stands, and murmurs—

"I SAID I WOULD REACH FORT BROWN IF I LIVED, AND I AM HERE!"

---

13 Faneuil Hall is in Boston. In this quote, Lippard is likely paraphrasing Senator Daniel Webster (1782–1852), who gave a speech similar in tone and verbiage at Faneuil Hall on November 8, 1844. *The Writings and Speeches of Daniel Webster Hitherto Uncollected Volume One, Addresses on Various Occasions, National Edition* (Boston: Little, Brown, & Company, 1903), 301–305.

14 This reference is to the death of Dr. Joseph Warren (1741–1775) at the Battle of Bunker Hill (1775).

15 According to Timothy J. Henderson, Santa Anna "spent vast amounts of time and money at the cockfights and gambling tables." Timothy J. Henderson, *A Glorious Defeat: Mexico and Its War with the United States* (New York: Hill and Wang, 2007), 129.

VI

Monterey

They tell me that Monterey[1] is beautiful; that it lies among the snow-white mountains, whose summits reach the clouds.

It sleeps beneath us now.

While the moon, parting from the white mountain tops, sails in the serene upper air, we will stand among the trees of the Walnut Grove,[2] and behold the slumbering city.

These trees, beneath whose leaves we stand, speak of the ages that are gone. So massive in their trunks, so wide-spreading in their branches, so luxuriant in their foliage. The moonlight trembles through the quivering leaves, and reveals the rich garniture[3] of the soil. It blooms with tropical fruits and flowers. Around the giant columns of Walnut, the jessamine and the wild rose, the lily and the orange blossom, spread their tapestry of rainbow dyes. The air is drowsy with excess of perfume. And from the shadows, flash the mountain streams, singing the midnight anthem, ere they plunge below.

It is the Grove of the Walnut Springs in which we stand; a grand Cathedral of Nature, whose pillars are Walnut trees, five hundred years old, whose canopy is woven leaves and vines, whose baptismal font is the pure mountain spring, whose incense is perfume, that intoxicates every sense, and whose offerings are flowers, that bewilder the gaze, with their fresh, their virgin beauty.

And from the grove, by the light of the moon, we gaze upon the city, that Amazon Queen, who reclines so royally among her warrior mountains.

Chapter VI

1 Monterrey was a city in northeastern Mexico with an estimated population between "12,000 to 15,000." It was the capital of the Mexican state of Nuevo Leon. The city served as an outstanding defensive position due to its location, as the city was bordered by the Sierra Madre mountains, smaller hills, and the San Juan River. In addition, the city itself was highly defensible, as "The center of town was tightly packed with sturdy limestone houses and narrow streets arranged in a grid-like pattern." The modern spelling of the city is "Monterrey," but Lippard uses the nineteenth century spelling, "Monterey." Christopher Dishman, *A Perfect Gibraltar: The Battle for Monterrey, Mexico, 1846* (Norman: University of Oklahoma Press, 2010), 29–31. See William Henry, *Campaign Sketches of the War with Mexico* (New York: Harper & Brothers, 1847), 192–226.

2 Lippard is referring to the area where the U.S. Army camped before attacking Monterrey. No walnut trees were present at this location, but Lippard refers to walnut trees due to American troops naming the area "Walnut Springs" and "Walnut Grove." John S.D. Eisenhower, *So Far from God: The U.S. War with Mexico, 1846–1848* (Norman: University of Oklahoma Press, 2000), 126; Dishman, *A Perfect Gibraltar, 92;* Henry, Campaign Sketches, 192.

3 According to a contemporary source, "garniture" are "[o]rnamental appendages; embellishment; furniture; dress." Noah Webster, *An American Dictionary of the English Language* (New York: Harper & Brothers, 1844), 370.

4   The city of the Royal Mountain refers to Monterrey. In English, "monte" translates to "mountain" and "rey" to "king."
5   The San Juan River is located south of Monterrey. According to Dishman, "As it approached the southeastern corner of Monterrey, the river made a gradual turn to the northeast to form the rough shape of a hook, with the city located above the flat, east-to-west shank." The river was one of Monterrey's natural defenses, Dishman, *A Perfect Gibraltar*, 29–31.
6   The Bishop's Palace refers to the vacant building located atop Independence Hill that Mexican forces fortified with hastily constructed walls and cannons in preparation for the American assault on Monterrey. Capturing this fortification was one of the American military's main objectives. It fell to U.S. forces on September 22, 1846. Dishman, *A Perfect Gibraltar*, 34; Henry, *Campaign Sketches*, 34, 165-168.
7   A "castellated" structure is "[a]dorned with turrets and battlements like a castle." Webster, *An American Dictionary*, 127.
8   The Grand Plaza was located in southeastern Monterrey. General Ampudia used the cathedral located at one end of the plaza as his command center during the Battle of Monterrey and also placed military supplies and the city's civilians in the Plaza. Dishman, *A Perfect Gibraltar*, 31, 87, 196.

It is a city of singularly impressive features, that reposes yonder. To the north, to the south, to the west, the mountains rise, girdled with tropical fruits and foliage, and mantled on their brows, with glittering snow. On the east, green with cornfields, and beautiful with groves of orange trees, spreads a level plain.

Those orange groves, seem to love the city of the Royal Mountain.[4] For they girdle her dark stone walls, with their white blossoms, and hang their golden fruit above her battlemented roofs. From this elevated grove, toward the south, around the sleeping city, winds the beautiful river of San Juan,[5] now hidden among pomegranate trees, now sending a silvery branch into the town, again flashing on, beside its castled walls.

Below us, with its roofs laid bare to the moonlight, we behold each tower and dome, of the mountain city. It is a place of narrow streets, and one storied houses, with walls and floors of stone. Above each level roof, rises a battlement, breast high; the streets are crossed by huge piles of masonry, and the whole town, presents the appearance of an immense fortress, linked together by bands of stone, adorned with gardens, and gloomy with towers of rock and steel.

Far to the west, a huge steep, crowned with a mass of stone, varied with cannon, casts its heavy shadow,—a long belt of blackness—over the town. That is the Bishop's Palace.[6]

Here, before us, east of the city, their outlines seen above the river, and the groves of orange blossoms, these castleated[7] mounds, rise clearly in the air. Yonder, on the north, glooms the massive citadel. Thus girdled by defenses of stone, iron and steel, thus sheltered by its mountains of fruit and snow, the city of the Royal Mountain, may well seem impregnable.

Yonder, toward the south, among its homes of stone, you behold an open space; the grand Plaza of Monterey.[8] There rise the cathedral towers, heaving above their peaks, and domes of stone, the golden cross into the midnight sky. Look! How it glitters above the town, smiling back to heaven, the beams of the rising moon.

It is impregnable, this mountain city. No arms can take it; no cannon blast its impenetrable walls. The Bishop's Palace on one side, the three forts on the other, the citadel on the north, the river on the east and south; it is shut in by stone, by water, by iron and by flame.

And yet, not many months ago—sit by me, while the moon shines over the city, and I will tell you the story—there came to this grove, an old man, mounted on a grey charger, and clad in a plain brown coat. On the mountains that frown toward the east, through the ravines, that darken there, he came followed by six thousand men.[9] He encamped in this grove of walnut trees, and the arms of his soldiers shone gaily, from the white waste of orange blossoms. He stood, where now, we stand, he gazed first upon his men, his horses, his cannon, and then upon the city, which though it smiles to us, in the light of the morn, gloomed in his face, by the beams of day—from every roof, and rock and tower—with one deadly frown.

The old man saw it crowded by nine thousand armed men.[10] He saw every roof transformed into a castle, formidable with its death array of cannon and steel, the Cathedral,[11] with its cross, and image of Jesus, converted into a magazine of gunpowder—a silent volcano, that only wanted the impulse of a single spark, to make it blaze and thunder.

And yet the old man, after his silent gaze, turned to his brother heroes, among whom Butler and Twiggs, and Worth of the Waving Plume, stood prominent, and said in his quiet way:

"The town is before us. We will take it."

Then every soldier in that army of six thousand men, took his comrade by the hand and said: *"If I fall, swear that you will bury my corse!"*

9 When General Taylor departed the town of Camargo in August, 1846, his army consisted of "3,000 regulars and 3,200 volunteers" and reached Monterrey in September. Ibid., 75.

10 While camped in Marin, Mexico in mid-September, 1846, Taylor's army received reports that Mexican forces in Monterrey consisted of "9,000 men—6,000 rancheros and 3,000 regulars." Ampudia had 7,303 men at Monterrey. Karl Bauer, *The Mexican War, 1846–1848* (Lincoln: University of Nebraska Press, 1974), 93; Dishman, *A Perfect Gibraltar*, 82.

11 The cathedral refers to the Catholic church in the Grand Plaza of Monterrey. In addition to using the building as his command center, Ampudia stored 17,000 pounds of gunpowder and munitions in the church. This choice influenced Ampudia's surrender. As the American artillery bombardment grew closer to the cathedral, Ampudia was forced to consider the possibility of an artillery strike hitting his munitions, which would have resulted in hundreds of civilian deaths. After moving within artillery range of the cathedral, U.S. Lieutenant Dana described the bombardment: "The shells all burst beautifully right in the plaza, scattering death and devastation" and "making them tremble lest one should go into the cathedral." Napoleon Dana, *Monterrey Is Ours!: The Mexican War Letters of Lieutenant Dana, 1845–1847*, ed. Robert Ferrell (Lexington: The University Press of Kentucky, 1990), 138; Henry, Campaign Sketches, *221–222*; Dishman, *A Perfect Gibraltar*, 87, 196; Eisenhower, *So Far from God*, 142–143.

For every heart felt that the contest must be horrible and deadly.

The heroes of the prairie, the Men of Palo Alto and Resaca de la Palma, were there. Mingled with these iron soldiers, you might see the men of Mississippi and Louisiana, Maryland, Tennessee and Ohio, Kentucky and Texas. The farms and the work-shops of the American Union, had heard the cry, which shrieked from the twin-battle-fields of Palo Alto, and Resaca de la Palma, heard it, and sent forth their beardless boys, their grey haired men, to the rescue. The sugar and the cotton plantations of the south, the prairies of the north, the mountains of Pennsylvania, the blue-hills of Kentucky, that dark and bloody ground, the massacre fields of Texas, all sent their men to swell the ranks of the New Crusade. The same Banner that waved over Bunker Hill, and Saratoga and Brandywine, from the Walnut Grove, flashed the light of its stars over Monterey.

The fight began on the Twenty-First of September, 1847, and tracked its bloody course, over the Twenty-Second, and did not cease its howl of murder, when the sun went down, on the Twenty-Third.[12]

You may be sure that it was horrible, this battle of street and square, of roof and cliff, of mountain and gorge. It was a storm—hurled from the mouths of musquets, cannon and mortar, wrapping cliff and dome in its dark pall, and flashing its lightning in the face of Sun, Moon, and Stars, for three days. You may be sure, that the orange groves, mowed down by the cannons blaze, showered their white blossoms over the faces of the dead. That the San Juan, sparkling in the moon, like silver now, then blushed crimson, as if in shame, for the horrible work that was going on. That nothing but shots, groans, shouts, yells, the sharp crack of the rifle, the deep boom of the cannon, was heard throughout those three days of blood. That in the battle trenches, lay the dead men, American and Mexican, their silent groups swelled every moment by new corses, looking with glassy

---

12 The Battle of Monterrey occurred between September 20 and September 24. Ampudia requested a truce on the 23rd, though skirmishes continued through the next day. Ampudia officially surrendered on September 25, 1846. According to Dishman, the Americans "reported losses of sixteen officers, 120 men killed, and 368 wounded," while the Mexicans "suffered losses of 122 killed and 316 wounded. Skeptics believe that casualties for both sides were much higher than either general admitted." Ampudia was allowed to take his remaining troops and leave the city. Dishman, *A Perfect Gibraltar*, 199; Eisenhower, *So Far from God*, 144–147; Henry, *Campaign Sketches*, 213–214.

eyes into each other's faces. That many a beautiful woman, nestling in her darkened home, was crushed in her white bosom by the cannon ball, or splintered in the forehead, just above the dark eyes, by the musquet shot.

And amid the fight, whether it blazed in volumes of flame, or rolled in waves of smoke, you may be sure two objects were distinctly seen—the white plume of the chivalrous Worth, and the familiar brown coat of stout Zachary Taylor.

It was on the morning of the Twenty-First, when the rising sun shone over the groves of orange and pomegranate, the fields of corn, and the girdle of rocks and waves, encircling the mountain city, that suddenly, a mass of white smoke heaved upward from the ravines, yawning about the Bishop's Palace, and rolling cloud on cloud, wrapt those towers in its folds, and stretched like an immense shroud along the western sky.

Beneath that smoke, Worth and his Men were commencing the Battle of Monterey, on the West of the town.

At the same moment, around these forts on the east, a cloud of smoke arose, it swept away toward the citadel, and soon melted into the cloud on the west.

Under its pall, Taylor and his men were advancing upon the town from the north and east. Thus the city of the Royal Mountain, was girdled by a pall of battle-smoke, and thus, from opposite sides of the town, Taylor and Worth fought their ways of blood, toward each other, driving nine thousand Mexicans, with AMPUDIA[13] at their head, into a centre of death and flame.[14]

Night came and went and came again, and still the fight went on. One by one, the three batteries on the east, fell before the arms of Taylor. Over the impregnable heights of the Bishop's Palace, waved the Banner of the Stars. The city saw not a glimpse of blue sky, for in the air hung a canopy

13 Major General Pedro de Ampudia (1805–1868) was the Mexican commander of the "Army of the North" and the leader of the Mexican forces at the Battle of Monterrey. He surrendered to Zachary Taylor on September 25, 1846. See Anderson Chenault Quisenberry, "History by Illustration: Gen. Zachary Taylor, and the Mexican War," *Register of Kentucky State Historical Society* 9, no. 26 (1911): 7–40; Dishman, *A Perfect Gibraltar*, 35–36, 39–42.

14 Lippard is describing Taylor's strategic maneuvers; he attacked from the east, while General William J. Worth (1794–1849) attacked from the west. Both units converged on the Grand Plaza of Monterrey. Eisenhower, *So Far from God*, 127–143.

of battle-cloud, and over the roofs the gunpowder spread its pestilential mist. There was neither food, nor shelter anywhere. God pity the women then, who, shuddering in cellars and burrowing in dark rooms, clutched to their breasts the children of their love! In the Cathedral no prayer was spoken, no mass sung the deep anthem, or waved from censers the snowy incense. The Image of Jesus was wrapt in the battle-cloud; that divine face, for once, seemed to frown. Mild Mother Mary, above the altar, was clad in a robe of smoke, and her sad and tender face grew livid, ghastly, with gleams of battle flame.

There was no rest for the sole of human foot, no slumber but the slumber of the bloody ditch, or dark ravine. None slept but the dead.

And still, from the west, the cannon of Worth hurled their message to Taylor on the east, and evermore the cannon of Taylor thundered their reply. Nearer grew those sounds to each other, and closer in the fiery circle, Ampudia and his Mexicans were hemmed. Over the roofs, through the battered houses, beyond their battered barricades, they were driven by Worth and Taylor, until the battle gathered to one point, and above the main plaza where the moon shines so calmly now, on Cathedral and Cross, hung the accumulated cloud of three day's agony.

And to this grove of the Walnut Springs, where at this hour, the moon breaks in tender light, on each massive tree and perfumed flower, the battle mangled were brought to bleed and die. The sod, spreading so thick with blossoms all around us, grew purple with a bath of blood. Hearts, that had once quivered to the pressure of a woman's bosom, were frozen in this grove, and eyes, that had looked tenderly into the eyes of Wife, Mother, Child, grew glassy beneath the walnut leaves.

But amid all the horror of the fight, the Mountains yonder,—like calm Demons, impenetrable to the yell of slaughter, or the howl of agony,—lifted their snowy tops, and shone on, whether lighted by the sun, or moon, or stars, or battle-flash.

Crouching in a darkened chamber, two Mexican girls flung their arms about each other's necks, and buried their faces in their flowing hair. Through the small window toward the west, half-covered with vines, a few wandering gleams of sunlight shone. Ever and again, a red flash bathed the room in crimson light. It was a spacious room, with stone walls, hidden in purple hangings, and a marble floor, strewn with the wrecks of books and harps and flowers.

In one corner stood a small couch, its ruffled pillows, yet bearing the outlines of those two virgin forms.

From that couch they had darted suddenly, and with their half-naked forms quivering with affright, flung themselves on the marble floor, near the window, where a Cross glittered in its shadowy recess.

And now, as their white shoulders and uncovered feet glowed in the feeble light, their faces were hidden on each other's breasts among their luxuriant hair.

You may see their limbs quiver, you may see the scanty robe, which but half-conceals each virgin form, move tremulously with each movement of their bodies, but their faces you cannot see.

It is now near sunset, on this fearful Twenty-Third of September, 1846. For three days, these girls have awaited the return of their father from the battle. Three days ago, they saw him go forth on his grey war-horse, an old but muscular man, whose olive cheek, seamed with wrinkles, and dark hair mingled with the snowy flakes of age, were shadowed by plumes of fiery crimson. They saw him, in his costume of national green, dash from the door of their home toward the battle. By his side, their brother rode; a manly boy of nineteen, whose jet-black hair, gathered in thick curls around his young forehead, while his sinewy arm waved his sword in the morning air.

So gallantly, from their garden-encircled home of Monterey, they went forth together, the father and son, their uniform flashing back the light, from every star of gold, while the necks of their steeds proudly arched, their plumes fluttering in the breeze, their figures quivering with the impulse of the fight—all gave omen of a bloody battle and a certain triumph.

For three days the maidens had waited for them, but they came not. For three days and nights, the roar of the night swelling afar, had startled slumber from their eyes. But now that roar grew nearer; it deepened into thunder; it spoke more plainly. Quivering in every nerve, as they knelt on the floor, they could distinctly hear the separate voices of the battle—now the rifle's shriek, now the musquet's peal, now the cannon's thunder shout.

And the storm grew nearer their house; it seemed to rage all around them, for those terrible sounds never for one moment ceased, and the red flash poured through the narrow window, in one incessant sheet of battle lightning.

Still the Father, the Brother came not!

Hark! That crash, which shakes the chamber, like an earthquake! The girls lift their faces, from among their flowing hair, and you may read the volume of their contrasted loveliness.

This, with her warm, voluptuous bosom, and the rich brown cheek, shadowed by the raven hair—Ximena. The other, with the fair cheek, and snowy breast, and large eyes, that remind you of the deep azure of a starry midnight, the hair that floats, in curls of chesnut brown—Teresa.

Their beautiful tresses twining together, in mingled dyes of light and shade, the full, luxuriant form of Ximena, contrasted with the more delicate figure of Teresa, those dark eyes, swimming in tears, the maidens half-starting from their knees, presented a picture of touching loveliness.

Around them strewn, their torn books, broken harps and withered flowers; before them, smiling from its dark recess, that solitary cross!

Again that crash, again that red light streaming through the window! With one bound the girls sprang to their feet, and gazed upon the door, whose panels you may distinguish yonder, among the purple curtaining.

"They come!" shrieked Ximena, and gathered her Sister to her heart.

Deep shouts were heard, the tramp of armed men, resounding through a narrow passage—another crash! The door gave way, and the red battle light rushed into the place. The door gave way, and as it clanged upon the floor, a dying man fell backward upon its panels, the broken sword, firmly clutched in his hand, the blood, pouring in a stream from the wound in his chest.

His throat bare, his dark hair sprinkled with silver, hanging damp and clotted above his wrinkled brow, he glared upward with his glazing eyes—made an effort to rise—and fell back, writhing in his death agony.

Above him, the foremost of a band, attired in blue, stood a slender, but athletic form, his upraised arm, still waving its sword, red with the blood of the prostrate enemy. His face, was very pale, but his hazel eye, shone with the mad light of carnage.

At a glance, the girls behold the form of that dying man, the figure of Murderer—and a shriek, that made his blood grow chill, though it raged with the battle fever—filled the place.

The American, in the doorway, felt his nerveless arm drop by his side. Even as the sword dripped its red tears upon the floor, he beheld those girls, kneeling beside the dying man, and heard one word quiver from their lips—

"Father!"

It was in the Spanish tongue, but he read its meaning in their extended arms, in their faces, stamped with agony, in their bared bosoms, wildly pressed against the bleeding chest of his foe.

They looked up into his face; they raised their eyes to this young pale brow, and spoke once more—

"Our Father!"

The young American felt his fingers stiffen, heard his bloody sword clatter on the floor.

"His pistol it was, that shot my comrade by my side, even as we came charging up the Plaza, his—"

He shrieked these words, driven to madness, by their accusing looks, but he could say no more. For he too had a grey-haired father, he too, among the hills of Pennsylvania, in the old farm house, at the end of the lane, where mill-stream wind among the woods, had two sisters! That father blessed him when he left home for the wars, those sisters pressed their warm kisses on his lips, as they gasped farewell!

Now, upon the threshhold of the Mexican home he stood, the dying father, writhing before his eyes, while his daughters, with their bared bosoms, sought to staunch the flowing of the blood, which hissed, warm and smoking from his heart. There, he stood, the Murderer, in presence of his victim, with the eyes of those beautiful sisters upon his face!

The sight was too much for him.

Waving his comrades back—they were all young men, like him, unused to scenes of blood, their veins fired for the first time, with the lust of carnage[15]—he flung himself upon the floor, and with his hands, pressed over the wound, madly endeavored to stop the blood, that glided through his fingers, and dashed into his face.

---

15 According to David Reynolds, Lippard viewed combat as an occasion "when man was exhilaratingly free to vent his most savage impulses." In *Blanche of Brandywine* (1846), Lippard described the power of carnage, "most horrible of all, is the instinct of Carnage! Yes, that Instinct which makes a man thirst for blood, which makes him mad with joy, when he steeps his arms to the elbows in his foeman's gore, which makes him shout and halloo, and laugh, as he goes murdering on over piles of dead!" David S. Reynolds, *George Lippard* (Boston: Twayne Publishers, 1982), 40; George Lippard, *Blanche of Brandywine* (Philadelphia: G.B. Zieber & Co., 1846), 223.

But the dying old Mexican, with distorted features and glazing eyes, muttered a curse with his livid lips, and feebly endeavored to withdraw himself, from the touch of the American.

Those half-clad maidens, with frenzy in their eyes, tore their glossy hair, and beat their breasts with their clenched hands, as they felt, that there was no longer a hope for the old man, their father.

The American, on his knees, beside them, saw the unspeakable agony, written on each face, and knew himself, a guilty and blood-stained man.

"*He* shot my comrade," the words came faintly from his lips—"My blood was up—I pursued him—we fought—fought on over heaps of dead, to the door—and—but I did not think of this! To stab an old man, on the threshhold of his home, in the presence of his children!"

Again he sank beside the dying man, but those lips, now changed to a clayish blue, only moved to curse again. With extended arms, he fell before the maidens, but their looks of horror, as they shrank from him with outspread arms, gave no hope of forgiveness.

At last he rose, and standing among the curtains, near the doorway, where the shadows were thickest, folded his arms and contemplated the scene.

Here Ximena, chafing with her warm palms the chilled hands of her father, her hair, streaming wildly over her shoulders, stained with the warm blood of his heart; there, Teresa, with the head of the dying man, on her lap, her fingers pressed upon his clammy brow, her blue eyes weeping their tears like rain, on his glassy eye-balls.

"It cuts my heart like a dagger"—the American forced the words between his set teeth—"I have a father too, away in Pennsylvania, and sisters too, that resemble these girls.—"

16 Lippard is referring to American efforts near the end of the battle to capture the cathedral located in the Grand Plaza of Monterrey. This phase of the battle was defined by artillery bombardment and urban combat. According to Dishman, the Battle of Monterrey was the "first time in U.S. history [that] large numbers of regular troops engaged in house-to-house combat." Dishman, *A Perfect Gibraltar*, xvi, 175–195.

He could bear it no longer. Scarce knowing what he did, only wishing to turn his eyes away from that sight, he plunged among the hangings, and found himself at the foot of a narrow stairway. A moment had not passed, when he emerged upon the flat roof, with its battlement of stone. His cheek was pale as death—before the battle he had suffered much with fever—and the emotions, fast crowding round his heart, gave an unnatural gleam to this eye.

He approached the battlement, and started away. The scene beneath, was at once horrible and sublime. That roof, commanded a free view of the Plaza of the city and all the avenues leading to it. Again he approached, and gazed upon the Last Fight of Monterey.[16]

Imagine a space, two hundred yards square, walled in by houses, one story high, frowning with battlements. This space is packed with one dense mass of infuriated soldiers, half naked, their faces scarce distinguishable beneath the stain of powder and blood. They shout, they yell, they roll to and fro, like the waves of a whirlpool. Here you may distinguish the American, there the Mexican uniform.

From every battlement, lined with frenzied Mexicans, pours the blaze of musquetry, hurling the death, alike on friend and foe. Beneath, bayonet to bayonet, and knife to knife, over the pavement, slippery with blood, the contest is maintained. As the ranks of the battling legions, move aside, or part for a moment, you may behold, the cold faces of the dead, amid their fiercest roar, you hear the deep piercing yell of the wounded.

Over this scene, glooms the Cathedral, its towers only half seen amid the clouds of smoke which toss around them.

That cross glitters in the setting sun, but all below is dim, dark, bloody. Just as you have seen, a mist hover above a summit, so that thick cloud, glooms over the grand Plaza of Monterey, its edges tinted with sunset gold, while all beside is dark.

And toward this Plaza, like separate streams of blood, rushing from north and south and east and west, toward one great lake of carnage, the three days battle rolls by every street and avenue, along these roofs, and through yonder smoking ruins.

Yonder to the west, far over the heads of advancing Americans cast your gaze, among the whirling combatants, you see the White Plume, waving in the battle light. WORTH is there! Like a cavalier of old he rides to battle, his graceful and commanding figure, clad in full uniform, his head placed proudly on his shoulders, his broad chest, thrown forward, as if in defiance of the danger and the death, around him.

To the east, turn your eye! Down, this avenue, where the cannon's blaze their fire, into the faces of the recoiling Mexicans, where the clouds now come down like Night, and now roll away, leaving the scene, to the warm glow of the setting sun, down this lane of blood, amid the charging squadrons, you behold a warrior, on a grey horse, with a brown coat, thrown back from his broad chest, while a plain cap, surmounts his bronzed face and flashing eyes. TAYLOR is there!

They hear each other's shouts, the Men of Worth and Taylor, charging from east and west, toward the Grand Plaza, their cannon balls encounter each other, in the ranks of the foe; crushing men and horses, firm masonry and battlemented walls before them, they fight on, toward the centre, where gleams the Cathedral cross over masses of cloud!

This was the scene, which the young American, sick of the battle, and thinking of his dear Pennsylvanian home, beheld, but it was not all! No—no!

Between the rolling clouds, the sky smiled so calmly down upon him; beneath in the bloody Plaza, the dead looked so ghastly up in his face! Not twenty yards from the place where he stood, a dead woman lay, her mangled breasts, clotted with blood, while her frozen features, knit so darkly in the brow, and distorted along the lips, told how fierce the struggle in which she died.

O, it would have made your blood dance, to stand there, and see how, wave on wave, the Americans rolled their flood of bayonets toward the Plaza, how flash on flash, their cannon lighted up the battle, whirling around the cathedral, how yell on yell, the stern hunters of the west, with clenched bowie knives, in their brawny arms, came rushing on, to the last act of the three day's drama of blood!

At last, as if the day light was sick of the scene, the night fell—a starless, moonless night—and in the darkness, the fight went horribly forward.

Then, through the pall that hung above the Cathedral, a mass of fire, came blazing on, like the bloody moon in the Book of Revelations, blazing on, with its fiery mane, flung far along the sky.

It comes from the mortar of Worth, and hisses down, among the Mexicans, in front of the Cathedral. Old Zachary, gazing from the east, sees that bomb, as it flashes on its meteor way, and knows that the end of the battle is near.

Weary of the darkness and the blood, the young American tottered, from the battlement and down the stairway, into the chamber, where he had left the sisters and their dying father.

A darkness, so dense, that it seemed to press upon the eyeballs, lay upon the place.

The American soldier, stood among the purple curtains, listening in awe for the faintest sound.

It was still—terribly still. To the excited fancy of the battle-worn Volunteer, it seemed a death vault, gloomy with the darkness of ages. The very atmosphere seemed thick with Death.

He advanced—a single step—and then, even as he could distinctly hear the beatings of his heart—he spread forth his arms, sank on his knees, and felt his way, through that darkened chamber.

His extended hands touched the cold face of the dead. There was something so loathsome, in that clammy pressure, which left his fingers, wet with clotted blood, that he started back, and remained for a moment, motionless as the dead, as if rooted to the stone, on which he knelt.

Then, dashing forward with trembling hands, he felt the cold face again, and another, and yet one more clammy brow. He was alone in that room, with the dead. Three corses lay on the stone floor, beside the kneeling man.

This was the work of War! War on the battle field, where the yell of the dying, rings its defiance to the charging legions, wears on its bloodiest plume, some gleam of chivalry, but War in the Home, scattering its corses, beside the holiest altars of life, and mingling the household gods, with bleeding hearts and shattered skulls—this, indeed, is a fearful thing.

As the American, sank back, shuddering and cold—for he, too had a father, he too, had sisters—a glare like lightning, illumined the chamber, laying bare, every nook and crevice, and tinting every object, with its red and murderous light. In a moment it died away, but that moment of sudden light, revealed this battle picture, to the eyes of the American soldier:

The Father, dead, upon the prostrate door, his distorted features, scowling curses, even as he lay, with his hands, clenched over his mangled breast. By his side, two forms, their arms about each other's necks, their lips close together, their young faces, even in that battle light, wearing a smile, serene, as a cloudless heaven. It was the Brother and his Sister, sleeping their last sleep. One bullet, had pierced their skulls through the temple—she, with her glassy blue eyes and brown hair, lay with her cheek to his, as the brother's lip, darkened by a slight mustache, was curved in a joyous smile.

So, by their dead father, the dead children lay, crushed into eternal silence, even as they had embraced each other, over his lifeless body.

It was evident that the young Mexican, came home from the fight, without a wound, and died in the act of consoling his fatherless sisters.

But Ximena—where is she?

Look, beside the bodies of the dead, and tremble, as you behold that kneeling woman, gazing fixedly, upon the three corses, her eyes dilating, until the white circle, is seen distinctly, around each burning pupil, while her death-like face and uncovered bosom, are darkly relieved by the volume of her luxuriant hair.

Was she dead?

A convulsive quivering of the lip, alone bore witness, to the miserable life, that still dwelt, in her maddened brain, a slight—almost imperceptible heaving of her white bosom—told that her torn heart, still throbbed on.

For a moment the American saw this picture—only one of the thousand horrible sights, which the light of battle, revealed in the Homes of Monterey—and the darkness, fell like a pall, upon the living and the dead.

It was on the Twenty-Fourth of September, when the battle clouds had rolled away, and the setting sun, shone over the wreck of the devastated city, that AMPUDIA, surrendered into the hands of the old man in the brown coat, his sword, and saw the Banner of the Stars, float into heaven, from every dome and peak of the city.

In a town, that resembled one immense castle, hemmed in by fortified mountains, and defended by forty-two pieces of cannon, with at least nine thousand, brave men, under his command, he had been conquered by this plain warrior, on the old grey horse, who had only six thousand men, one mortar, two howitzers and four light field batteries.

History does not tell of many deeds like that!

Well might the old man gaze proudly round him, as he felt the sword of AMPUDIA in his grasp! For encircled by his own gallant officers—Worth of the Waving Plume was foremost there—he saw the mountains, with their white tops, glittering in the setting sun. He saw the Cathedral Cross, shining like a point of flame, as the Banner of the Stars, floated around its dome. The orange groves, whose white blossoms, could not conceal the dead, the River of San Juan, red with blood, the gloomy Bishop's Palace, frowning under the victorious flag, the city, littered with corses,—he saw it all, that scene, where he had fought and won!

Gaze upon the old man, as he stands triumphant, among the wrecks of Monterey, the glow of the setting sun, upon his bronzed face, the sword of Ampudia in his hand. His Army—his People, not his Slaves—are there, with their tried bayonets, shining on every side. There are taller warriors, who wear gayer uniforms, and go to the fight, in more elegant costume, but this familiar man, in that unadorned attire, wears his battle jewels, in the hearts of six thousand men.

And as he stands before us, the object of ten thousand eyes, yonder, far away, in the City of Washington, the pismires[17] of Faction, are already busy with the Mound of his Fame. That Mound, built of the trophies of Palo Alto, Resaca de la Palma, Monterey, and cemented with the blood of at least one thousand heroes.

Toil on, heroic Insects of the Cabinet and Council! For work like this, you were born; it is your destiny, to gnaw holes in the drapery of greatness, and burrow hiding places, for your mighty insignificance, beneath

17 According to a contemporary source, "pismire" is "[t]he insect called the *ant* or *emmet*." Webster, *An American Dictionary*, 613.

the Monument of Genius. Toil on! In the olden times, Pismires, as brave as you,—although not born in the miasmatic[18] air of caucus and convention—swarmed over the drapery of a man, called Washington, and went terribly to work, beneath the granite mountain of his fame.

Where are they now? Where will you be, ten years hence?

Toil on, heroic Insects, of the Cabinet and Council! But be very careful how you annoy heroes like Washington or Taylor—a single flutter of their drapery will scatter you; a solitary pebble, falling from the Monument of their fame, crush you, into dust.

These Politicians, who scheme in dark holes, while brave men, do heroic deeds, in the face of day, are interesting personages.

Behold them, in the Continental Congress, lay their plans and weave their plots, against one WASHINGTON, now battling hunger, cold and pestilence among the hills of Valley Forge![19] Yet this same WASHINGTON, with the ant-hills of party reared all about him, to block his way and precipitate him into the dust, comes forth serenely from Valley Forge, and fights the BATTLE OF MONMOUTH.[20]

Behold them, after the Battle of Monterey, sever old ZACHARY TAYLOR from his tried veterans, leave him at the City of his Conquest, with only six hundred men, which at last are swelled by new recruits, into four thousand. Immortal Insects! What matter if the old man and his four thousand are massacred?[21]

The whole Union palpitates with quivering anxiety for the old man and his soldiers. Superseded in his command, stripped of his veterans, he is left among the mountains, with only four thousand, while Santa Anna[22] seeks for him, with twenty thousand men, eager for the fight, and confident of victory.

---

18 According to a contemporary source, "miasmatic" "pertain[s] to miasma; parting of the qualities of noxious effluvia." Ibid., 529.

19 Valley Forge refers to the location of the 1777–1778 winter camp of the Continental Army during the Revolutionary War. James K. Martin and Mark Lender, *A Respectable Army: The Military Origins of the Republic, 1763–1789* (Malden: Harlan David Inc., 2015), 102.

20 The Battle of Monmouth (1778) took place during the Revolutionary War and ended with no clear victor.

21 Lippard is referring to the large portion of Zachary Taylor's army placed under the command of General Winfield Scott (1786–1866) for the attack on Veracruz. According to Dishman, "Ultimately Scott acquired 4,000 regulars and 3,200 volunteers from Taylor" and with the reinforcements provided by General Wool (1784–1869), Taylor's remaining force consisted of "about 4,500 troops, almost all volunteers." Lippard believed this decision was enacted by Taylor's political enemies to reduce his role in the war and curtail his rising popularity. Dishman, *A Perfect Gibraltar*, 202–203.

22 Antonio López de Santa Anna (1794–1876) was the Mexican military leader and President from December 1846 to September 1847. Santa Anna was Mexico's most well-known military hero and political leader, but his political allegiances changed repeatedly throughout his career, and he was exiled from Mexico in 1845. After the commencement of hostilities with the United States, he returned to Mexico and quickly resumed power. See Timothy J. Henderson, *A Glorious Defeat: Mexico and Its War with the United States* (New York: Hill and Wang, 2007).

Who cares for old Taylor? Let him retreat; he has won glory enough; we Insects of Politics are afraid of his fame. Let him retreat or die.

And, even as the Insects talk thus, there came a Rumor that the old man has discovered a path through the very dangers which threaten him, a Beautiful Prospect through the very clouds which frown upon his head, or to speak it in Spanish, a—Buena Vista.

Toil on heroic Pismires of the cabinet and council!

Still we stand in the shadows of the Walnut Grove, gazing by the light of the moon, on slumbering Monterey. To see it sleep so calmly, in the embrace of its warrior mountains, who would dream that it had ever been the scene of a three day's battle? Gloomily above the town, the Bishop's Palace towers, but its guns are voiceless now. Beautifully through the night, the silvery San Juan gleams, but its waves no longer blush with blood. The orange groves are there, with their golden fruit mantled in snowy blossoms; there, the cornfields waving their long emerald leaves and tossing their silver tassels on the breeze, there the homes of stone, with battlemented roofs, framed in gardens of flowers—Beautiful Monterey! From the Cathedral tower, the Cross glitters through the night, emblem of that Faith—though clouded by priests and creeds—which says forever, "All men are alike the children of God." Over the Bishop's Palace waves the Banner of the Stars, symbol of that Democratic truth, which never for a moment ceases to speak, "This Continent is the Homestead of free and honest men. Kings have no business here. Hasten to possess it, Children of Washington!"

—While the moon rises over Monterey, let me take you to the fireside of yonder distant Home, in the land of Penn, among the mountains.

There is snow upon the ground, not only on the summit of the hill, but in the deep gorges, and chasm-like ravines. Over the mantle of snow, a ray of light quivers like a flaming arrow. It comes from yonder window; you see it, with its deep frame sunken in the thick walls of the old farm-house. With leafless trees around it, that pile of dark stone, with steep roof and many chimneys, breaks on your eye. The barn is near, one of those massive structures, which speak of glorious harvests, and shame the Slave House of the Factory[23] into nothingness.

By the light of the fireside, which sends its flaming arrow through the window, into the dark night—like a ray from heaven, blessing a dark world—behold this picture of Christmas Night.

A spacious room, its floor and ceiling white as snow, and a wide hearth, smoking and blazing with huge hickory logs. Above the hearth, a Rifle hangs, which blazed in the Revolution at Germantown.[24] Altogether, this hall of the old farm-house, with its ancient furniture, its heavy rafters, and joyous hearth, appeals to your heart; it is such a picture of Home.

Near the fire, on one of those oaken arm-chairs, sits an old man, with a rosy-cheeked damsel on either side. They clasp his hands and smooth the white hairs aside from his wrinkled brow,—their fresh young faces contrasting with his aged visage—but the old man, with his grey eyes fixed on the fire coals, bends his head and does not breathe a word.

It is the Christmas Night, and the Christmas Fire lights his face, but there is one absent from its glow. He is thinking of the absent one, picturing among the fire-coals, the image of his manly form, and repeating to himself, the last words which he said, ere he left his home:

"Father, I will come back covered with glory. I will bring you a trophy from the fields of Mexico!"

Now, it may be, he lies writhing with battle wounds or dying in the slow agonies of the tropical fever.

The daughters read the sorrow written in the aged lineaments[25] of their father, and cast their tearful eyes upon the Christmas Fire. Mary, with

---

23 According to Reynolds, "Lippard was more concerned with the white slavery in northern factories than with black slavery on southern plantations." Lippard used his fiction to protest the factory system and advocate for reforms that would aid the poor. Reynolds, *George Lippard*, 19–21, 51–58.

24 The Battle at Germantown (1777) was a turning point in the Revolutionary War where Washington sought to cut off the British supply lines outside of Philadelphia but was stalled due to Hessian resistance. This battle, along with the Battle of Saratoga, convinced the French to ally with the Americans the following year. See Friedrich Ernst Von Muenchausen, "Notes on the Battle of Germantown," *The Pennsylvania Magazine of History and Biography* 23, no. 4 (1899): 483–87.

25 According to a contemporary source, "lineament" is "a mark in the hand or face," Webster, *An American Dictionary*, 498.

the soft brown hair, and bosom that swells beneath its 'kerchief covering, dreams a half-waking dream of that golden and bloody land called Mexico, and sees her brother toiling through the wastes of chaparral. Anna, with hair golden as the beams of the setting sun, and a pale cheek, tinted with a solitary rose-bud, also dreams, but in her vision beholds her brother's brow, bathed with the red flush of victory.

And so they dream on, the father and his two mountain flowers, while the dismal wind, howling through the deep ravines, only serves to render more dear, more holy, the light, the blessing of that Christmas Fire.

At last a step is heard; through the opened door, a gust of wind and sleet rushes toward the fire. With one bound, the old man and his daughters start to their feet.

In the doorway, they behold a tall, slender form attired in a plain blue overcoat; they see that pale face, lighted by the eyes that flash with vivid light, they know those curls of chesnut brown, clustering beneath the military cap, around the white forehead.

"My Son!" and the old man spreads forth his arms.

"Brother!"—the Sisters are clinging round his neck.

Wasted by the deadly fever, the young Soldier bore in his pale cheek and scarred brow, the stern testimonials of Monterey. He stood in the centre of the group, his heart too full for words, gazing now upon his white-haired father, now into the faces of those blooming sisters. It was not very singular, but still the door remained open, and the wind and sleet still rushed upon the Christmas Fire.

"You've come back, Harry,"—the Father surveyed his son with a look of pride—"You've seen hard fightin' I don't doubt! A terrible scrimmage, that of Monterey! Come sit by the fire; the girls will get you something to

26 According to a contemporary source, "cumbrous" is "[b]urdensome; troublesome; rendering action difficult or toilsome; oppressive," Webster, *An American Dictionary* 213.

eat. An' as you eat, tell us all about it—what do you think of the old man, Zachary Taylor?"

At that name the young soldier uncovered his head; the tears started to his eyes.

"He is the Father, the Brother of his soldiers, as much as their General!" he said, with deep emotion.—So I have seen, time and again, the heads of returned soldiers uncover at the name of Taylor, while the tears in their eyes, the tremor in their voices, told how deeply in their heart the memory of the old man's kindness had taken root and flourished.

"But come," said the Father—"The night is bitter cold; close the door and sit near the fire—"

The Soldier did not move toward the fire, but stayed his father's hands as they were extended to close the door.

"When I left for Mexico, I told you I would bring back with me a Trophy of the War. That Trophy is here!"

Flinging the door yet wider open, he led the Trophy forward to the light. Behold it! A young, a beautiful girl, whose voluptuous outline of form, is not altogether hidden in her cumbrous[26] dress of furs, whose clear olive cheek, jet black hair and dazzling eyes, glow in the light, as they are framed in the close-fitting hood.

The snow was upon her dress, and melted in pearl drops in her hair. She stood gazing around the place with a half-frightened glance; then raising her large eyes to her Husband's face, she came tremulously forward and knelt at the old man's feet and kissed his hand. With one impulse, the Sisters flung themselves beside her, and kissed the snow drops from her raven hair.

"It's a long story, father—" gasped the Soldier, in a voice choked by emotion—"But I saw her father, her sister, her brother—together—dead upon the floor of their home, at Monterey. She was without a friend—and I had killed—"

He abruptly paused, and turned his face away. As if his soul was in his words, he gasped again—

"I can't tell it now father! But there she is, a true woman, who has nursed me in sickness, and followed me from her land of orange blossoms and flowers, into this land of winter and snow. She is my wife! Your child, father! Your sister, my sisters! Be very kind to her, for she has suffered much, and deserves all the love in your hearts! True, she doesn't understand English, but—"

There was a language which she understood! It spoke from her large beautiful eyes, it heaved with the pulsations of her young bosom, it wreathed in her red, warm lips, and shone in every blush of her glowing countenance.

As though she had been a gift, sent to them from Paradise, the old man and his daughters took that warm southern flower to their hearts, and from that moment she grew there!

Beautiful Ximena! Shaking the glittering snow drops from her hair, as it fell in dark masses from her raised hood, she advanced toward the Christmas Fire, and its warm glow bathed her cheeks as with a blessing. The old man looked smilingly into her face. On her right stood Mary, taking her silently by the hand, on the left her other sister, Anna, threading her jet-black hair with her fingers.

Somewhat in the rear, stood the pale Soldier, his arms folded on his breast, his head downcast, his eyes flashing with deep emotion as they rested on his wife.—That beautiful Trophy, from the battle-rent walls of Monterey.

VII

Buena Vista

A mother, with her mild blue eyes shining with a joy too deep for words, was gazing upon the face of her new-born child. Through the curtained windows of her Virginian home, shone the clear calm light of the setting sun. A mass of golden beams fell like a glory upon her down-cast head, and baptized with warm radiance, the face of her slumbering babe. In that darkened room, crowded with antique furniture, the bed-curtains crimsoned by the glow of the winter fire, you might distinguish through the twilight gloom which filled the place, those two faces, one eloquent with a Mother's love, the other calm as a cloudless sunset, and fresh from the hands of God.

The name of that new-born babe, slumbering so like a dreaming Angel, beneath its Mother's gaze, was GEORGE WASHINGTON.

The winter day, on which the Mother pressed her new-born child to her bosom, was the TWENTY-SECOND OF FEBRUARY, 1732.[1]

Time passed on, and that child's name became a holy word in the hearts of millions: the day of his birth a holy day, celebrated with solemn prayers, with glad hosannahs, in all the homes of a redeemed People.

But there came a day, when it was celebrated with offerings of blood. When the cannon, crushing hundreds with its thunderbolt, sung the anthem to its praise, and the white lips of dying men—dying afar from country and home, in the depths of bloody ravines—gasped with the last impulse of life, these holy words—*The twenty-second of February—Washington.*

Chapter VII

1   The battle of Buena Vista took place February 22–23, 1847, which was 115 years after the birth of George Washington. On February 20, Lieutenant Colonel May dispatched a reconnaissance team who set up camp at the hacienda of Buena Vista. James Henry Carleton, *The Battle of Buena Vista: With the Operations of the "Army of Occupation" for One Month* (New York: Harper and Brothers, 1848), 16.

It was on the Twenty-Second of February, 1847, just one hundred and fifteen years from the day when the Mother gazed upon her new-born child, that the same sun which had baptized their faces with tender light, shone over a far different scene.

It was sunset among the mountains of Mexico.

Wild and rugged mountains were those, which rose against the clear winter sky, terrible ravines yawned in the light, dreary and inhospitable wastes wearied the eye, with their desert loneliness. It looked—that desolate view—like the Chaos of a former world.

Through these colossal steeps, hideous with piles of rock, tossed into the sky in every fantastic variety of form, wound a narrow defile.

It was the road from Buena Vista—a hacienda, or mansion yonder on those northern hills,—to Agua Nueva, some miles to the South.[2]

To the left of this defile, the valley of cliffs is broken by ridges, stretching away, peak on peak, until they walled in by the colossal mountain, in the east. On the right of the defile, deep gullies yawn in the light, their almost perpendicular sides rough with rocks, glowing redly in the light of the winter sun.

And on those ridges, stretching away toward the eastern mountain—each ridge separated from the other, by a hideous ravine—and above those gullies, breaking the valley, into every chaotic shape, to the right of the defile, arrayed in battle order, you behold an army of four thousand men.

Their arms glitter in the light, with the dark mountain waste all around them. And between their regiments and companies, the ravines darken; among their ranks, huge granite rocks arise; they are extended, at intervals to the right and to the left of the defile, masses of men, horses, cannon and steel, broken by columns of shadow.

---

2   Agua Nueva is a village approximately thirty miles south of Buena Vista in the Mexican state of Coahuila.

In their midst—you see him yonder, on the ridge that towers directly to the left of the defile—sits an old man on his grey steed, his right leg carelessly crossed over the pommel of his saddle, while his plain brown coat, and unpretending military cap, are distinctly revealed in the light of the setting sun.

His bronzed face, warms with a deep glow, as his grey eyes traverse that wilderness of Mountains to the south.

The foe is there; Waterloo never beheld, gathered in one view, a more beautiful or terrible array.

As far as eye can see, the wilderness is one dense mass of men and horses, with cannon glooming in the intervals of their firm ranks, and steel blazing over their heads.

The setting sun lights up that quivering mass of steel, with a red glow. You see it blazing everywhere. Yonder, up the mountain side, it shines, circle of steel, piled on glittering circle, until that mass of rugged rock, flames like an immense altar, lighted for some Demon Festival. From the depths of the ravine, those glittering points, burst into the sunset, and far down the valley of ridges and gullies, rank on rank, column on column, regiment on regiment, that dense and formidable array seems to grow larger, blacker, brighter, as it melts into twilight distance. Twenty thousand men are there, upon the mountains, and in the ravines, arrayed in battle order.

It looks like the army of a Persian despot, so gaily flutters its innumerable red flags, from their flag-staffs of sharpened steel, so far, so wide it grows into space, so triumphantly it looks down, upon the little army, arrayed upon these northern ridges.

Yonder, on that solitary ridge, towering some hundred yards to the left of the defile—one long wave of bayonets tossing tremulously beneath him—behold the soul of this immense mass. In the centre of a circle, formed by the gorgeous costumes of his officers, behold, mounted on a dark charger, a man, whose breast, blazing with stars and orders, cannot divert your eye, from the melancholy grandeur of his face. His head is uncovered. His strongly defined profile, is marked upon the sunset sky. There is intellect in every line of his bold forehead; his mouth, wears an expression of almost painful melancholy, his dark eye, shines with deep and steady light.

As his olive cheek, glows in the sunset, while his eye roves over the legions of his twenty thousand men, can you call to mind his past life? By turns, President, Dictator, Exile, for twenty years and more, the great impulse, of his country's destiny; now lording in a royal state, in his Palace, reared upon the very spot, where stood, Montezuma's luxurious home; now looking with tiger-like ferocity upon the corses of slaughtered Alamo; again a miserable outcast, resorting to opium, for oblivion of his defeat, by a few hundred Texan hunters—behold the Man of Mexico, covered as he is with stars, and bearing the marks of battle, in his maimed limb—Antonio Lopez Santa Anna.

But a few months ago, sitting in the Havanna theatre, he smiled carelessly at the dance and song, and with his young wife by his side, did not seem to think, that among the nations of the earth, there was a land, called Mexico.[3]

Now—upon these wintry mountains, some thousand feet above the sea—with twenty thousand men, one irresistable mass of horse and foot, he proudly surveys plain Zachary Taylor, and his four thousand volunteers.

What does it mean, this terrible, this sublime spectacle?

The same power which brought Santa Anna from his place of exile in Havana, stripped Zachary Taylor of his veterans after the three day's fight of Monterey, and left him, to retreat or die.

---

3   In May, 1845, Santa Anna was deposed by General Paredes and exiled to Havana. His exile ended in December, 1846, when the Mexican congress appointed him president. Jeffrey Dixon and Meredith Sarkees, *Guide to Intra-state War: An Examination of Civil Wars, 1816–2014* (Los Angeles: Sage, 2016), 45.

Let us behold the array of the great old man.

Yonder, above the defile, frowns Captain Washington's[4] battery.—WASHINGTON? Yes, it is a glorious omen! On the 22nd of February, the Name and the Blood of the Continental General, are here!—The crests of the ridges on the left and to the rear, are occupied by one company and three regiments.[5] There you may see the First and Second Regiments of Illinois, with their commanders, Harden[6] and Bissell[7]; a company of Texans under Captain Connor[8]; the Second Regiment of Kentucky, headed by M'Kee. All volunteers, commanded by volunteers. All citizen soldiers, summoned from their fire-sides, by the war-cry of Zachary Taylor. And amid that crowd of gallant men you distinguish one manly form, and chivalric face, shown distinctly in the level sunlight. The blood of a great man throbs in that soldier's veins; his name is Henry Clay.[9]

On the extreme left, beneath the shadow of the mountain, behold the mounted men of Arkansas, with their leader, Colonel Yell,[10] and the cavalry of Kentucky, with their commander Humphrey Marshall.[11] Two regiments of men, horses and scimitars.

The reserve, you see it yonder, on the hills to the rear, a gallant band, formed of the Indiana Brigade, under Brigadier Lane,[12] its two regiments commanded by Colonels Bowles[13] and Lane—the Mississippi Riflemen, with their leader Colonel Davis,[14] all heroes of Monterey—May of Resaca de la Palma, with his dragoons, side by side, and another squadron under Captain Steen[15]—the cannon of Bragg[16] and Sherman[17] completes the array.

These men, with but few exceptions are untried soldiers. Yesterday Zachary Taylor, retreated from Agua Nueva, (some few miles to the south,) and on these hills, he has determined to meet the twenty thousand men, and thirty two pieces of cannon, in battle.

4   John Macrae Washington (1798–1853) graduated from West Point and fought in the First and Second Seminole Wars (1816–1819, 1835–1842). After, he taught at West Point until the U.S.-Mexico War. During the war he served under Brigadier General John Ellis Wool as leader of the 4th U.S. Artillery Regiment. After the war he became the governor of Saltillo, Texas. Washington went on to serve as the military governor of the New Mexico Territory. In 1853, while en route to California in rough seas, he was thrown from the deck and drowned. Spencer C. Tucker, *The Encyclopedia of the Mexican-American War: A Political, Social, and Military History*, vol. 1 (Santa Barbara: ABC-CLIO, 2013), 720, 721.

5   Taylor positioned these men and their units strategically with the aim to "paralyze the artillery and cavalry of the enemy." Major General Zachary Taylor to William L. Marcy, Secretary of War, March 6, 1847, accessed October 17, 2018, http://www.dmwv.org/mexwar/docs/bvista.htm.

6   John J. Hardin (1818–1847) was a lawyer, politician, and colonel of the 1st Regiment, Illinois Volunteer Infantry. Harden was killed during the battle of Buena Vista. Franklin William Scott, *Newspapers and Periodicals of Illinois 1814–1879* (Springfield: Illinois State Historical Library, 1910), 203.

7   William Henry Bissell (1811–1860) was a doctor, lawyer, and politician who served during the Battle of Buena Vista as colonel to the 2nd Regiment, Illinois Volunteer Infantry. Robert Howard, *Mostly Good and Competent Men* (Springfield: Illinois State Historical Society, 1988), 397.

8   Patrick Edward Connor (1820–1891), first lieutenant under Colonel Bissell in the Battle of Buena Vista, reached the rank of brigadier general for his efforts in the Powder River Expedition. Thomas F. Prendergast, *Forgotten Pioneers: Irish Leaders in Early California* (Honolulu: University Press of the Pacific, 2001), 250–257.

9 Henry Clay Jr. (1811–1847) was the third son of U.S. Senator Henry Clay. After graduating from West Point, Clay became a lawyer and politician. When the war with Mexico began, he entered the U.S. Army as lieutenant colonel of the 2nd Regiment Kentucky Volunteers. He died in the Battle of Buena Vista. James C. Klotter, *Henry Clay: The Man Who Would Be President* (New York: Oxford University Press, 2018), 332.

10 Archibald Yell (1797–1847) was a judge, governor of Arkansas, and soldier. Yell fought in the War of 1812, the 1st Seminole War, and the U.S.-Mexico War. At the Battle of Buena Vista Colonel Yell led the Arkansas Volunteers and was killed in action. *The New Age Magazine* 14, no. 1 (January 1916): 533–557.

11 Humphrey Marshall (1812–1872) graduated from West Point and fought in the Black Hawk War, achieved the rank of colonel, and led the 1st Kentucky Cavalry during the Battle of Buena Vista. After the war, he became a congressman and the minister to China. During the Civil War, Marshall achieved the rank of brigadier general in the Confederate Army. John E. Kieber, *The Kentucky Encyclopedia* (Lexington: University of Kentucky Press, 1992), 610.

12 James Henry Lane (1814–1866) fought in the Battle of Buena Vista as the brigadier general to the 3rd and 4th Indian Regiment. After the battle he became a U.S. senator and, later, a Union general during the Civil War. Lane committed suicide in 1866. Ian Michael Spurgeon, *Man of Douglas, Man of Lincoln: The Political Odyssey of James Henry Lane* (Columbia: University of Missouri Press, 2008).

13 William A. Bowles (1799–1873) served as a politician from Indiana and served as a colonel of the 2nd Indiana Regiment during the Battle of Buena Vista. Samuel Ryan Curtis, *Mexico Under Fire: Being the Diary of Samuel Ryan Curtis, 3rd Ohio Volunteer Regiment*

At eleven o'clock there came from Santa Anna, a messenger of peace, bearing a white flag. He found the old General quietly seated on his grey steed, and placed in his hand the letter of Santa Anna. The Mexican General announced that he was surrounded by twenty thousand men, and summoned him to surrender.[18]

The reply of Zachary Taylor, has already become battle scripture in the pages of history. Its succinctness and brevity, are eminently refreshing:

Head Quarters, Army of Occupation.
Near Buena Vista, Feb. 22, 1847.

S<small>IR</small>—In reply to your note of this date, summoning me to surrender my forces at discretion, I beg leave to say, that I decline acceding to your request.

With high respect, I am Sir,
Your obedient Servant,
Z. T<small>AYLOR</small>.[19]

The day is now wearing toward its close, and a pillar of white smoke suddenly towers upward, along yonder mountain. It is the Shroud of Buena Vista, enfolding the first dead men of the battle. Beneath that cloud, the men of Kentucky, Indiana and Arkansaw, are engaged: you see their arms glitter on the mountain side; they hurl the Mexican light troops before them, and the battery of W<small>ASHINGTON</small> whirling from the centre to the left, pours its thunder, upon the flying foe.

The battle has begun, but night closes in, and the voice of the fight, is stilled until the rising of the sun.

The Americans slumber upon the field, without fires—although the air is bitter cold, and slumber upon their arms. Through the midnight shadow the mountains rise, girdling the slumbering heroes with their wall of rock, mantling the glitter of their arms, with immense masses of shadow.

Zachary Taylor, is summoned to the north, from Buena Vista to Saltillo.[20] General Minon,[21] with a formidable mass of cavalry, hangs round that town, like a cloud, ready to burst upon it, with a hurricane of flame and steel. The veteran WOOL[22] remains at Buena Vista, and the Mississippi regiment, with the second squadron of dragoons, guard old Taylor on his way. By his side, he beholds Colonel Davis, and Lieutenant Colonel May, brilliant with the glory of Monterey and Resaca de la Palma.

When Zachary Taylor, came to the field of Buena Vista, on the morning of the twenty-third; the scene, that awaited him, was stirring and sublime.

The day had dawned in cloudless beauty, the mountain tops, breaking without a frown, into the serene sky. But now, Buena Vista, lay wrapt in one dense mass of smoke, that hung from mountain to mountain, over a space of three miles. The roofs of the Hacienda, from which the field takes its name, were hidden in cloud and flame. Under the shadow of that pall, Santa Anna hurled the terror of his force, upon the American volunteers, and bathed the mountain sides, in fire.

From rank to rank, hurried the heroic Wool, his breast exposed to the enemy's deadliest fire, his horse, seen glancing through the clouds of battle. His tall athletic form, rose proudly in every part of the field, as with his hawk eye, gleaming with battle light, he hurried his men to the charge.

When riding from Saltillo, old Taylor came to Buena Vista, and reined his grey, on the ridge, near the defile, this was the sight which he saw:

During the American Military Occupation of Northern Mexico 1846–1847 (Fort Worth: Texas Christian University Press, 1994), 272.

14 Jefferson Davis (1808–1889) graduated from West Point and served as second lieutenant of the 1st Infantry Regiment. During the Battle of Buena Vista, Davis achieved the rank of colonel and led the 1st Volunteer Mississippi Rifles alongside his father-in-law, Zachary Taylor. After the war, Davis became a senator and served as the President of the Confederate States of America. William James Cooper. *Jefferson Davis, American* (New York: Vintage Books, 2001).

15 Captain Enoch Steen (1800–1880) was a western explorer and military officer. He led two companies under General John Ellis Wool during the Battle of Buena Vista, where he was injured. Steen received a promotion to major on the field at Buena Vista and led troops for the Union during the U.S. Civil War. Edwin Russell Sweeney, *Mangas Coloradas, Chief of the Chiricahua Apaches* (Norman: University of Oklahoma Press, 1998), 498.

16 Captain Braxton Bragg (1817–1876) was a West Point graduate. During the Battle of Buena Vista, he was promoted to the rank of lieutenant colonel. Bragg served as a Confederate general during the U.S. Civil War. Earl J. Hess, *Braxton Bragg: The Most Hated Man of the Confederacy* (Chapel Hill: University of North Carolina Press, 2016).

17 Thomas Sherman (1813–1879) was a West Point graduate who fought in the Second Seminole War (1835–1842) and was promoted to major at the Battle of Buena Vista. Sherman served as a Union officer during the Civil War. John S.D. Eisenhower, *So Far from God: The U.S. War with Mexico, 1846–1848* (Norman: University of Oklahoma Press, 2000), 183–185, 190.

18 According to a translation in the *Natchez Weekly Courier* dated April 21, 1847, Santa Anna's letter read, "You are surrounded by

twenty thousand men, and cannot, in any human probability avoid suffering a rout and being cut to pieces with your troops.... I wish to save you from a catastrophe ... [and] give you this notice in order that you may surrender at discretion, under the assurance that you will be treated with the consideration belonging to the Mexican character." *Natchez Weekly Courier,* April 21, 1847, 3, col. 4.
19 This letter was widely reprinted in the national press.
20 Saltillo is about ten miles north of Buena Vista in the Mexican state of Coahuila.
21 Jose Vicente Minon (1802–1878) was born in Caldiz, Spain, where he joined the military, but later switched sides and helped Mexico fight for independence. During the Battle of Buena Vista, he was out-numbered and overrun. Santa Anna lambasted Minon in the press, stating the loss at Buena Vista was Minon's fault. Tucker, *Encyclopedia of the Mexican-American War,* 431.
22 John Ellis Wool (1784–1869) fought in the war of 1812 before the U.S.-Mexico War. Due to his experience, he trained 10 volunteer regiments for Zachary Taylor. Wool earned the rank of major during the conflict and continued his military career by becoming the commander of the U.S. Army Department of Virginia during the Civil War. Wool served 51 years in the U.S. Army. Ibid., 735, 736.
23 John Paul Jones O'Brien (1818–1859) was a West Point graduate and served in the Second Seminole War (1835–1842). During the U.S.-Mexico War he was first lieutenant under Captain John M. Washington and led the 4th U.S. Artillery Regiment. O'Brien's troops held their positions during the Battle of Buena Vista, for which he was promoted to major. After the war, O'Brien earned the rank of captain and served out his military career in Texas until his death. Ibid., 471.
24 George Lincoln held the rank of captain and led the 8th Infantry Regiment during

Frowning upon the left flank, the Mexicans appeared in overwhelming force, upon the mountain side, their bayonets and lances, shining away, one dazzling flood of steel, until they were lost in the distance.

While that belt of glittering arms was seen, girdling the mountain's base, they poured their hail of copper and iron from every ridge, and wrapt the Americans in a sheet of flame. The carnage was horrible. One brave captain—O'Brien[23]—saw every man and horse, around his cannon, crushed with the same fire, into dust. The second Indiana regiment, broke their ranks, and fled towards the Hacienda.

In vain the gallant Lincoln,[24] a brave descendant of the Revolutionary hero, endeavors to stay their flight! In vain their own commander, Colonel Bowles, with a small and faithful band, who defy the panic and the foe, places himself in the path, waves the flag of their Regiment, beseeches them to turn and meet the Mexicans with firm ranks and woven steel!

Seized with one of those sudden panics, which render powerless, the bravest armies, they retreat and do not pause in their flight, until the Hacienda of Buena Vista breaks on their eyes.

Meanwhile the battery of Washington, threatened by a steady column, advancing along the centre, did its work, upon their ranks, and scattered their beautiful array, into the shadows of the ravines.

Colonel Bissell's men, the second Illinois regiment—you behold them yonder upon the broad plateau, beneath the mountain—perform deeds worthy of the days of old. While Sherman's battery, aids them in the bloody task, they face that sea of flame and steel, rushing upon them, from the mountain side—fight step by step, as they are driven backward—wave their banner and rush to the certain death once more.

At this moment, in fact, the army of Santa Anna, have poured their overwhelming force from the mountain side, turned the American flank, and girdled our rear, with one dense mass of lance and bayonet.

The moment is critical, the danger imminent. Zachary Taylor feels that the arm which shielded him, at Palo Alto, Resaca de la Palma and Monterey, will not fail him now.

At his word, Colonel Davis, with his Mississippians, hurries to the left, and the deadly rifles of the west, mow down the advancing Mexicans by hundreds. At his word, Captain Bragg, thunders away, confronts the formidable horde, as it pours from the mountain side, and pours his grape, into their closely-woven ranks. The second Kentucky Regiment, with its commander McKee, fought side by side with Hardin and his Illinois volunteers. Amid the very thickest of the fight, the Second Henry Clay, was seen, urging his countrymen forward, as he led the way, and rushed into the Mexican battle, sword in hand.

As we gaze upon this fight of the mountain and ravine, we see the Mississippi Regiment, completely encircled by the Mexicans, who only pour onward, the faster, as their ranks are blocked with dead. The third Indiana regiment, headed by Col. Lane, come rushing to its aid, and while Sherman and Bragg pour their blaze from the plateau, a glittering bolt of battle, with young May, dashing in its van, separates from the American army, and sweeps toward the mountain, where the Mexican lances flash like a shower of meteors.

In that battle bolt, you may distinguish the regular dragoons, Pike's[25] Arkansaw horse, and the cavalry of Kentucky and Arkansaw headed by Marshall and Yell. The whole fire of the American army was now concentrated upon the base of the mountain: the dead bodies of the Mexicans began to bridge the smaller gullies, and flood them with a red torrent.

the Battle of Buena Vista. *The Mexican War and Its Heroes: Being a Complete History of the Mexican War* (Philadelphia: Grigg, Elliot and Co., 1849), 266.

25 Albert Pike (1809–1891), a school teacher who "became a well-regarded attorney, poet, planter, and newspaper publisher," joined the military in 1836. He served as a captain under Brigadier General Wool at the Battle of Buena Vista. On July 19, 1847, Colonel John S. Roanne challenged Pike to a duel due to Pike's criticism of Roane's "poor performance" during the battle. Neither man was wounded in the duel. Tucker, *Encyclopedia of the Mexican-American War*, 508.

As the smoke, ascending pile on pile, from the ravine to the mountain, rolled aside, old Taylor saw the work go steadily on, and saw the Banner of the Stars, flash beautifully where the spears and bayonets, joined in their deadliest conflict.

The battle whirls away toward the Hacienda of Buena Vista: you see the smoke tossing above its roof: Santa Anna would possess the train of the American army. But May comes gallantly to the rescue, and Reynolds[26] with two pieces of cannon, meet the lancers, as they come, and hews them into dust, as they fly.

Yell, of Arkansas and Marshall of Kentucky are there, battling with the Mexicans, horse to horse, and sword to sword. That firm column is broken, one portion rushes by the Hacienda, toward the opposite mountain, while the other retracing its steps, seeks to gain the mountain on our left.

As they receive the fire, pouring from every point of the field, near the Hacienda, a brave soldier, creeps from beneath his dead horse, springs on his feet, his lower jaw, torn away, by the blow of a murderous lance. For a moment he stands gazing upon the divided array of the Mexicans, and he then falls to rise no more. The gallant YELL had fought his last battle.

Look, through the mists of the battle, and behold that band of Mexicans, at least one thousand strong, crowded in the narrow gorge, which is raked by the American cannon. In vain they attempt to fly; their ranks become entangled; they are crushed into the bed of the ravine; a wild and affrighted Mob, scatters through the pass; where a moment ago, was but one glittering array of steel, now is only a dark and hideous Golgotha.[27]

It was at this moment, that the old General, calmly surveying the fight,—his brown coat, visible from every part or the field, a mark for the

---

26 John Fulton Reynolds (1820–1863) graduated from West Point in 1841 and was a career military officer. During the Battle of Buena Vista, Reynolds flanked Santa Anna, forcing him to withdraw. His efforts earned him a promotion to the rank of major. After the war, Reynolds fought for the Union in the Civil War. Ibid., 556.

27 "Golgotha" is a reference to the "place of the skull" where Jesus was crucified, a hill outside the walls of Jerusalem used by the Romans for executions during the first century AD.

musquets and cannon of the enemy—was surprised by the appearance of another messenger from Santa Anna, bearing a White Flag.

"His Excellency General Santa Anna," said the officer bowing—

"Desires to know, what General Taylor wants?"

"Wants?" echoed the veteran—"I want him to surrender!"

This was bold language from the leader of four thousand volunteers, to the General of twenty thousand brave Mexicans.

Willing however, even amid that hour of havoc, to hear the propositions of the Mexican Chief, he silenced the American fire. At his command, the second General of the day, the brave WOOL, rode toward the Mexican line, seeking an interview with Santa Anna, but was greeted with a treacherous fire. The White Flag, was but a trick of the Mexican, to save the portion of his force, which had been divided near the Hacienda.

Amid the clouds which rolled to the right, young CRITTENDEN[28] of Kentucky, a volunteer, for that day, near the person of Taylor, rode forward, with a summons to the commander of that immense body of Mexican cavalry, which had been cut off from the main body of the Mexican army.

He summoned the commander of this force to surrender, in the name of Taylor, and was led blind-folded, through ravine and gully, until a loud flourish of drums and trumpets, announced that he was in the presence of Santa Anna.

"Your mission?"

—"To demand the surrender of a portion of your force, separated by our soldiers, from your army."

"But Taylor"—said the Mexican Chief, in abrupt tones: his words were translated by an officer, who stood by his side—"What does he mean to do? Surrounded by twenty thousand men, he must surrender?"

28 Thomas L. Crittenden (1819–1893) served as a volunteer aide to Zachary Taylor during the U.S.-Mexico War. *The Mexican War and Its Heroes*, 74.

29 This is a loose translation of *molon labe*, or "Come and take them," from Plutarch's *Sayings of the Spartans*, spoken by King Leonidas at Thermopylae in response to Xerxes' demand, "Hand over your arms." Plutarch, *Moralia*, vol. III (Chicago: Loeb Classical Library edition, 1931), 350. "Come and take it" was also displayed on a Texas flag at the Battle of Gonzales (1835), the first battle of the Texas War for Independence. William C. Davis, *Lone Star Rising* (New York: Simon and Schuster, 2017), 124–146.

30 This anecdote was widely reprinted in the national press soon after the battle. Its origins are likely a report by Second Lieutenant John J.C. Bibbs for the *New Orleans Picayune*, dated March 22, 1847. *Vicksburg Weekly Sentinel*, March 31, 1847, 1, col. 2. John J.C. Bibbs fought at the battles of Palo Alto, Resaca de la Palma, and Monterey, and was forced to resign from the army having "forgotten his pledge, [and] got on a frolic." Bibbs likely served as a reporter for the *Picayune* thereafter and followed Taylor's forces as a correspondent. George W. Cullum, *Biographical Register of the Officers and Graduates of the United States Military Academy* (Boston: Houghton, Mifflin, 1891), vol. II, 208; Philip Norbourne Barbour, *Journal* (New York: G.P Putnam's Sons, 1936), 87.

31 Vaughan was a young officer who died during the Battle of Buena Vista. *The Mexican War and its Heroes*, 67.

Francis T. Bryan (1823–1917) graduated from West Point in 1842. During the Battle of Buena Vista, he served as the first Lieutenant of the Topographical Engineers attached to O'Brien's section of Washington's battery. Bryan retired from the army in 1861 at the rank of captain and resided in St. Louis, Missouri until his death. *Forty-Sixth Annual Reunion of the Association of the Graduates of the United States Military Academy at West Point, New York* (Saginaw: Sermann & Pethers, Inc., 1915), 67.

Then it was, that this young Kentuckian, born of the land of Boone, and Taylor and Clay, felt the blood rush to his cheek, as looking the Mexican Dictator in the eye, he uttered the phrase, which has already, been linked with the '*Come and take me*!'[29] of ancient story:

"GENERAL TAYLOR NEVER SURRENDERS!"[30]

But why need we picture, the course of those ten hours of Buena Vista, in all their details of agony and glory? Where twenty thousand men, advancing around the base of mountains, and dashing from ravines, level their forest of steel, their volcano of flame, upon a band, only four thousand strong, you may be sure, that the carnage is horrible.

But when we remember, the wild and broken nature of the ground, that valley of ridges and chasms, three miles in extent, almost impracticable, for artillery or cavalry, it becomes plain, that there was much of the silent butchery of bayonet to lance, and sword to sword, and breast to breast.

To speak of all the heroes of the band of Buena Vista, as they deserve, would fill a volume. Their conduct, forever frowns into oblivion, the silly lie, uttered by silly men, that the Citizen Soldier, is not to be depended upon in the hour of need. These brilliant names, were that day, painted in blood, on the American Banner—Davis, McKee, Clay, Marshall, Hardin, Yell and Vaughan, Lincoln, Pike, Lane and Wool, O'Brien and Bryan, Bissell and Sherman, Bragg and Reynolds, Steen and McCullouch, Bowles and Gorman, Kilburn and Rucker, Monroe and Morrison, Brent, Whiting and Couch; Thomas, French, Shover, Donaldson, May, Washington, Taylor[31]—all brave, some wounded, some killed, some of the regular, others of the Volunteer force, but all glorious, as were a thousand other heroes, with the halo of Buena Vista.

From the scenes of the bloody day, let us select but two, as memorable examples of the stern daring of Taylor and his men.

———

Mounted on his grey steed with one leg crossed over the saddle, the old Man beholds the Mexicans emerge from yonder ravine, their numbers, marked by their lances and bayonets.

Near Zachary Taylor, glooms the battery of Captain Bragg; a cool soldier, who never fires, until he sees the color of the enemy's faces. On come the Mexicans—on, with their lances flashing, their war-horses, beating the earth, with a sound like thunder, their entire array, closing in the prospect, with one dazzling battle barricade.

Taylor's grey eye begins to look, as it looked at Palo Alto!

Then the battery speaks out, and you may read the faces of a hundred dying men by its light. Do you see that glimpse of clear sky through their ranks? Do you hear the horrible howl of horse and man, go up to God together?

Taylor bends forward; he sees those columns quiver, but still the moment is one of absorbing interest. That cannister, hurled from the muzzle of Bragg's cannon is deadly—as they press on, with but a few yards between, it crashes them down as though a bolt from heaven had blasted their flags and lances into blood.

Still they come on; the old man can maintain his silence no longer; leaning forward, with every vein in his bronzed face glowing and swelling with the impulse of that terrible hour, he lays his hand on the shoulder of the undaunted Captain—

Ben McCulloch (1811–1862) grew up a protégé and neighbor of Davy Crockett. McCulloch fought in the battle for Texas Independence and earned the rank of first lieutenant. During the Battle of Buena Vista he commanded John Hays' first Texas Mounted Rifle Regiment. Later, he was assigned to Zachary Taylor as a scout. Under Taylor his company became known as "the spy company." Tucker, *Encyclopedia of the Mexican-American War,* 393.

Willis A. Gorman (1816–1876) enlisted into the army in 1846 as a private, and by the Battle of Buena Vista, had achieved the rank of major and led a rifle regiment. After he retired from service he practiced law in St. Paul, Minnesota. *The Mexican War and Its Heroes,* 61.

Charles Lawrence Kilburn (1819–1899) graduated from West Point in 1842 and served as an officer in the U.S. Army. At the Battle of Buena Vista, he achieved the rank of captain. *Thirtieth Annual Reunion of the Association of the Graduates of the United States Military Academy* (Saginaw: Sermann & Pethers, Inc., 1899), 146–148.

Daniel Henry Rucker (1812–1910) served during the Battle of Buena Vista and earned the rank of captain. Michael Robert Patterson, "Daniel Henry Rucker," Arlington National Cemetery, accessed October 18, 2018, http://www.arlingtoncemetery.net.

John Monroe was in charge of Zachary Taylor's "sea tail," which consisted of quartermasters, engineers, artillery, and others "that would travel by water." According to various sources, Major Monroe was in charge of supply movement. Eisenhower, *So Far from God,* 52.

Alexander Ferguson Morrison (1804–1857) served as a politician and editor before becoming a major in the U.S.-Mexico War. He served under Zachary Taylor and sent correspondence informing individuals about the progress of the war. During the

Battle of Buena Vista, he was severely injured and blinded. Ida Morrison (Murphy) Shirk, *Descendants of Richard and Elizabeth (Ewen) Talbott,* (Baltimore: Day Printing, 1927), 17.

Thomas Lee Brent (1810–1858) graduated from West Point in 1835. He served as second lieutenant in the Second Seminole War (1835–1842). He was promoted to the rank of captain for his service as quartermaster. Bill Thayer, "Class of 1835," *Cullum's Register* online, vol. 1, 628, accessed October 18, 2018, http://penelope.uchicago.edu/Thayer/E/home.html.

Henry M. Whiting (1821–1853) served in the Battle of Buena Vista as Assistant Quarter Master. After the war he held the rank of lieutenant of artillery until he died at Fort Brown, Texas. Charles Lanman, *The Red Book of Michigan: A Civil, Military and Biographical History* (Detroit: E.B. Smith & Company, 1871), 497.

Darius N. Couch (1822–1897) was promoted to first lieutenant during the Battle of Buena Vista. He became a major general in the Union Army during the Civil War. Tucker, *Encyclopedia of the Mexican-American War,* 178.

George H. Thomas (1816–1870) graduated from West Point in 1840 and earned the brevet rank of major duing the Battle of Buena Vista. After the U.S.-Mexico War he fought for the Union during the U.S. Civil War and became known as "the rock of Chickamauga." Freeman Cleaves, *Rock of Chickamauga: The Life of General George H. Thomas* (Norman: University of Oklahoma Press, 1948).

Samuel Gibbs French (1818–1910) graduated from West Point in 1843. During the Battle of Buena Vista, he was shot in the thigh while mounting his horse. After the U.S.-Mexico War, he held the rank of brigadier general in the Confederate Army during the Civil War. Tucker, *Encyclopedia of the Mexican-American War,* 252.

"A little more grape, Captain Bragg!"[32]

He says it in a whisper, but the Soldier hears him, and feels that voice stir his blood like a trumpet peal. Turning away with a flushed forehead, he obeys the mild request of his General, and as the Mexicans come up to the muzzles once more, he speaks to them with grape!

When the smoke clears away, you see the edge of the ravine lined with dead men, and the arms of the retreating Mexicans, glittering from the shades below.

———

It was near the setting of the sun, when the Man of Palo Alto, Resaca de la Palma, and Monterey, saw the clouds come down on the last charge of Buena Vista, that a scene, worthy of the days of Washington, closed the day in glory.

Do you behold that dark ravine, deep sunken between these precipitous banks? Here no sunlight comes, for these walls of rock wrap the pass in eternal twilight. Withered trees grow between the masses of granite, and scattered stones make the bed of the ravine uncertain and difficult for the tread.

Hark! That cry, that rush like a mountain torrent bursting its barriers, and quick as the lightning flashes from darkness, the dismal ravine is bathed in red battle light. From its northern extremity, a confused band of Mexicans, an army in itself, come yelling along the pass, treading one another down as they fly, their banners, spears, horses and men, tossed together in inextricable confusion.

By thousands they rush into the shadows of the pass, their dark faces reddened by the sheeted blaze of musquetry. The caverns of the ravine sends back the roar of the panic, and the grey rocks are washed by their blood.

But the little band who pursues this army? Who are they? You may see in their firm heroic ranks, the volunteer costume of Illinois and Kentucky. At their head, urging his men with shouts, rides the gallant M'Kee, by his side young Henry Clay, that broad forehead, which reminds you of his father, bathed in the glare, as his sword quivers on high ere it falls to kill. There too, a wild figure, red with his own blood and the blood of Mexican foes, his uniform rent in tatters, his arm bared to the shoulder, striking terrible blows with his good sword—Hardin of Illinois, comes gallantly forward.

This small, but iron band, hurl the Mexicans from the heights into the ravine, and follow up the chase, far down into the eternal twilight of that mountain pass.

Look! As their musquetry streams its steady blaze, you would think that one ceaseless sheet of lightning bathed these rocks in flame!

Over the Mexicans, man and horse, hurled back in mad disorder, the Americans dash on their way, never heeding the overwhelming numbers of their foes, never heeding the palpitating forms beneath their feet, with bayonet, and rifle, and sword, they press steadily on, their well-known banner streaming evermore overhead.

The howl of the dying war-horse—hark! Does it not chill your blood to hear it? The bubbling cry of the wounded man, with the horse's hoof upon his mouth, trampling his face into a hideous wreck—does it not sicken your soul to hear it?

A hundred yards or more, into the pass the Americans have penetrated, when suddenly a young Mexican, rushing back upon their ranks, seizes the fallen flag of Anahuac, and dashes to his death!

William H. Shover (1814–1850) graduated from West Point in 1838 and upon graduation fought in the Second Seminole War (1835–1842). Shover was promoted to the rank of major for his valor at the Battle of Buena Vista. Bill Thayer, "Class of 1838," Cullum's *Register* online, vol. 1, 703, accessed October 18, 2018, http://penelope.uchicago.edu/Thayer/E/home.html.

James L. Donaldson (1814–1855) graduated from West Point in 1836 and served during the Second Seminole War. Donaldson was promoted to the rank of major during the Battle of Buena Vista, then served as quartermaster for the Union during the Civil War. Bill Thayer, "Class of 1836," Cullum's *Register* online, vol. 1, 637, accessed October 18, 2018, http://penelope.uchicago.edu/Thayer/E/home.html.

32 The quote itself is apocryphal and, according to another source, actually was, "Captain, Give them Hell." Ethan Allen Hitchcock, *Fifty Years in Camp and Field: Diary of Major-General Ethan Allen Hitchcock, U.S.A.* (New York: G.P. Putnam's Sons, 1909), 349.

To see him, young and beardless, a very boy, rush with his country's flag, with his bared breast, upon that line of sharp steel—it was a sight to stir cowards into manhood, and it shot into the Mexican hearts like an electric flame.

Even in their panic-stricken disorder, they turned; by hundreds they grasped their arms, and rolled in one long wave of lance and bayonet, upon the foe. Woe to the brave men of Illinois and Kentucky now! Locked in that deadly pass, a wall of infuriated Mexicans between them and that wall of rocks—above their heads, through every aperture among the cliffs, the blaze of musquets pouring a shower of bullets in their faces—wherever they turned, the long and deadly lance poised at their throats—it was a moment to think once of Home and die!

Those who survived that fearful moment, tell with shuddering triumph of the deeds of the three heroes—M'Kee, Hardin and Clay.

M'Kee, you see him yonder, with his shattered sword dripping blood, he endeavors to ward off the aim of those deadly lances, and fights on his knees when he can stand no longer, and then the combatants close over him and you see him no more.

Hardin, rose from a heap of slaughtered foes, his face streaming from its hideous lance wounds, and waved a Mexican flag, in triumph, as his life blood gushed in a torrent over his muscular form. That instant, the full light of battle was upon his mangled face. Then, flinging the captured flag to a brother soldier, he shouted—"Give it to her, as a memorial of Buena Vista! My Wife!" It was his last word. Upon his bared breast, the fury of ten lances rushed, and the horses' hoofs trampled him into the heap of dead.

But most sad and yet most glorious of all, it was, to see the death of the Second HENRY CLAY! You should have seen him, with his back against yonder rock, his sword grasped firmly, as the consciousness that he bore a name that must not die ingloriously, seemed to fill his every vein, and dart a deadly fire from his eyes!

At that moment he looked like the old Man.

For his brow, high and retreating, with the blood-clotted hair waving back from its outline, was swollen in every vein, as though his Soul shone from it, ere she fled forever. Lips set, brows knit, hand firm—a circle of his men fighting round him—he dashed into the Mexicans, until his sword was wet, his arm weary with blood.

At last, with his thigh splintered by a ball, he gathered his proud form to its full height, and fell. His face, ashy with intense agony, he bade his comrades to leave him there to die. That ravine, should be the bed of his glory.

But gathering round him, a guard of breasts and steel—while two of their number bore him tenderly along—those men of Kentucky fought round their fallen hero, and as retreating step by step, they launched their swords and bayonets into the faces of the foe, they said with every blow—"Henry Clay!"

It was wonderful to see how that name nerved their arms, and called a smile to the face of the dying hero. How it would have made the heart of the old man of Ashland throb, to have heard his name, yelling as a battle cry, down the shadows of that lonely pass!

Along the ravine, and up this narrow path! The Hero bleeds as they bear him on, and tracks the way with his blood. Faster and thicker the Mexicans swarm—they see the circle around the fallen man, even see his pale face, uplifted, as a smile crosses it fading lineaments, and like a pack of wolves scenting the frozen traveller at dead of night, they come howling up the rocks, and charge the devoted band with one dense mass of bayonets.

33 According to a letter dated July 23, 1847 from Senator Henry Clay (1777–1852) to Thomas B. Stevenson, editor of the *Cincinnati Atlas*, Captain George Washington Cutter (1801–1865) "was among the persons who last spoke to … my lamented son" and "received from him a brace of pistols which he has safely delivered to me." Clay asked Stevenson to have a ring made in Cincinnati for Cutter with a piece of Henry Clay Jr.'s hair "placed in it." Henry Clay, *The Papers of Henry Clay*, vol. 10, ed. Melba Porter Hay (Lexington: University Press of Kentucky, 2015), 341.

Up and on! The light shines yonder, on the topmost rocks of the ravine.—It is the light of the setting sun. Old Taylor's eye is upon that rock, and there we will fight our way, and die in the old man's sight!

It was a murderous way, that path up the steep bank of the ravine! Littered with dead, slippery with blood, it grew blacker every moment with swarming Mexicans, and the defenders of the wounded hero, fell one by one, into the chasms yawning all around.

At last they reach the light, the swords and bayonets glitter in sight of the contending armies, and the bloody contest roars towards the topmost rock.

Then it was, that gathering up his dying frame—armed with supernatural vigor—young Clay started from the arms of his supporters, and stood with outstretched hands, in the light of the setting sun. It was a glorious sight which he saw there, amid the rolling battle clouds; Santa Anna's formidable array hurled back into ravine and gorge, by Taylor's little band! But a more glorious thing it was to see, that dying man, standing for the last time, in the light of that sun, which never shall rise for him again!

"Leave me!" he shrieked, as he fell back on the sod—"I must die and I will die here! Peril your lives no longer for me! Go! There is work for you yonder!"

The Mexicans crowding on, hungry for slaughter, left no time for thought. Even as he spoke, their bayonets, glistening by hundreds, were levelled at the throats of the devoted band. By the mere force of their overwhelming numbers, they crushed them back from the side of the dying Clay.

One, only lingered; a brave man, who had known the chivalric Soldier, and loved him long; he stood there, and covered as he was with blood, heard these last words:

"*Tell my Father how I died, and give him these pistols!*"[33]

Lifting his ashy face, into light, he turned his eyes, upon his comrade's face—placed the pistols in his hand—and fell back to his death.

That Comrade, with the pistols in his grasp, fought his way alone to the topmost rock of the path, and only once looked back. He saw, a quivering form, canopied by bayonets—he saw those outstretched hands grappling with points of steel—he saw a pale face lifted once, in the light, and then darkness, rushed upon the life of the young HENRY CLAY.[34]

Placing his hands behind his back, with his head on his breast, a tall old man, strode thoughtfully along the carpet, of his chamber. It was near the evening hour, and the blush of summer, was upon those woods and hills, which you may see through the uncurtained window.

Were you to meet this old man among ten thousand you would know him when you saw him again, and did you once behold that wide mouth, wreathe in a smile, that grey eye, fire with soul, that brow, high and relenting, glow with his heart, you would be very sure to love him.

But the voice, that rings from those lips, and swells from that chest—you should hear it, melt in pity, or hiss in scorn, or thunder forth the frenzy of a great soul!

Plainly clad in a dark dress, his face covered with the large wrinkles of seventy years, this old man, is thinking over his life. From a log hut into a Senate, from the arms of a widowed mother, into the love of a nation—an impressive life, wild, vivid startling, in on every line, with Genius.

But he is old now. Those grey hairs, tell of the coming on of the fast crowding years. The things of political strife, who loved the old man, as a miser loves a diamond, not on account of its pure and beautiful light, but

---

34   While much of Lippard's description here is fanciful, the death of Henry Clay, Jr. (1811–1847) was widely reported. One correspondent reported Clay "received five wounds—three of them gunshot, and two bayonet or lance wounds." *Louisville Daily Courier,* December 2, 1848, 2, col. 2. In an open letter to Clay's father, General Taylor wrote, "Manly and honorable in every impulse, … he gave every assurance that in the hour of need I could lean with confidence on his support." *Poughkeepsie Journal,* April 17, 1847, 2, col. 4.

from the great query—*how much will it bring?*—seem to have forgotten him. They have left him, to the Hearts of the People.

He paces the floor, and thinks of the days he has seen. Born in the Revolution, he grew up among its memories and saw the greatest among its great men.

Where are they now? Where the comrades of his earlier days? Where the compeers of his manhood? Where the most gallant of all his foes, whose soul, was warmed with fire, like that which gave his own heart its energy, its love and its fate, where the Man of New Orleans and the Hermitage?

There is grass above his grave.

Like the last column, standing erect, in a desert of ruins, the old man is left alone.

You may take my word for it, that his thoughts at this still hour, are strangled and contrasted in their hues, as the Ghosts of the Past, come crowding up to him, their faces looking sadly out from the shrouds of Memory.

The door is opened—a man appears, whose scarred face, and battle-worn figure, speak of the land of Mexico. You gaze upon the old man, as he motions the Stranger to a seat. He reads in that face, the volume of a sad yet heroic history. The Stranger does not move, but stands in the sunset glow, his nether lip, quivering faintly.

Advancing he endeavors to speak, but there is a spell on his tongue.

He can only place in the old man's hands a pair of pistols.

"Buena Vista!" he said, and turned away—unwilling to witness the tears and agony of the Father.

When he looked again—the twilight shadow was gathering fast—the old man, stood near the window gazing silently upon those eloquent memorials of Henry Clay, his Son.

We left the young hero, on his couch of stone, with twenty bayonets in his breast. That ravine, far down into the shadows, was lined with Mexicans, who came swarming towards, the topmost rock, glittering in the sunset glow. From every nook and cavern, they poured, like jackals to a warrior's corse, and—their overwhelming numbers, lighting the dark pass, with an endless blaze of steel—they advanced, to the topmost rock, and displayed in battle order, along the summit of the ridge.

But the battery yonder, stationed on a higher ridge—what does it mean? Washington and his sturdy cannoniers, are there! On the plateau, you see, the riflemen of Mississippi, stand shoulder to shoulder, with the volunteers of Indiana, with the cannon of Bragg, frowning through the intervals of their solid ranks.

The sun, was setting, and that firm array on the plateau, looked beautiful, as it stood prepared, to receive the last onset of the Mexican horde. Not a shout disturbed the silence, on the American side.

The Mexicans—you behold them by thousands, horse and foot, along the summit of this ridge—their banners, spears and bayonets, forming one glittering pageant, as far as eye can see.

Look on them well, in this moment of their glory, for a smoke rolls over the plateau, and the hurricane of death, is on its way!

When the smoke rolls up the Mountain side, you see the ridge heaped with dead, while far down the ravine, rushes the wreck of that formidable force, retreating from the last charge of Buena Vista.

Night on Buena Vista!

It was a sad, an awful night. The stars shone serenely on the mountain top, while all beneath was dim and dark. Through the gloom, at irregular intervals broke the glare of torch-light, only making the darkness more sad and dismal.

The Americans slept on their arms, without fire. The night was bitter cold; the moans of the dying, joined in chorus, from the depths of the ravines; and the living moved silently along, endeavoring to recognise, their own dead by the light of the stars.

From afar, the camp fires of Santa Anna's army, were seen, ever and again, as the battle vapor rolled aside. The Americans slept well, on their tired arms, but in the passes of the defile, upon the ridges and over the plateau, there were those who slumbered not.

The women of Mexico, soothing the agonies of the dying strangers!

Their garments, fluttered through the darkness, as they went to and fro, staunching the blood, placing to the feverish lip, the cup of water, bending beside the dying in prayer. Prayer in a strange tongue, prayer on a strange battle field, in a strange land—how it went to the hearts of the American soldiers, and made them remember the Homes, they should never see again!

There were others who slumbered not, but watched in anxious expectation, for the moment, when the conflict would begin again.

Amid the band of watchers, on the summit of yonder ridge, stands the old man, Zachary Taylor, his form dimly revealed in the light of the stars. Beside him his favorite grey; before him, the darkened field, yawning with chasms, he stands with uncovered head, his grey eyes uplifted to the sky. The morrow? What new danger will it bring, what new conflict in those hideous gorges of Buena Vista? Through the live-long night, the old warrior prepared for the worst.

The morning came at last, and looking to the south, far through the mountain pass, Zachary Taylor, beheld the retreating banners of Santa Anna.

Then it was, that sitting down amid the dead of that heroic fight, the old man penned his immortal despatch, and sent word to the Capitol, that with his four thousand untried volunteers, he had beaten Santa Anna and twenty thousand men, in the chasms of Buena Vista.[35]

That word rang through the American Union, like a voice from the grave of Washington, and thundering along the Gulf of Mexico, it nerved the arms of the brave men, who besieged the Castle of San Juan De Ulloa,[36] and found its glorious consummation in the fall of Vera Cruz[37] and route of CERRO GORDO.[38]

THE END

[35] Taylor's report to Secretary of War William Marcy, dated March 6, 1847 from U.S. headquarters at Agua Nueva, was widely reprinted in the press. See Major General Zachary Taylor to William L. Marcy, Secretary of War, March 6, 1847, accessed October 17, 2018, http://www.dmwv.org/mexwar/docs/bvista.htm.

[36] San Juan de Ulloa is a fortified island in the Gulf of Mexico that defended the city of Veracruz.

[37] General Winfield Scott (1786–1866) besieged Veracruz from March 9 to March 29, 1847, after an amphibious landing by U.S. forces.

[38] The Battle of Cerro Gordo took place on April 18, 1847 under the commands of Winfield Scott and Antonio López de Santa Anna.

To the Rev. C. Chauncey Burr:[39]

When first I determined to write the Legends of Mexico—ancient and modern, from the era of Scott and Taylor, back through the mists of ages, to Cortez and Montezuma—it was your generous sympathy with my purposes, that gave me strength and deepened my enthusiasm for the task. These works on Mexico—every one of which is intended to be distinct and separate, yet forming together, a complete book on the 'golden and bloody land'—I now dedicate to you, in this the first of the series, embodying the BATTLES OF TAYLOR. This Dedication, my tried friend, is no less a token of that brotherhood which I feel with you, than a tribute to your commanding Genius, which having ranked you among the first orators, will soon claim admiration for you, among the first Essayists of the Nineteenth Century.

> Your friend,
> GEORGE LIPPARD
> August 15, 1847
> Wissahikon

---

[39] Charles Chauncey Burr (1817–1883) was an essayist and political activist remembered as a friend of Edgar Allan Poe and a defender of Poe's legacy. Jay Hubbell notes that Burr was a Copperhead during the Civil War, a critic of abolitionists, the Union cause, and the policies of Abraham Lincoln. Jay B. Hubbell, "Charles Chauncey Burr: Friend of Poe," *PMLA* 69, no. 4 (September, 1954): 833–840. Burr officiated Lippard's marriage to Rose Newman in May, 1847.

Appendix

Contemporaneous Political Cartoons

Facing Page:

Strong, Thomas W., *Engraver. Union / Strong*, N.Y. ca. 1848. New York: Ackerman, 101 Nassau St. Poster. https://www.loc.gov/item/2003690755/.

Facing Page:
Jones, Alfred, Engraver, and Richard Caton Woodville. *Mexican News*. 1851. [?] Etching and Engraving. https://www.loc.gov/item/96509640/.

Facing Page:

N. Currier. *An available candidate–the one qualification for a Whig president.* United States, 1848. [New York: Nathaniel Currier] Lithograph. https://www.loc.gov/item/90708859/.

Facing Page:

Battle of Buena Vista. ca. 1848. Mar. 13. Print. https://www.loc.gov/item/2003654073/.

Facing Page:

N. Currier. *Battle of Monterey–The Americans forcing their way to the main plaza Sept. 23* Lith. by N. Currier. Mexico Monterrey, ca. 1846. New York: Published by N. Currier. Lithograph. https://www.loc.gov/item/90709071/.

Index

A

Aboukir, Battle of 84, 87
Adams, John 152
Adams-Onís Treaty xxvii
Adonai: The Pilgrim of Eternity xviii
Alexander I 84
Allen, George W. 66, 125–126
Ampudia, Pedro de 75, 100, 112, 134, 137, 142–143, 149, 155, 157, 158, 168–169
Anahuac 31, 38, 40, 59, 60, 68, 191
Anglo-Sikh War, First 3
Anti-Imperialist League xxxvii
Arista, Mariano 19–20, 54, 57, 65, 68, 74–75, 89, 96–103, 97, 111–116, 132, 134–136, 149
Army of Observation 15
Army of Occupation 12
Arnold, Benedict 149
Arrillaga, Mariano Paredes y 13
Austerlitz, Battle of 84–86, 87

B

Barbour, Philip Nathan 125–126
Battalon de Tampico 113, 125, 137–141
Beauregard, Pierre Gustave Toutant xxxii
Belknap, William Goldsmith 66–67, 125, 125–126
Beveridge, Albert xxxiv
Bibbs, John J.C. 188
Bissell, William Henry 181, 184, 188
Black Hawk War 14, 25
Blake, Jacob E. 67–68, 110–111
Bonaparte, Napoleon 3, 29, 68, 82–87, 103
Boone, Daniel 188
Bourbon, House of 83
Bowles, William A. 181, 182, 184, 188
Bragg, Braxton xxxii, 181, 183, 185, 188, 189–190, 197
Brandywine Creek, Battle of 9, 12, 66, 156
Brent, Thomas Lee 188, 190
Brotherhood of the Union x–xii, xix, 9
Brown, Jacob 15–17, 104, 132–133, 144–146
Bryan, Francis T. 188
Buchanan, James 125–126, 151

Buena Vista, Battle of x, xxix, xxxi, 6, 14, 177–200
Bunker Hill, Battle of 9, 152, 156
Burr, Charles Chauncey xi, 200
Bush, George W. xxxvii
Butler, William O. 155

C

Cadwalader, John 14, 62, 71, 93
Castle of Otranto, The xiii
Cerro Gordo, Battle of xxix, 7, 199
Chadbourne, Theodore Lincoln 62, 125–126
Charles I 18
Charles II 18
Chase, Salmon P. xxxi
Childs, Thomas 66–67
Churchill, William H. 66, 67, 80, 89, 90–93, 106–107
Churubusco, Battle of xxix
Civil War, American xxxi, xxxiii, 122, 123, 182, 183, 184, 186, 190, 191, 200
Civil War, English 18
Clay, Henry 148, 194, 195–196
Clay Jr., Henry 181, 182, 185, 188, 191–197, 195
Cochrane, Richard E. 135
Cold War xxxvi
Colt, Samuel 14
Connor, Patrick Edward 181
Contreras, Battle of xxix
Cortés, Hernán 4, 38–40, 200
Corwin, Thomas 9, 150
Costilla, Miguel Hidalgo y 40
Couch, Darius N. 188, 190
Crittenden, Thomas L. 187
Crockett, Davy 189
Cromwell, Oliver 18
Crosman, George H. 66–67
Currier, N. 206, 210
Cutter, George Washington 194

D

Dana, Napoleon Jackson Tecumseh 155
Davis, Jefferson xxxii, 181, 183, 185, 188

Democratic Review xxvi, xxvii, xxxiv
Donaldson, James L. 188, 191
Duncan, James 66–68, 70, 72, 79–80, 89, 97–103, 100, 106–107, 110, 114–116, 131–132, 136, 141–142, 144
Duyckinck, Evert Augustus xiv

F

Félix, José Miguel Ramón Adaucto Fernández y 75
Foltz, J.M. 92
Fontainebleau, Treaty of 82
Fort Brown 15–18, 35, 37, 45, 62, 63, 65, 92, 103–107, 111–113, 131–134, 141, 142–145, 152
Fort Texas. *See* Fort Brown
Four Freedoms xxxv
French, Samuel Gibbs 188, 190

G

Garland, John 66
German Confederation 3
Germantown, Battle of 172
Gist, Christopher 29
Global War on Terror xxxvii
Golgotha 6, 186
Gorman, Willis A. 188, 189
Gothic xii
Graham, William M. 123
Grant, Ulysses S. xxxii, xxxiii
Great Depression xxxv
Guadalupe Hidalgo, Treaty of xxx

H

Hancock, John 152
Hardin, John J. 181, 185, 188, 191–192
Hawkins, Edgar 132–134, 144
Hawthorne, Nathaniel xiii
Hays, John Coffee "Jack" 14, 125–126, 189
Holy Roman Empire 3
Hooker, Joe xxxii
Huamantla, Battle of 14

I

Inez 27–60
Inge, Zebulon M.P. 121–122, 124
Iraq, invasion of xxxvii
Iraq War xxxvii

J

Jackson, Andrew xxvii, 14, 116–119, 120, 148
Jackson, Thomas "Stonewall" xxxii
Jefferson, Thomas xxv–xxvii, 146
Jesus 31, 32, 39, 75, 155, 158
Jones, Alfred 204
Jordan, C.D. 125–126

K

Kansas-Nebraska Act xxxi
Kelly, Patrick 92
Kennan, George xxxvi
Ker, Croghan 66, 67, 79, 131
Kilburn, Charles Lawrence 188, 189
Korean War xxxvi

L

Ladye Annabel, The viii
Land Ordinance of 1785 xxv
Land Ordinances of 1784 xxv
Lane, James Henry 182, 185, 188
La Pagerie, Marie Josèphe Rose Tascher de 29, 86
La Vega, Rómulo Díaz de 19, 67, 112, 123–124
League of Nations xxxv, xxxvi
Lee, Robert E. xxxii
Lincoln, Abraham xxx, xxxvii, 200
Lincoln, Benjamin 62
Lincoln, George 125–126, 184, 188
Lippard, George vii–xxix
Lippard, Mima xi
Lippard, Paul xi
Longstreet, James xxxii
Louisiana Purchase xxv–xxvii
Luther, Roland A. 97

M

Mahitili 56–58
manifest destiny xii, xiv–xvi, xix, xxiv–xxviii, xxxii–xxxvi, 7, 15
Marcy, William 181, 199
Marengo, Battle of 87
Maria Louisa. *See* La Pagerie, Marie Josèphe Rose Tascher de
Marshall, Humphrey 181, 182, 185–186, 188
Mary, Virgin 31, 35, 57, 158
Matthews, Cornelius xiv
May, Charles A. 13–15, 20, 63, 66, 106–107, 117–125, 136, 142, 177, 181, 183, 185–186, 188
McClellan, George xxxii
McCulloch, Ben 188, 189
McIntosh, James S. 66, 106–107, 115, 125, 128–132
McKee, William R. 181, 185, 188, 191–192
McKinley, William xxxiii
Meade, George xxxii
Mejía, Francisco 19, 75
Minon, Jose Vicente 183, 184
Missouri Compromise xxxi
Molino del Rey, Battle of xxx, 66, 123
Monmouth, Battle of 170
Monroe Doctrine xxxiv
Monroe, John 188, 189
Montero, don Cayetano 97–103
Monterrey, Battle of xxix, 6, 66, 76, 153–175, 180, 181, 183, 185, 190
Montezuma 4, 31, 32, 33, 34, 38–42, 51, 53, 55, 56, 59–60, 180, 200
Montgomery, Cora xiv
Montgomery, John B. 66, 141
Morgan, Daniel 77
Morris, Lewis N. 66, 125–126
Morrison, Alexander Ferguson 188, 189
Moscow, Battle of 84–85, 87
Myers, Abraham C. 66–67
Mysteries of Paris, The xiii

N

New Crusade 1–10, 27, 156
Newman, Rose xi
Northwest Ordinance of 1787 xxv
Nuestra Señora de Guadalupe 75

O

O'Brien, John Paul Jones 184, 188
O'Sullivan, John xiv, xix, xxx, xxxiv, xxxv

P

Page, John 93–96, 97
Palo Alto, Battle of xxix, 6, 15, 20, 37, 40, 43–44, 54, 61–108, 111, 131, 146, 147, 149, 156, 169, 185, 189, 190
Paredes 180
Payne, Matthew M. 90–93, 125
penny dreadful xiii
Peterson, T.B. xxxviii
Pike, Albert 185, 188
Pleasanton, Alfred 123
Plutarch 188
Poe, Edgar Allan xiii, 200
Polk, James K. xxviii, xxix, 5, 9
Pratt, J.S. xxxviii
Punic Wars 3

Q

Quaker City, The vii, ix, x, xiii
Quetzalcoatl 38

R

Resaca de la Palma, Battle of xxix, xxx, 6, 20, 54, 57, 109–152, 156, 169, 181, 183, 185, 190
Revolution, American vii, xxiv, 3, 7, 9, 14, 15, 27, 62, 71, 93, 146, 149, 152, 170, 172, 184, 196
Revolution, French 83
Reynolds, John Fulton 186, 188
Ridgely, Randolph 76–81, 106–107, 114–116, 121, 131, 133, 136, 141–142, 144
Ringgold, Samuel 13–15, 20, 62, 66, 70–72, 75–81, 89–94, 96, 97, 99, 114, 121, 125

216   Legends of Mexico

Roanne, John S. 185
roman-feuilleton xiii
Roosevelt Corollary xxxiv
Roosevelt, Franklin xxxv
Roosevelt, Theodore xxxiii
Rucker, Daniel Henry 188, 189

S

Sacket, Delos Bennet 122
Santa Anna, Antonio López de 1, 5, 13, 20, 149, 150, 151–152, 170, 179–187, 194, 198–199
Saratoga, Battle of 9, 156, 172
Saturday Courier xxxviii
Scott's Weekly xxxviii
Scott, Winfield xxx, 68, 170, 199, 200
Seminole Wars 14, 15, 25, 61, 66, 121, 123, 181, 183, 184, 191
Sentmanat, Francisco 75, 142
Sepoy Rebellion 3
Shelley, Mary xiii
Sherman, Thomas 181, 183, 184–185, 188
Sherman, William T. xxxii
Shover, William H. 188, 191
Slidell, John 5
Smith, E. Kirby 131
Spanish-American War xxxiii, xxxvii
Spirit of the Times viii
Steen, Enoch 181, 183, 188
Stephanson, Anders xxxiii
Stephens, George 124
Stevenson, Thomas B. 194
Strong, Thomas 202
Sue, Eugene xiii
Sword of Washington 10, 69, 146

T

Taliban xxxvi
Taylor, Zachary ix–x, xxviii, xxix–xxxi, 12, 13–15, 18, 20–25, 29, 37, 53–54, 61–66, 74, 76, 79–80, 90, 97–107, 109–116, 119–124, 126–128, 132–134, 136, 141–152, 155, 157–158, 165–166, 168–171, 174, 179–190, 193, 195, 198–199, 200

Texas Rangers 13
Thomas, George H. 188, 190
Tilghman, Lloyd 68
Torrejón, Anastasio 75–77
Truman, Harry xxxvi
Twiggs, David E. 62, 66, 77–80, 106–107, 124, 155
Twiggs, John 62
Tyler, John xxviii

U

Uncle Tom's Cabin vii
United Nations xxxvi

V

Valley Forge 12, 170
Vaughn, Edward M. 188
Velasco, Treaties of 1
Veracruz, Battle of xxix, 66, 68, 199
Vietnam War xxxvi, xxxvii

W

Walker, Samuel 13–15, 20, 63, 76–77, 100, 106–107, 111, 114–116, 136, 142
Walpole, Horace xiii
War for Texas Independence 5
War of 1812 xxvi, 3, 14
War of Reform xxxi
Warren, Joseph 152
Washington and His Generals xiii
Washington, George xx, xxiv, xxvii, xxviii, 1, 2, 5, 6, 9, 12, 14, 15, 28, 32, 66, 103, 146, 148, 149, 150, 170, 171, 177, 190, 199
Washington, John Macrae 181–182, 184, 188, 197
Waterloo, Battle of 3, 83, 84, 85, 87, 179
Webster, Daniel 152
Wellesley, Arthur 83
Wellington, Duke of 83, 84
Whiting, Henry M. 188, 190
Wilson, Woodrow xxxiv
Winship, Oscar F. 123
Woods, James S. 125–126

Woodville, Richard Caton 204
Wool, John Ellis 181, 183, 184, 185, 187, 188
World War I xxxiv, xxxv
World War II xxxv, xxxvi
Worth, William J. 155, 157–158, 165–166, 169

X

Ximena 159–175

Y

Yell, Archibald 181–182, 185–186, 188
Yorktown, Battle of 9
Young America xii–xvi

www.ingramcontent.com/pod-product-compliance
Lightning Source LLC
Chambersburg PA
CBHW081719100526
44591CB00016B/2425